Ruth Petrovna

REACHING
RUSSIANS

Ruth Petrovna

REACHING RUSSIANS

THE INSPIRING STORY
OF LIFELONG MISSIONARY
RUTH DEYNEKA SHALANKO ERDEL

BY ERIC AND GILLIAN BARRETT

Copyright © 1998 Slavic Gospel Association
6151 Commonwealth Drive
Loves Park, Illinois 61111

All rights reserved.

Printed in the United States of America.

ISBN 1-56773-002-7

No part of this publication may be reproduced or transmitted in any form
or by any means, electronic or mechanical, including photocopying, recording, or any information storage and retrieval system, without permission
from the publisher.

All Scripture quotations in this book, except those noted otherwise, are
from the New International Version, copyright © 1973, 1978, 1984 by
New York International Bible society, and are used by permission.

Special thanks to Elisabeth Elliot for permission to quote directly from
Through Gates of Splendor.

Place name spellings are taken, whenever possible, from *Philip's Atlas of
the World*.

Photographs on pages 67 and 98 provided by the Billy Graham Center,
Wheaton College, Wheaton, Illinois. All other photographs courtesy of Ruth
Deyneka Shalanko Erdel and Slavic Gospel Association.

Cover photograph of Peter and Vera Deyneka with Ruth, age nine months.

This book being Ruth's story, it is right that its dedication be hers . . .

—◆◇◆—

In loving memory
and with deepest gratitude
to my parents
Peter and Vera Deyneka
who taught me to love God

—◆◇◆—

Contents

Foreword

Few women in today's Christian world have made an impact on the Slavic nations of the Eastern bloc as compared to Ruth Deyneka Shalanko Erdel, daughter of Peter and Vera Deyneka (whose names are synonymous with Russian ministries). Born in White Russia (Belarus) myself, I recall the childhood thrill of serving as a flower boy at Peter and Vera's wedding in the little town of Chomsk . . . of emigrating with my family to the United States when I was seven years old . . . and of first seeing Ruth when she was just about one year old. Thus, I know very well how she grew up under constant exposure to the news of the suffering and persecution of her parents' countrymen. Their pain became hers, and their problems and needs her prime concern. Little wonder that she gave up potentially lucrative opportunities for a leisurely and comfortable lifestyle in America to go to the mission field of Europe!

Following World War II, in the early days of her ministry with the door to Russia closed, she labored among the Russians who were living as displaced persons in the western countries of Europe. Upon her return to the United States and her marriage to missionary Jack Shalanko, the door suddenly opened for a far greater outreach — to reach millions in the Eastern bloc nations via radio. Ruth and Jack set their sights on HCJB in Ecuador. Blending their voices in song and speaking with a tone of urgency and concern, their programs became crucial to meeting the spiritual hunger of the struggling masses. Working night and day, they tried to read between the lines of mail which reached them and then respond to these inquiries via the airwaves, speaking with understanding and sincerity.

Though in God's timing the Lord saw fit to take her husband Jack home to Glory, Ruth continued with even greater determination to fulfill the task to which, early in life, she had committed herself. A frequent traveler to the land of her forefathers, where today she can speak person to person with those whom she was only able to reach by radio in years before, Ruth is a much-sought-after speaker at conferences, women's meetings and retreats throughout the CIS as well as in Europe, South America, Canada and the United States. It is truly amazing how God has used and blessed her ministries among Russians, but among so many other people too. Her enthusiasm becomes contagious, and her dedication to the cause of Christ is a driving force for others who see and hear her to follow her example.

In God's providence, Ruth is now married to Dr. Paul Erdel who has shared a lifetime of fellowship and ministry with the Shalankos in Ecuador. Ruth continues to reach Russians through radio, literature and trips to the CIS, and Paul trains church leaders.

It has been my joy to know Ruth throughout her lifetime as my cousin, but an even greater blessing to know her as a co-laborer in the greatest of life's pursuits — bringing others to the saving knowledge of Jesus Christ. I am sure that this fascinating and inspiring book will be used of God to pass the torch of evangelism to you, dear reader, as well.

DR. ALEX LEONOVICH
president, Russian-Ukrainian Evangelical Baptist Union of the United States
executive director, Slavic Missionary Service, Inc., New Jersey

Preface

So far as we can remember, we first met Ruth in 1977 at the U.S. office of Slavic Gospel Association, then in Wheaton, Illinois. We knew she was a special person by birth — the daughter of Rev. Peter Deyneka Sr., founder of SGA. We quickly began to discover that she is also a very special person by reason of her Christian character, and even above that, through her personal calling and commitment to the Lord's service as an SGA missionary. In the 1980s we came to see Ruth quite often, and our love for and appreciation of her grew all the time.

Today, two years after we began to explore with Ruth the possibility of sharing her story with a much wider audience, we have come to realize just how little we previously knew of this remarkable woman. By nature and instinct, Ruth is a humble, private person. She has had to be encouraged long and often to help bring this book to publication. Yet we, and SGA as a whole, are glad that she has helped so much with it because we believe her story will be both an inspiration and a challenge to many.

From the outset, all of us involved in this project, and most crucially Ruth herself, have been of the same mind — the book should have FOUR PURPOSES: *first*, to record and review how the Lord has spiritually blessed many Russian people, despite — and even in many ways because of — great persecution and suffering; *second*, to recall and reflect on how truly amazingly God has recently answered prayers for greater Christian freedom in Russia and other lands of the old Soviet empire; *third*, to inform and inspire others with an account of how the Lord has worked wonderfully in and through one particular child and servant of His; and *fourth*, to provoke thought and prayer in respect of the directions Christian life and witness should take as the 20th century closes and a new millennium opens before us all.

To support the text and advance these purposes, chapter-by-chapter lists of topics for thought and discussion can be found in Appendix 3. We hope these will further broaden the value of this book through encouraging individual readers to critically and constructively explore their own circumstances in light of Ruth's life, work and experiences. The same lists will facilitate the use of this volume as a study book for use by groups such as Sunday schools, missionary training classes, etc.

We pray and trust that this biography will be seen as a fitting tribute to a tremendous Christian and, therefore, as a tribute to her heavenly Lord and Master. Somewhat coincidentally, it is also a slice through the whole history and many of the ministries of SGA, for Ruth's life was bound up with these from early childhood and she has served with this mission all her working life. We are confident, therefore, that this book will be of great interest to all who have known Ruth, and many more who have supported the Lord's work through SGA. We cherish even more strongly the hope that her story will become a spur to others in the worldwide church today, to dedicate themselves anew to serve the Lord to the utmost of their ability, wherever He may choose.

Our thanks are due to the many friends of Ruth who have assisted in any way with the preparation of this book — especially those who have helped fill it with details she has been most reluctant to add about herself! We wish to also thank our many friends and colleagues at SGA, both past and present, who have been so generous with their help and encouragement. It has been an outstanding privilege for us to have been called (even if only on a part-time, honorary basis) to work for many years alongside Ruth and Jack Shalanko, Peter and Vera Deyneka, Peter and Anita Deyneka, Nick and Roz Leonovich, Const and Elizabeth Lewshenia, Andrew and Pauline Semenchuk, and many other SGA workers named or not named in this volume. We are so blessed to have been able to count them all among our best friends! We have recently come to appreciate, too, the friendship and warm, inspirational leadership of SGA in the United States by Dr. Bob Provost and his dear wife, Louetta. We also wish to express our deep appreciation to colleagues in the U.S. office of SGA who have helped bring the original manuscript to final fruition in this book form — especially because this is the first book we have attempted to write in "American" English as distinct from "British" English!

Despite the effort required by a project of this kind, some of our most blessed experiences recently have been times with Ruth and Paul Erdel, and members of their extended families, as we have worked together on this book. However, preparing it has been one of the most challenging writing tasks we have ever known. Through it all we have grown ever more conscious that we have been trying to craft the life story of one who is, without a doubt, one of the greatest lady missionaries of our time. Ruth's commitment to the Lord was made at a young age and has remained strong and secure ever since. Her call to serve Him in a particular context was accepted willingly and has been acted upon unswervingly, and her many gifts and talents have been applied unstintingly to honor Him. We trust her story will be an inspiration and a challenge to all who read it.

ERIC AND GILLIAN BARRETT
honorary SGA representatives
Backwell, North Somerset, United Kingdom

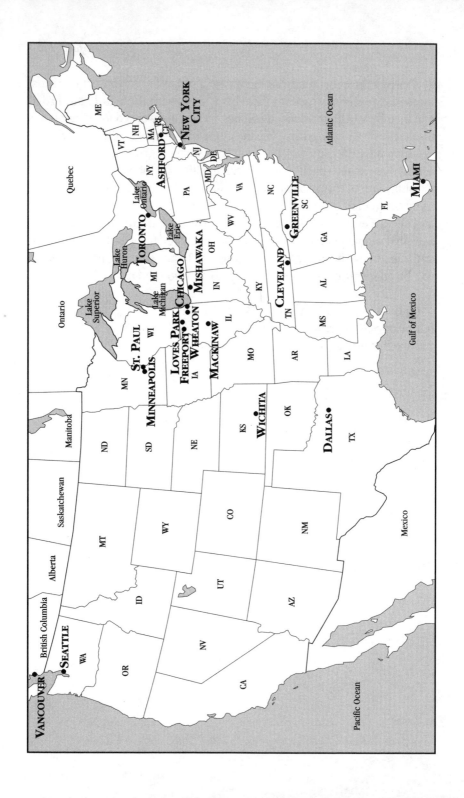

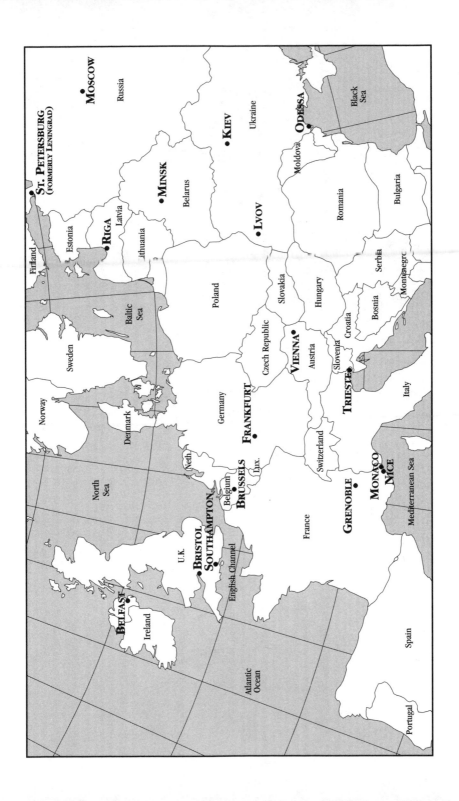

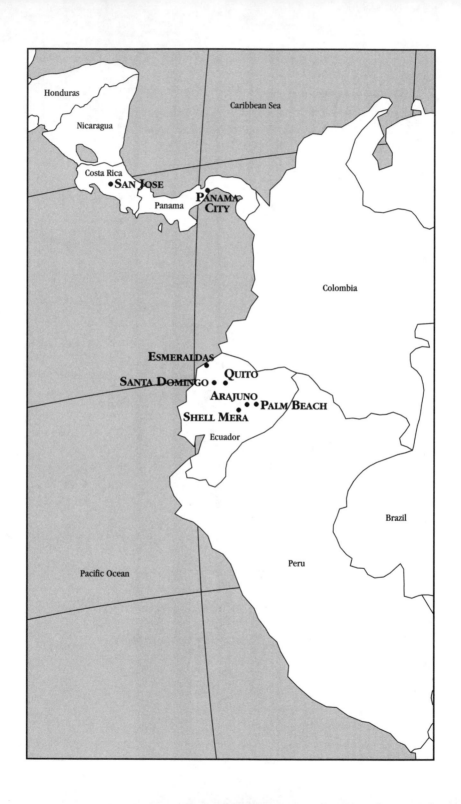

CHAPTER 1

Relationships and Roots
1993 - 1995

Ruth awoke to the rhythmic clatter of the big Russian train wheels. It was about 3 a.m. Peeping out through the curtained windows, she scanned the moonlit, icy landscape of Siberia. *Siberia!* The very name prompted her to shiver, and all the more so at the sight of the snowbound woods and fields glistening before her.

But Ruth Deyneka Shalanko Erdel shivered also with excitement and anticipation. A few days previously, in November 1995, she had been speaking at a major women's convention in Omsk, the regional capital of southwestern Siberia.

"Oh, *Ruth Petrovna,*" (as she is known in Russian) some ladies had pled, "*please* come to OUR village! We Christians there don't have a church. We just meet in a home. But, oh, how we want you to share the Word with the women in our area who love the Lord, and meet those who have listened to you on the radio broadcasts from Ecuador!"

So there she was, nearing that little settlement at the end of a 10-hour train journey from Omsk, eager to minister to that small group of believers in Jesus Christ. Ruth's Russian companion, Svetlana, soon awoke too, and at about 4:30 a.m. the carriage attendant tapped on their compartment door to say that they would shortly arrive at their destination, Vinzili.

Ruth and Svetlana took their bags with them along the corridor to the front of the train. It slowed and shuddered to a halt. The attendant lowered steps for them. Moments later as the train pulled away, they found themselves in almost complete darkness. Away to the left, a single naked light bulb swung to and fro in the icy wind. All of a sudden, Ruth and Svetlana realized they were *alone!* No one else had gotten off the train, and there was no one to meet them.

Ruth's next thoughts were chilling, like the wintry weather . . . "What if nobody comes to meet us? What will we do? Where will we go?" But she had known the presence and help of the Lord most of the 67 years of her life. This comforting fact kept panic at bay. And minutes later, any lingering fears were swept away by loving shouts of their names from the darkness . . . *"Ruth Petrovna! Svetlana! HELLO!"*

Ruth recalls her thoughts at that moment and what happened next: "Believe me, I was *thrilled* to hear those voices! The two ladies whom we had met at the convention in Omsk emerged from the darkness with one of their husbands, and greeted us with love and care and kisses. They took our small bags and we began to walk down the country lane. Crunch, crunch, crunch went our heels in the snow and ice. As our eyes adjusted to the darkness, we could see some one-story log houses with barns attached and smoke seeping from their chimneys. Our footsteps awakened roosters who spread the news of our approach with their discordant crowing. As we grew colder and colder, I began to look forward to the warmth inside one of the homes, even if it was shared with cows, pigs, chickens or rabbits! But I was marveling that the Lord had brought us so far, and was looking forward to being used of Him in that remote place."

Some 20 minutes later, they reached the home of one of the ladies. In the kitchen, a table was set for breakfast. After a hot cup of tea, some dark bread, sausage and cheese, Ruth was able to rest on the sofa, falling asleep almost immediately. Later that morning, much refreshed, Ruth and Svetlana were taken to a larger house where the second lady lived with her husband and eight children. Since its living room was bigger than most in the village, this was where the meeting was to be held. Men and women had already gathered for it, and others were crowding in.

Many of the ladies greeted Ruth warmly, hugging and kissing her as if she were a long-lost friend. "Oh, *Sister Ruth Petrovna*," they said, "We *recognize your voice!* We have listened to you for so many years on the radio — but now we can SEE you and TOUCH you!"

After they had all stood for opening prayers and a Bible reading, and had sung some hymns, Ruth was invited to begin her address.

Politely, she asked what time the meeting was to end. "Well," came the reply, "Why are you asking this? *You're* not going anywhere until tomorrow morning — and *we've* come to listen to *you!*"

This much was clear to Ruth — her hosts were expecting a good, long session! She quietly prayed to the Lord once more, seeking His help and wisdom as she opened His Word to those eager people. She scanned her audience. There were older women whose faces were careworn and deeply lined, whose hands and arms were rough and cracked from decades of hard labor — planting their vegetable gardens, milking the cows, and physically straining to prepare food and clothing for their children. And there were younger women with the greater parts of their lives ahead of them, but expecting little by way of comfort or personal success. Some, both men and women, were visibly unhappy and depressed. Ruth later learned that several in the meeting did not know the Lord. For them, life was not just tough; it was meaningless drudgery, which is much worse.

And some attending that crowded home meeting in the depths of Siberia were children. Bright-eyed, they gazed with wonder at the tall, graceful lady standing before them. She was speaking their language, Russian, but was an *American* — the first they had ever seen! Although Ruth was plainly and simply dressed, her clothes, boots and hairstyle were foreign to them, and the kids were fascinated. Even her nice, new Bible looked different from the few they had seen before.

Yes, great gulfs lay between Ruth and the members of this congregation . . . but the Lord had brought her together with them for His own special purposes. Of this she was very sure! More than 50 years before, she had committed herself to serving Him, especially as a missionary to Russian-speaking peoples. All her life had been a preparation for situations like this!

Drawing strength from her memories and from her Master, Ruth squared her shoulders, opened her Bible, smiled at the congregation, and began to share with them messages transcending time, culture, education and economic status. She had news of God's love for all, and encouragement from His Word for all who follow Him. Most particularly, she was able to develop lessons from the lives of women in the Bible, lessons relating to the most fundamental aspects of human life — relationships with one another, and above all, *relationships with God Himself.*

Looking back, Ruth affirms: "Two things that impressed me so much that Saturday afternoon were the *joy* on the faces of those who really knew Christ as their personal Savior . . . and the *sadness* of those who were without Him. My heart went out to them all as I tried to share God's Word with them, and as they faced the simple future of living there in that small community. Yes, it was a very cold, dreary, snowy winter's day in Siberia. But crowded together in that home, we felt the warm, loving presence of the Lord in our midst."

The chance for anyone to have made such a missionary journey to Siberia in 1995 was just one result of a late-20th-century miracle of truly epic proportions. By this time, the lands of the vast Union of Soviet Socialist Republics (U.S.S.R.) and several of its neighbors in Europe and Asia, had been freed from the yoke of communism. An era of new hope and opportunity for Bible-believing people and their churches had dawned at last. Many years had passed since Ruth had received a clear call to Russian Christian missionary work. But it had been only 10 years prior to her wintry trip to Vinzili that she had been able to pay her very first visit to Russia. And it had been merely two years previously that she had been able to set out from her home in the United States, hoping to see for the first time the home villages of her father and mother in the former Soviet republic of White Russia, now newly independent Belarus.

It had been in late May 1993 that Ruth had joined a special trip to the countries of Russia, Ukraine and Belarus. This had been organized by her mother's cousin, a favorite relative of hers, Dr. Alex Leonovich, president of Slavic Missionary Service (SMS). Its official culmination was to be the dedication service of a new church building in the Belarussian city of Kobryn. This ceremony had especially interested Ruth in advance, for it had been in that very area that her mother had first heard the Gospel of Jesus Christ. Furthermore, Kobryn was near the area where her parents had been born, grown up, met each other, and married. The trip might be an opportunity for Ruth and her younger brother, Peter Deyneka Jr., to visit the region of their roots!

What actually happened on the trip?

As it unfolded, Ruth was greatly encouraged by the visits to Moscow, Kiev and Minsk. Returning to churches she had last seen in 1985, she was thrilled to discover that they were at least as packed as before. Better still, believers could now witness freely and openly in their communities, and there were higher proportions of younger and professional people present in the congregations.

However, the Kobryn weekend was the time she had anticipated most eagerly of all. On Saturday, June 5, 1993, one final service was held in the little old Evangelical Baptist church building. It was so crowded that the congregation overflowed into the aisles, the porch, and even into the choir loft around the choir itself. When Sunday came, Ruth was overjoyed to see the big new church building next door rapidly filling for its dedication service. Nearly 4,000 people crowded into it, though it had been designed for just over half that number! The architect, the mayor, and other local dignitaries were in attendance. Ruth learned that the bricks had come from an old army barracks over 40 miles away — and marveled that each brick had been individually cleaned by members of the congregation. Also, the beautifully varnished floor, the benches, carved pulpit and railings, and all the other furnishings and fittings had been built and prepared by church members themselves. It was obvious that many had given sacrificially of their time, talents and meager money to complete this splendid new spiritual sanctuary.

Ruth was so glad that her brother-in-law, Tom Felter, was also present. Together, Tom, Ruth and her brother, Peter Jr., were able to give a gift to the church in memory of their parents, Peter and Vera Deyneka, who had come from that region of Belarus.

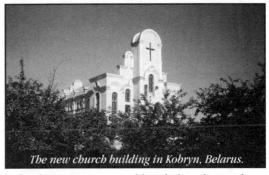

The new church building in Kobryn, Belarus.

Visitors and local church members witnessed several local people dedicate themselves to the Lord for the first time that weekend.

The next day dawned full of anticipation for Ruth and Peter Jr. as they set out to try to find the villages of their roots. Accompanied by Vanya Leonovich, a distant relative who lived locally, they soon neared the town of Chomsk.

Many people responded to the invitation to accept Christ as Savior during that service of dedication.

Being summertime, many people were busy in the fields. Passing the busy milking parlor of a collective farm, Vanya stopped the car to inquire where the village of Staramlynia might be. Workers pointed down the road to a building where they said someone would know — then spontaneously offered the American visitors some of the fresh, steaming milk scooped up in an aluminum cup. Ruth was the only one brave enough to accept their offer!

The someone down the road was not only able to help, but also *thrilled* to help! He was so excited Ruth and Peter were children of a native from that region that he insisted on going with them as a guide. Driving through the little town of Chomsk, he was able to take them to the site where its evangelical church had stood. In it, Ruth and Peter's parents had married in 1926, and their father had preached there many times. Two kilometers the other side of Chomsk they found a road sign pointing to the left: *STARAMLYNIA 0.8 km.* After a couple of twists in the lane, they suddenly reached the village. Ruth spotted a row of mail boxes by the roadside, each bearing a name. On the last one, DEYNEKA was painted! Their pulses raced — things were now happening so fast!

They stopped the car, and spoke to a couple who came out of the first wooden hut: "Could you show us the house where the Deynekas live?"

"Oh, yes," they said. "It's right over there, the yellow one. And Anastacia is at home!"

Ruth was startled, remembering she had a cousin of that name. She looked at Peter and said: "*Anastacia* — that's the name of our Uncle Andrei's daughter!"

Ruth knew that her father had four brothers and two sisters . . . but apart from her father, only Andrei had lived to adulthood. His married daughter, Anastacia, had been 30 years old when, in a drunken stupor, her husband had kicked her in the forehead, blinding her.

To confirm that the Anastacia who lived in the yellow hut was indeed her cousin, Ruth asked the couple if she was blind. They confirmed she was, but said: "It's all right, she gets along fine! We'll bring her out." They rushed ahead to do just that. So as Ruth and Peter crossed the dirt road toward the gate of the little home, they saw a lady in simple peasant clothing being led from the house to meet them.

There at the gate, Ruth stopped and stared at Anastacia. Remembering that memorable moment, she recalls: "The thing that shocked me most was that *we looked so much alike!* Her forehead, her eyes, were just like mine! I was soon hugging her, smiling and crying, and saying 'Anastacia, Anastacia, *I'm your cousin Ruth!'*"

"Oh," the woman inquired wonderingly, "*you're Uncle Peter's daughter?!*" and hugged and kissed Ruth back.

"Yes," Ruth replied. "And I'm not alone. Here's Peter Jr., his son." She took Peter's hand and placed it on Anastacia's.

After some hectic minutes of happy confusion, Anastacia invited the visitors into her two-room hut. Chickens ran out squawking as they entered. There, in what had been their grandmother's home, Ruth and Peter sat on the sofa. It was the very room where their father had been born, nearly a century before!

There was much to talk about, and things to see both inside and out. Ruth and Peter were especially interested in the well in the yard. Their father had often mentioned it, how drawing water had been one of his daily chores.

Ruth and Peter Jr. with Anastacia's granddaughter by the Deynekas' well.

Anastacia had sent her neighbors to fetch her daughter, Valya, as well as her three grandchildren from the vegetable fields so they too could meet the unexpected visitors and all have their pictures taken together. Peter talked to the children and gave them a copy of an illustrated New Testament in the Russian language. Other people from the little village gathered around, particularly intrigued by the foreigners when they learned who they were. One couple brought out a photo of Peter Deyneka, Ruth and Peter's papa, taken in 1925. That was the year he had returned home from America, had married a girl from another village nearby, and had told many of the local people how he had come to personal faith in Jesus Christ after he had left the area 12 years earlier!

Ruth and Peter Jr. with relatives and villagers outside the Deyneka home in Staramlynia, Belarus.

One elderly man gruffly confessed to Ruth and Peter that his own father had been a Christian. "I guess I used to be one myself," he continued. "But when the communists came, I changed and became a communist too."

Ruth looked at him, smiled, and said: "You know, I think God has sent us here today to help you change back once again. *HE* has not changed. He still loves you as much now as when you were a young man!"

"Oh, no, no," the man replied, "I can't change again. I'm too old now. I can't even think of doing so!"

Peter took this as a cue. There in his father's village, in front of the parental house, he told the crowd about the boy who had been born in that very place, who had drawn water from its well, and kicked the dirt in the lane . . . the boy whose life had been greatly changed by leaving home, but who had gained most by accepting the love of the Lord Jesus Christ — love that is available to *all* who trust in Him . . . a boy whose new desire had been to live for the Lord, and whose most frequent prayer until he went to Heaven was that his own people would also come to know and love the Lord.

As Ruth and Peter hugged and kissed everybody farewell, she kept thinking how easily her father, like his father before him, could have lived out his life as a freshwater fisherman in that quiet corner of Belarus — but the Lord had led him out to give him a victorious life as a fisher of men! As a result, many millions of Russian and other Slavic people had heard, and were still hearing, the Gospel of Jesus Christ.

And Ruth and Peter's great day was not over yet.

Where was the village of Ruth and Peter's mother? Their self-appointed guide was not sure. He suggested they stop in Makarevich, a few kilometers from Staramlynia, to make inquiries. Arriving there, they drew up by a particular house. On a bench in front sat a middle-aged couple. Ruth and Peter got out of the car and approached the gate.

As they did so, to their amazement the woman began calling out Ruth's name: "*Ruthia, RUTHIA*, you're HERE!"

Ruth looked at her in astonishment. She had never been to that village before and was sure she had never previously met the woman. She asked her how she knew who she was.

"Come, Ruthia," she replied, "and I will show you!"

The woman had a lame foot, and picked up a roughly trimmed branch which served as her walking stick. Hobbling, she led her guests into the small, but clean, one-room hut.

There in a corner, almost like a shrine, sat a shortwave radio receiver surrounded by two framed collages of pictures.

Ruth with Evgeni and Nadia Klimovitch, HCJB radio listeners in Makarevich, Belarus.

Ruth remembers: "As we inspected the little gallery, we saw pictures of my brother Peter, my sister Lydia, pictures of our relatives the Leonovich family, of the Christian radio station HCJB . . . and a picture of *myself!*"

"Of course I know you, Ruthia," the woman insisted. "We listen to you on the radio from Ecuador. We have written to you and the Leonovichs there. That's how we've gotten many of these pictures and feel just like we've known you a long time!"

Once they had all recovered from their astonishment at this unexpected meeting, they sat and talked for a while. At one point Peter said to the man, "Well, dear brother . . . " but was interrupted by the woman.

"No, no, don't call him brother. He won't accept the Lord! I *can't* go to church now because of my bad foot. The church is 30 kilometers away. But my husband *won't* go to church because he has never trusted Christ!"

Peter looked at the man. "My friend," he said, "why haven't you prepared your heart to meet the Lord, as your wife has? You know you should! You know that Jesus died on the cross for you. You should accept Him as your personal Savior too!"

The man started to cry. "Yes, yes, I know," he said. So Peter prayed for him, and their time together ended happily.

But the woman then reflected rather negatively on their remaining quest. "You won't find your mother's village, Borisovka," she said. "The

Germans burned it down in World War II, when they were retreating from this area! And since the villagers all left, it was never rebuilt. But my husband can show you where the village was, and your grandfather's grave. It's in the cemetery which still exists."

So Ruth, Peter Jr., Vanya Leonovich and their guides drove off across fields which were fortunately dry, for no roads remained to the former village. Elderly trees of Borisovka could soon be seen . . . cherry trees which had survived the fires started by the German army . . . cherry trees of which Mrs. Vera Deyneka had spoken so often to her children in faraway Chicago. In the old overgrown cemetery, Ruth and Peter were shown the grave of Vera's father, Ivan Demidovich, plus the graves of two more cousins.

Ruth confesses: "It is so difficult to explain how we felt as we left that spot. But Peter and I were glad to have been able to visit the places where our parents had grown up, and where they had started their life together. Although both Mama and Papa were enjoying Heaven, that day in June 1993 we had been following their early footsteps here on Earth.

"I shall always remember looking back down the dusty lane in Staramlynia as we left my father's birthplace and thinking: *I could have been born here too!* But in the PURPOSES OF GOD, my Papa was able to emigrate to America where he found Jesus Christ.

"From the United States, he was able to effectively serve his Lord all over the world! And because of my Papa's and Mama's love, prayers and encouragement, *I myself was to hear and respond to a similar call to share God's love with Russian people in many lands!*

"I just marveled then, and STILL MARVEL at the amazing ways in which He works!"

CHAPTER 2

Twice Born, Twice Saved
1928 - 1940

Ruth Deyneka was born of Russian Christian parents in the United States on March 29, 1928. How had her parents, Peter and Vera Deyneka, become Christians . . . married in what is today Chomsk, Belarus . . . and come to establish the home in Chicago where Ruth first greeted the world?

Ruth's father, Peter Naumovich Deyneka, had arrived in the United States in March 1914 — alone, unable to speak English, a mere lad of 15 years of age. On his slender shoulders rested this great weight of responsibility — not only to earn enough money to support himself, but also to help support his parents and siblings 6,000 miles away. It says much for his youthful determination that he was to succeed in both.

Eleven years later, Peter returned home for the first time. Much had changed. Peter himself was no longer a hesitant teen-ager, but a confident, determined young man. He had also become a Christian believer. In his biography *Peter Dynamite: Twice Born Russian*, the immediate change his conversion had brought to him is reported through the conversation with his landlord in Chicago, when Peter had returned to his lodgings that memorable night in January 1920. Noticing his broad smile, his landlord had inquired, "What's wrong with you, Peter? Are you drunk?"

"No, I'm not drunk, I'm *saved!*"

"Go to bed. You'll feel all right in the morning."

Peter had been unable to sleep all night — for joy — so he still wore the same smile the next day.

"Peter," his landlord then objected, "you're still drunk!"

"No, I'm not," Peter had insisted, "I'm a *new person!*" And he was. The old Peter Deyneka was gone forever. The new "Peter Dynamite" had found explosive new life in Christ!

Peter grew quickly as a Christian, witnessing to others and developing a heavy burden for his own people. Less than three years after his conversion, he had entered Bible school in St. Paul, Minnesota. Less than six years later, he was on his way back home to the Chomsk area — as a highly energetic evangelist.

But other things had changed, too, in the years which had inter-

Recently born again Peter Deyneka wearing his broad, conversion smile.

vened between Peter's first departure for the United States and his return to Chomsk. World War I had shifted some national frontiers. Peter's home district fell within the tract of country which had been ceded from Russia to Poland. It was to remain Polish until after World War II. Meanwhile, World War I and the famine which followed it had ravaged the region. Many buildings had been destroyed. Worse still, in European Russia as a whole, more than five million people had died of starvation. For four long years, from 1918 to 1922, Peter received no letters from his parents. When at last he did hear from them, their tragic news was that three of his brothers and two sisters had starved to death. Peter had been devastated by this disclosure. He could hardly eat or sleep and spent entire nights in prayer for the remainder of his family, for he knew that his relatives had never heard the Gospel which had so revolutionized his own life. That was when he first began to pray for an opportunity to become a missionary to his own people.

Peter's reunion with his family in the village of Staramlynia in 1925 was therefore a highly emotional occasion. Only his mother Anastacia, and one brother, Andrei, had survived the famine. Peter shared his faith with them, plus many others in that village and its surrounding areas. Many trusted in Christ. But his mother and brother were not ready to do so.

However, despite the great pain and disappointment Peter suffered at the hands of these, his nearest relatives — who insisted they did not even want to hear about the Lord — he came to praise and thank God greatly on that trip . . . for the unexpected, priceless gift of a *wife!* Peter had mentioned to church leaders in his home region that he was praying for a helpmate, one who loved the Lord, who spoke the Russian language, and who shared the same values as himself. Some brethren warmly recommended a girl who, despite opposition from her own family, was living faithfully for God. Vera Demidovich was eight years younger than Peter, but had already been a Christian three years when Peter visited her village of Borisovka to preach in December 1925. Peter quickly became impressed by the 20-year-old girl's devotion to the Lord, and his friendship with her deepened. Six months later, on May 23, 1926, they were married.

The pattern for their whole married life was to be set immediately. The Lord had called Peter to a public ministry involving much travel. Vera's role would be to establish and maintain a home for Peter, and in due course, their children. She was to support her husband in every practical way possible, not the least of which was prayer. Thus, their wedding day found Peter preaching in both their home villages, Staramlynia and Borisovka! Peter's biographers say:

> The sun had long since disappeared when the singing and preaching came to an end on that momentous day.
>
> Peter and Vera desired more than anything else to put the Lord's work ahead of their own ease, so they traveled on foot in pouring rain for 16 miles to the homes of Vera's relatives to distribute Gospel portions and tell them about Jesus Christ. They arrived at 11:00 in the morning the following day and found that a crowd of eager people had gathered. The crowd would not even let the bride and groom dry their clothes. They wanted them to begin the service immediately.
>
> Peter preached from 11:00 to 1:00, thinking that would suffice. "You're not going to go, giving just a two-hour service!" exclaimed one mother with a six-month-old baby. "I walked 20 miles to this place to hear God's Word, and you want to quit so soon?"
>
> There was nothing to do but have a short recess and continue another service, lasting until 5 p.m.
>
> The newlyweds stayed the night with relatives. In the morning the rain poured down again, but they set their faces toward a village 12 miles away through a woodland. They borrowed a team of horses and a horse blanket to cover their heads. Before they arrived, however, the blanket had become soaked and the dirt began

to trickle down their faces. They were cold but supremely happy, doing the work of the Lord on their honeymoon.

"In the afternoon we reached the village where a crowd was waiting for us," Peter wrote. "We had a wonderful Gospel service even though we were cold and tired. It was a great encouragement to witness for the Lord."

A spirit of revival followed them. Russian people eagerly responded to the message of salvation, and believers were stirred in their zeal to follow the Lord more closely.

Shortly afterward came the first of Peter and Vera's many times apart. Worn down by the antagonism of his mother and brother, and in need of both a rest and time to consider carefully how best to share the Gospel with the Russian people, Peter returned to the United States. His wife would not be able to follow until nearly six months later, for it took that long to procure all the necessary documents and tickets for her. Even before Vera arrived in Chicago, Peter had new responsibilities: on November 1, 1926, he was appointed field secretary of the All-Russian Evangelical Christian Union, one of the two largest Protestant denominations in the U.S.S.R. His immediate duties were to serve as a traveling Russian evangelist in the United States and Canada, and to raise financial support for evangelism within the U.S.S.R. itself.

Although the Bolshevik Revolution of 1917 in Russia had been followed by many unpopular social and economic measures, by the time of Peter's return home in late 1925 the nation was firmly under communist control. However, with the possible exception of the modern era, the period from 1923 to 1928 is now seen to have been marked by some of the best opportunities for evangelism in the whole of Russian history. This was due to the 1923 Lenin Constitution which provided freedom for both religious and antireligious groups to proselytize. Such freedom had not been guaranteed previously under the Tsars, and was not to be available in practice again under the communists, from 1928 right through to the early 1990s. These were to be long, hard decades indeed for Russian churches and their members.

From the time of his return to the United States in 1926 until 1934 when he founded a new missionary society — and even more so thereafter — Peter was very often away from the home he and Vera had set up in Chicago. His absences were thus part of little Ruth's life from the very day of her birth.

On March 29, 1928, when Vera went into labor, Peter was away in North Dakota, sharing the Gospel and telling of the needs of the people of Russia. Vera, as yet knowing little English, called in a Russian-Jewish midwife when she realized her baby was about to be born.

Immediately after the delivery, a telegram was sent to Peter. When this reached him at the farm where he was staying, he began to pray about a name for his new daughter. Peter and Vera had already decided that if they had a boy, his name would be Peter too. But they had never discussed what name they would choose if they had a girl! So Peter leafed through his Bible. It kept opening to the Old Testament book of Ruth. Peter thought about the biblical Ruth — a shining example of personal commitment and obedience, she was therefore a woman much used of God. Peter prayed that his daughter would follow her example and also be true to the Lord. And so when he arrived home in Chicago soon afterward, he told his wife: "We will call this child RUTH."

In the Russian culture, every person takes on the first name of their father. Thus, Ruth would become known as *Ruth Petrovna Deyneka*, or Ruth Deyneka, daughter of Peter. But because they were living in the United States and friends said that most American children have second names of their own, another name was chosen accordingly. The English translation of Mrs. Deyneka's Russian first name, Vera, is faith. This seemed a good name for the new baby, so in English she became Ruth Faith Deyneka.

When Ruth's sister was born six years later, she was named Lydia Hope. And so it was that their poor brother, Peter Jr., in age midway between his two sisters, came to be told often — and teasingly — that he was the Charity which ensured there was Faith, Hope and Charity in the Deyneka household!

Ruth grew up a very active, vigorous child. She was lively, inquisitive, and quickly learned to walk and talk, easily tiring her small, slight mother. And because Peter Sr. was so often away on his travels, it was Vera who carried most of the responsibility for ensuring that the three children were raised in a Godly environment. But her husband's frequent absences were sometimes painful for him as well as for Ruth. Once when Ruth was only three years old, her father was

Ruth at age two.

packing his case before leaving for a speaking engagement. Little Ruthie knew this meant he would be going away, so she clung to the case and cried "No, Papa! I won't let you go! *I won't let you go!*"

Peter Sr. later recalled that moment with tears. "I had to jerk my suitcase out of Ruth's hands. She wouldn't let me go! It nearly broke my heart. But when you say yes to Jesus, you *have* to go. I could hear her a block away, crying and calling out to me. It was not easy. My wife cried too — many times. When you say yes to Jesus, you HAVE TO PAY THE PRICE!"

But the time soon came when Ruth was old enough to travel with her father on school holidays or weekends. Her first clear memories of childhood involve an amusing little incident during what she describes as the "outstanding adventure of being taken by my father on an all-night train trip to the city of St. Paul, Minnesota. My Papa had graduated from the St. Paul Bible Institute, a Christian Missionary Alliance Bible training center. There were many churches in the twin cities of Minneapolis and St. Paul that remembered my father and would invite him to speak. Being a clergyman, he was given a free pass on the Milwaukee Road train, and he frequently traveled to speak at missionary conferences and special services. But this trip is the first one I remember — for more reasons than one! I was only five or six years old at the time. When we woke in the morning, it was vividly brought home to me that my father was different from most other men. I suddenly realized my hair was tousled and I had forgotten my comb. 'But its all right, Papa,' I said, 'I'll use yours!' And I remember so well that he replied, 'But Ruthie, I *don't use* a comb. I just use a wash rag on my head.' For even by then he was mostly bald! Somehow in those circumstances I managed to look halfway decent as we went to visit other people, and they helped by getting me a comb for the rest of the trip!"

Thereafter, the realization that her parents were also different from most other people in much more basic and important ways grew rapidly in Ruth. On the last day of 1933, Peter shared with a special friend his growing burden to organize a missionary outreach among Slavic people throughout the world. That friend was Dr. Paul Rood, then pastor of Chicago's Lake View Mission Covenant Church, later to become president of the Bible Institute of Los Angeles in Biola, California. After prayer, the date was set for an inaugural committee meeting one week later.

So it was that the historic first meeting of the new Russian Gospel Association was held in a dingy back room of C.B. Hedstrom's suburban shoe store. In addition to Peter, at that meeting were Dr. Rood, Dr. Arthur Brown (a medical doctor and surgeon), C.B. Hedstrom himself, and George Benson (another businessman). The new mission had been born. Soon renamed Slavic Gospel Association, SGA has come to do more than any other mission to encourage Christian believers and share the Gospel with unbelievers across the whole Slavic-speaking world. Peter's new responsibilities as general director of SGA were to take him away from home even more frequently than before.

Ruth was generally a happy child, but sometimes fretted to her mother when her father was absent. She often missed him and wished they could all be together more often. She would point out how other families spent holidays together, and how her friends had fathers who would come home by 6 p.m. and spend quiet evenings with them. But she recalls how her brave mother often gathered the three children to her and said, "Children, WE are the privileged ones, because God is using our dear Papa in His service." And instead of complaining as a lesser person might have done, she would say: "All of us, let's get down on our knees and praise God for our Papa, and pray for him where he is today" — naming whichever place or country he was in — "so that God will give him a special blessing, that God will protect him, and above all, *that people will be saved.*" Ruth remembers the three children being gently and lovingly pulled down onto their knees by a bed, or chair, or sofa,

Ruth at age four and a half, with her parents and Peter Jr.

just where they were, so that they and their Mama could kneel down and pray for their Papa. This would always make Ruth happy again.

Prayer was absolutely central to all the Deyneka family did. *"Much Prayer — Much POWER!"* was not just a slogan Peter coined. It was something frequently uttered to encourage or challenge others throughout the 60-plus years of his Christian ministry. Nor was it just the title of a book he wrote in 1958. Rather, it was one of his own most profound experiences and therefore one on which his whole life in all its different facets — personal, domestic, public and spiritual — became firmly based.

Ruth comments: "We did everything with prayer. We never began a meal without praying. Then when we had finished our meal, we would say a very loving phrase my mother taught us. Translated into English it would be: '*Praise be to God for this food, and thank you Mama and Papa.*' Afterward we would pick up our plates, glasses, knives, forks and spoons, and carry them into the kitchen as we had been instructed. These were routines of life that we were taught, very simply without ceremony, and something which we always did. But of all such routines, prayer was by far the most important."

As the Deynekas always thanked God for their food, so they always prayed when they went shopping for it. Shopping expeditions for other items, such as footwear, were also special subjects for prayer, largely because Ruth wore out her shoes very quickly. Mrs. Deyneka would always ask the Lord's help to find good, strong pairs that were relatively inexpensive! It was through things like this that Ruth became aware that their whole family was different from many others in relation to money. In the Deyneka household, this was always tight!

In the meantime, God had been blessing their new mission and its support base was gradually growing. Work inside the U.S.S.R. itself was becoming more and more difficult as Josef Stalin's grip tightened, both on the country and its Communist Party. But simultaneously, opportunities to share the Gospel with Slavs in the Americas and Western Europe were great and rapidly expanding. In order that SGA could do as much as possible to reach others for the kingdom of God, Peter further espoused careful, frugal living in his own home. In fact, in the interests of good stewardship of donations, it even housed the first SGA office.

In domestic budgeting, Vera's approach was consistent and exemplary. Ruth has no childhood recollection of the family buying new clothing. Their wardrobe consisted of articles given by other Christians. Far from being fazed by this, though, Ruth recalls the frequent thrills of inspecting the contents of boxes of used clothes brought by friends! Ruth always looked forward to rummaging around to see if perhaps there was a little garment that would be her size and which she could have. If there was something suitable, then for her, at least, it was new! To this day Ruth enjoys sewing, a pleasure she says dates from her early childhood memories of watching her mother convert old garments to fit one or another of the family. It has always seemed to her that old clothes take on a new lease of life after such attention! Ruth's family still regularly saves items for her to work on, and so renew, when she goes to visit. She considers such activities not as unwanted chores, but as creative and challenging tasks through which value can be added to things which otherwise might be thrown away.

Because of the limited funds available to the Deyneka family, they lived in low-cost apartments, usually in buildings which housed other Russian and Russian-Jewish residents. This was good for Vera, who spoke little English. In some ways it was not so good for the children, for their playmates included some about whom their parents had anxieties. Therefore Peter Sr. and Vera always carefully watched to make sure they knew what their children were doing and where they were. It was certainly a rule that they would always let their mother know where they would be at any time.

One day, though, little Peter Jr. went out to play without telling his mother where he was going. Temporarily, he was LOST! Vera became quite frantic as she searched for him, asking everyone if they had seen him. Even then, he could not be found. Peter Sr. even reported to the police station that his son was missing. But what impressed Ruth most of all was that Mama and Papa called her and her little sister, Lydia, together to commit the problem to the Lord. He was the One in whom they had greatest confidence of all. Shortly afterward, their prayers were answered, for Peter Jr. came home, safe and sound. He had simply gone out with another lad, for once forgetting to tell his mother, and had had such a good time that he had lost all awareness of the time!

Ruth began to be aware of still more differences between the Deynekas and many other families she knew. Although born an American citizen in Chicago, Ruth's Russian heritage was indelible from the very beginning. Thus another vivid, early childhood memory springs from her first day at school. This was, as she has put it, "very definitely an OUTSTANDING DAY" — not only because almost all her previous childhood acquaintances had been Russian, but even more because she herself did not yet speak English! At home, the Deynekas only used Russian. Ruth had been taught by Vera to read in the Russian language and write in the Cyrillic alphabet. And so from the day she started school at age six, she not only had new friends to play with, but also a new language to learn and even a strange new alphabet to decipher and memorize!

Food in the Deyneka home was always typically Russian. Little wonder that among Ruth's favorite dishes today are Russian-style potato pancakes, the beet vegetable soup called *borscht*, as well as *blintzes* (crepes), and *vareneke* — dough filled with cheese or meat, then boiled and served with sour cream. Even the food Ruth was given to take to school for lunch was different from the food the more American children had. She recalls that theirs included delicate little sandwiches made of soft white bread and processed lunch meats or cheese. Meanwhile, hers were made from dark, whole wheat or rye bread, cut more informally and filled with cottage cheese and jam, accompanied by celery or carrot sticks. Although her lunches were less expensive, they were considerably healthier than those of many of her friends. However, Ruth can be forgiven for having been conscious of the differences and even somewhat embarrassed by them.

To make matters worse for her, the lunches most of the other children took to school were wrapped in brand-new waxed paper, whereas Ruth's were packed in leftover bags in which bread or other items had been bought. Ruth, wishing to conceal such contrasts, would find some little corner away from the other children, get through her meal as rapidly as possible, then throw away the remaining evidence that she was different before rejoining her friends to run around and play!

In view of all these circumstances, Ruth could have been resentful of the differences between her parents and American parents and upset by the variances she felt between herself and other kids. She affirms, though, that neither was the case. "I remember being rather shy and embarrassed by the fact that I was different from others," she says. "But I accepted our situation, and because my parents would point out all the positive things, I was satisfied with life. I had a bed, I had a nice home, and parents who loved me. If I went home and asked Mama why I could not have all the things other children had, like bicycles, roller skates, fancy clothes, even nice lunch boxes, she would lovingly reply that things like that weren't important and we didn't need them."

It was important, though, for Mama and Papa to show their love to their children in some very tangible ways. This they did all the more effectively because they did not do so too extravagantly. Almost always when Peter Sr. had been away he would bring home each of his children a Hershey candybar — a simple gift from a frugal parent who used everything he had for the Lord, but a very meaningful gift for it confirmed that he loved and remembered his children. Today whenever Ruth sees a Hershey bar in a grocery store, she still thinks of her father's love for them.

Even at Christmas — when Peter Sr. would always try to be at home — the children did not receive big gifts. But the presents under their Christmas tree were very thoughtful. Ruth remembers with special fondness the "fluffiest, warmest pair of mittens imaginable!" which were her present from her parents one Christmas. She remembers them with special fondness because her mother confided afterward that it had been her intention to buy Ruth a plain, practical pair of gloves. It was her father who had insisted on those warm, exotic mittens instead — he knew she would enjoy them so much! So the love Peter Sr. had for his wife and his children, as well as for his ministry, communicated to his family and they appreciated it and responded with love of their own.

Thus the Deynekas owned little in the material sense, and even though Ruth, Peter Jr. and Lydia did not at first understand either the needs of others or how they might best be met, Peter Sr. and Vera were quick to obey the instructions in Romans 12:13 — *"Share with God's people who are in need. Practice hospitality."* Through prayer and practical kindnesses, Peter Sr. and Vera helped many in their own home. One memorable visitor was a man whose life had fallen apart because of a misplaced faith. He had come to believe that a particular world leader was the Antichrist prophesied in the book of Revelation, and had therefore spent a long time researching and writing a book to share that belief with others. When his ungodly hero had confirmed his actual mortality by dying, the man's life had fallen apart and he had become acutely depressed. A soul in deep need, he was welcomed into the Deyneka home to be cared for, both physically and spiritually.

For several years the little Deyneka apartment served as home not only to the family, but also the headquarters of the fledgling SGA mission. This had several interesting consequences. One was that when Ruth's sister, Lydia, was small, the SGA mail would be transported to the post office every day in her baby buggy because the mission did not own a car.

Another effect involved sleeping arrangements for the children. In their three-bedroom flat, Mama and Papa slept in one bedroom. The second was used as the SGA office, and the third as the guest room, always kept ready for visitors. Ruth, Peter and Lydia could sleep in this room when none were staying, but that was not very often. When guests came, the three children would sleep on the pull-down sofa bed in the dining room. The window faced a streetlight, and people passing it cast shadows on the pull-down blind. Ruth found these frightening, for sometimes to this imaginative little girl they would look more like threatening hands or even wild animals than umbra and penumbra of innocent people. But the family talked freely about the Lord in their home and were conscious of His presence at all times. Thus, Ruth knew He was always close, and if she ever became concerned by those misshapen silhouettes on the window shade, she would quickly close her eyes and say, "Lord Jesus, I know You are here. And if these things I see are really threatening me, You are greater than whatever they are! Please help me not to be afraid." She would then draw up her sheet over her head and quickly fall asleep.

As Ruth grew older, she became increasingly aware that she needed to ask God to cleanse her own sinful, human nature so she could enter a real personal relationship with Him. One related incident, when she was six or seven years old, remains particularly clear in her mind. It was a bright, sunny day. She was watching Mama on her hands and knees, scrubbing the kitchen floor. As Ruth leaned against the frame of the open doorway leading from the sitting room, Vera used what she was doing to illustrate the words of Jesus in Matthew 5:8 — *"Blessed are the PURE IN HEART, for they will see God."* She taught her daughter that verse, stressing that if Ruth wished to someday see God herself, her heart would have to be made pure first. Ruth often remembered this as her mother continued to encourage her to holy living.

Thus, Ruth was to be merely nine years old when the Protector of her early childhood years became her personal Savior and Friend too. Her birthday had come and gone the day before. Papa, having been away on a speaking engagement, had missed it. Ruth describes the red-letter day which followed: "I remember so vividly Mama in the kitchen working at the stove and Papa sitting on an upright chair in the dining room, facing the kitchen so he could watch Mama work. I was sitting near him when he began talking to me. 'Ruthie, yesterday was your ninth birthday. You are getting to be a very big girl now. I was just wondering, when are you going to celebrate your *spiritual* birthday?' And he explained once more the way of salvation and the joy I could have through knowing Jesus personally. I had the opportunity to know that He was mine and I was His — the opportunity to commit myself to Him.

"In my mind right now I can clearly picture the scene. I can see myself getting down on my knees beside my father, putting my head down on his leg, and praying to Jesus to save me from my sins, to forgive me for them, to purify my heart, and to come and live within me. I remember also my mother coming from the kitchen, laying down the spoon she had been using, and joining us on her knees on the other side of Papa. All three of us prayed aloud to God . . . and I remember thinking as I opened my eyes, how *bright* was the yellow linoleum on the floor! I have never forgotten this whole scene from the day I committed myself — as much as I understood at the age of nine — to follow Jesus."

Ruth had always enjoyed going to church. Even the journey to and from their Russian church on Crystal Street in Chicago was exciting because the distance was considerable and required one or two streetcars. The family always went to church together, and if Peter Sr. was taking a service elsewhere in the Chicago area, the family would accompany him and the children would participate. Even when quite small, they recited verses of Scripture in Russian or English and sang choruses, standing on chairs to make them taller. Now, after the momentous event of her conversion, Ruth's enthusiasm for attending church grew even greater and she would sometimes be asked to give a short testimony.

As their childhood years passed, Ruth, Peter Jr. and Lydia were also encouraged to develop their musical gifts. There were many young people in their church, including many of Ruth's age. The church ran children's as well as adult choirs. A brother and sister, Nick and Mary Beechik, were leaders of the children's work. Very spiritual, they encouraged the growing generation to follow Christ. Very musical, they taught the use of several instruments. Nick was particularly talented with brass and taught Ruth to play the trumpet so she could play in the church band. Mary taught the guitar and mandolin for use in the church youth orchestra.

Later, both Mary Beechik and Ruth became SGA missionaries and have been lifelong friends. Mary Fewchuck (as Mary Beechik was to become) was to work most of her missionary life in Argentina and then Australia where she now lives. But she remembers well those early days. "I used to be Ruth's Sunday school teacher, then her brother Peter's too," she says. "On Sunday evenings during the sermons, the children would run downstairs for children's church. Some of the kiddies were unruly. I used to wish all would be like dear Ruth Deyneka!" And of Ruth's musical endeavors in those days, Mary says, "Ruth had to regularly attend piano lessons, and as in other areas of her life, she learned to *discipline* herself. Indeed, she would prove to be most faithful in anything the Lord led her to do."

As she grew older, Ruth increasingly came to recognize the overwhelming desire of her parents to prepare her to serve God, perhaps even as a missionary if He should call her in that way. Therefore, more emphasis was placed on Ruth learning to play the piano than other instruments because Mama and Papa thought the piano might be the most useful in Christian service.

Much later, Ruth's own daughter, Lydia — now married with children of her own — asked how Baba (Grandma) Deyneka had gotten her to practice, to really settle down and learn her music? In reply, Ruth confessed that in the early days her Mama had to sit beside her on the piano stool, sometimes even with a menacing strap within easy reach! The very threat this potential weapon represented was enough to remind her how seriously her parents considered the daily half-hour or so of practice to be! Later on, however, Ruth had been stimulated more constructively by "a very inspirational teacher" and piano practice became an enjoyable and important element of her young life.

In reply to further quizzing by daughter Lydia, Ruth admitted that she had still not enjoyed piano practice at all times and was sometimes annoyed that she could not be doing other things of her own choice. "Didn't you sometimes pout and perhaps complain, talking back, and even refuse to practice?" persisted Lydia.

"No," replied Ruth, in a more telling answer, "I don't think so, because I *respected* my parents so much! Ours was a household of *love*. There was just nothing I would want to do to hurt my parents, for they were so kind and loving to me. If I ever felt unhappy or disgruntled, I definitely kept these feelings to myself and did not express them aloud to my parents.

"This doesn't mean, though, that I was a model child! I knew I was the cause of many problems and heartaches. But I loved my parents in return, and to this day I am very grateful for the discipline they exercised generally — and for their insistence that I learned not only the Russian language, but music also."

Of the problems Ruth presented, one event is especially noteworthy — for although short-lived, she learned much from it. It happened on one of the family's quite numerous pseudo-holidays.

In place of true vacations, the family often accompanied Peter Sr. when he traveled to special services elsewhere in the United States. Each summer, he did what he could to ensure the children had some fun at the same time, and always chose to take the family to some out-of-town conferences where he was speaking and where they could stay for as long as a week. For much of each day the children were able to play or participate in the often varied activities provided in the conference center grounds — many of which, even in those days, were very well-equipped for fun for everyone. However, Ruth, Peter Jr. and Lydia were also expected to attend all the worship services.

When Ruth was about twelve years old, the Deynekas traveled to the northwestern corner of the United States to the Lake Sammamish Bible Conference near Seattle, Washington. At the beginning of one of the services, Ruth grew unusually restless. She simply could neither concentrate nor even just sit still! She begged her mother to let her miss that meeting, arguing that she had been to every other one. Surely she could be excused *just once?* Unusually exasperated, Vera finally whispered her consent.

Ruth tiptoed out, and soon found herself by the lakeside at the swimming area. Once or twice each summer, Vera would take the children by bus to Chicago's shoreline on Lake Michigan for a day in the sun, to build sandcastles and play on the beach. But she had never tried to teach them to swim. Now by Lake Sammamish, camp assistants were in the water, tutoring some children in swimming. Seeing Ruth, they invited her to join them. "Don't worry if you don't know how to swim," they said, "we will teach you!"

Ruth quickly went and changed into her swimsuit, then ran down to join them in the water. The instructors showed her how to float, then how to kick the water, and then how to use her hands and arms as paddles. Soon Ruth and her helper were in quite deep water and the girl said, "Come on, you're doing fine! Let's swim to that raft. I'll be right beside you!"

All went well for a few strokes. Then for some reason, Ruth lost her confidence: "I did something wrong! I can remember as clearly as today, going down, my eyes wide open, soon feeling the seaweed at the bottom of the lake." Ruth shudders, "I also saw the bubbles from my mouth and realized I was DROWNING! My twelve years of life flashed before me . . . but in those seconds I also felt a *sweet peace* as I said to myself, 'I know that Jesus is in my heart, and if anything happens to me I will be with Him.'"

Abruptly, everything became brighter above and in front of her . . . and she became aware that she was lying on the raft with someone giving her artificial respiration.

"I didn't really need that," Ruth continues, "I was all right. But I did notice they were also working on a bigger girl, the one who had saved me, and they had more trouble bringing her around. I was so relieved when she recovered too!

"But I was *very scared!* I knew this had happened because I had been disobedient and had talked my way out of that church service. I ran back to our cabin, got dressed, dashed back to the meeting place, and slipped into the seat by my mother. I had quickly combed and braided my hair, but it was still very wet. Mama's eyebrows raised as she stared at me . . . but she never asked me what I had been doing, and I was *so ashamed of myself* that I never did tell Mama or Papa what had happened!"

From that episode, two things ensued. Several years later, when Ruth was a camp counselor at an AWANA (*"Approved workmen are not ashamed"* — 2 Timothy 2:15) camp in Wisconsin, she submitted enough to the insistence of friends for them to be able to train her for the Red Cross medium swimming award — the only other time she has been swimming since that frightening experience at Lake Sammamish. The other, more lasting, thing is that she has never enjoyed the water since that time, and admits to even now having "*absolutely no interest in swimming!*"

More positively, her near-drowning experience deeply impressed upon her the need not only to obey her Christian parents at all times, but also to do everything possible to honor God since He may call any of us to be with Him at any time.

So Ruth, like her beloved Papa, and many more to whom they were to minister in years to come, became a "twice-born Russian." By the time she reached her teens, she had been spiritually saved from her sins, as well as physically preserved from possible drowning. She had long been consciously aware that her family was different from many others by reason of its Russian background and all that flowed from that. But she had also come to realize that she was now different from many of her school and neighborhood friends by reason of her membership in the family of God and her total accountability to Him.

More than 50 years later, thinking over those earliest years and her coming to personal faith in God, Ruth speaks warmly of her loving home and her father's challenge to commit her young life to Jesus Christ. From a very small child, Ruth had learned that God loves His children and delights to adopt more of them into His family. Her father, when preaching on how to be saved from the consequences of sin, often impressed upon his hearers the Bible-based analogy between his own family and God's family. With Vera, Ruth, Peter Jr. and Lydia in the congregation, he would explain that just as he was the father of his own children and would always love them because they had been born into his family, so God would always love and care for any who were born again through faith in Christ — for in this way they became permanent members of the family of God.

Ruth found these thoughts highly appealing, for she had had such a happy upbringing with such wonderful family relationships. She is sure that through her own family situation from the very time she was born, she was being prepared for faith in God. Many times before the red-letter day of her conversion when she was nine years and one day old, she had thought about her personal relationship with Him. But for one reason or another, she had put off seeking His forgiveness for the wrong things in her life and His help and guidance for the years ahead.

It says much for the spiritual sensitivity and discernment of her father that at the very moment he pointedly challenged Ruth about her need to be born again, she was not only ready, but even *very happy* to positively respond to that invitation. At that precise moment, she was glad to commit her own life to the Lord forever, without further delay.

CHAPTER 3

Early Whispers
1940 - 1950

"Probably a *missionary!*"

From a young age, this is how Ruth had almost always answered questions about what she wanted to be when she was older. And this was understandable, for she was growing up in the company of missionaries and was deeply impressed by what they did and what they were like. "Even when I was young I saw the value of missionary work," she says. "I saw the reasons for it. I saw it in practice. My parents were missionaries and I saw that they had a good and happy life with peace in their hearts. What child does not want these things? It was natural for me to want to be a missionary too."

Ruth tells of the joy and excitement the Deyneka children felt when missionaries were visiting their home. Such visits became more and more frequent as SGA grew larger. Visiting missionaries were interesting and kind to the Deyneka kids! They had inspiring stories to tell of the countries from which they had come, the people they had met, and how God was blessing them.

By nature, Ruth is a sympathetic person. From early childhood, she had been greatly moved by human suffering. Often she heard her father speak of her own Russian relatives in those earlier years in Eastern Europe, telling of those young men and women who had died so tragically of starvation. This was sad enough in itself. But Peter Sr. would go on to say that it was not so much the horror of the deaths of his brothers and sisters for lack of food that had been so hard for him to bear, but the eternal tragedy that they had died *never having heard of the love of God.* They had died in their sins, not knowing that God had sent Jesus to die for them on the cross of Calvary. Every time Ruth heard all this, from one church pew to another, she would sit and weep for the aunts and uncles she had never met, tears rolling down her cheeks because of the many in the U.S.S.R. who had never even heard of the Lord Jesus Christ.

By the time Ruth entered her teens, there were also compelling reasons for the family to feel deep sadness for those in Russia who already knew and loved the Lord. Under the dictatorship of Josef Stalin, life for Christian believers in the Soviet Union had become very difficult indeed. This was the period dubbed "The Age of Terror" by Alexander de Chalandeau. In his classic review of *The Christians in the U.S.S.R.*, Chalandeau records that after the passing of new laws by Stalin in 1929, "a great persecution followed, which was worse than anything known up to that time." To make matters even worse for many European Christians and non-Christians alike, World War II had begun to blight much of their continent.

Understandably, missionary work in many parts of Europe therefore became impossible. However, even as some major arenas for Slavic missionary work were closing down, new ones were opening up. Large numbers of Russians and other Slavs — seeking new lives after the ravages of World War I and the Great Depression which followed it a decade later — had emigrated from Eastern and Central Europe to the Americas. The South American nations of Argentina, Paraguay and Uruguay had been particularly favored by the refugees. These fast-developing countries had opened their doors to people of pioneering spirit who were prepared to homestead in marginal areas. Growing communities of Slavic settlers in South America were claiming new farmland from thick jungles and forests by felling trees, clearing undergrowth, pulling out roots and tree stumps, gathering up rocks and boulders, and painstakingly preparing the soil for ranching or agriculture. While this was a tough challenge for anyone, the freedoms from war and personal oppression proffered by the New World were easily incentive enough for literally millions of newcomers. Christians among them were meeting together and forming new churches.

In late 1940 and early 1941, Peter Deyneka Sr. visited South America to help spread the Gospel among new Slavic immigrants. And in a most unexpected way, before her father was able to return home, 13-year-old Ruth was to play a vital part in a new venture for him and SGA. This part seemed small to her at the time, but was important to her family. Moreover, through it the Lord breathed into her own heart and mind the first little whisper of a specific ministry call. Later, in obedience to this, she was to commit many years of her own life to a particular place and certain types of work for the Lord.

It was in the fall of 1940 that Peter Deyneka Sr. set out on his marathon missionary journey, several months long. He traveled to South America by ship, then moved from one community to another by whatever means of transport was available. Often this was a train or bus, but not infrequently a horse and cart, trundling over rough dirt roads. Many of the homes he visited were very humble, mud-walled with tin roofs. Before he returned home, the fruitful southern hemisphere harvest season had come. Many fields were golden with grain and food was plentiful. But Peter's travel diary shows that food for the spirit was uncomfortably scarce. He found a "GREAT HUNGER for the Bread of Life." In one meeting after another at which he spoke, "Hearts were melted, believers revived, backsliders redeemed, and sinners converted."

Peter Deyneka en route to a meeting in a remote corner of South America.

The strain of tedious travel, all-day counseling, and frequent preaching physically exhausted Peter. But each time he looked into the face of a spiritually needy Russian, he felt an overpowering urge to do all he could to ensure he or she found peace with God. Buoyed up by God's evident blessing on his ministry, Peter wrote home that his "heart was overflowing with joy" as he began his arduous journey back to the United States where his family was eagerly awaiting his return.

However, long before they were able to welcome him home they would be able to hear his voice — through a series of historic broadcasts from a pioneering Christian radio station in Quito, Ecuador.

Soon after Peter's conversion at the Moody Memorial Church in downtown Chicago, a young Christian draftsman-turned-missionary trainee,

Clarence Jones, had become one of his best friends. Together they had witnessed for the Lord. Together they had heard His call to serve Him wherever He chose, a call channeled through the forceful ministry of the then senior pastor at Moody, Rev. Paul Rader, who had challenged many to step out in faith into full-time missionary work. So together, Peter and Clarence had begun to venture out for the Lord with real vision and true Holy Spirit zeal. Some inspired by Paul Rader were to move quickly from his plainly furnished church with its sawdusted floors and simple wooden benches into much more modern environments, equipped with the very latest in high-technology devices. Clarence Jones became one such pioneer — his vision would soon be to found a missionary shortwave radio station.

At that time in the very early 1930s, radio stations — and even radio receivers — were still quite rare. Many governments had been unsure how they should respond to the unprecedented challenges and opportunities which the revolutionary new medium of radio was promising. Therefore, as Dr. Clarence Jones (as he had become by then) and another missionary friend of his, Dr. Reuben Larson, had traveled through South America seeking a suitable location for a new Christian radio transmitter, one country after another had been reluctant and said no. At last in Ecuador, where Dr. Larson had been based, they found the Ecuadorian government not only interested in such a scheme but also very willing for such a station to be established just outside their capital, Quito. Negatively, it was reckoned that there were so few radio receivers in Ecuador that they could be counted on the fingers of one hand! Positively, although God alone knew this at the time, the high Andean location would eventually come to yield some notable blessings. One was abundant water. This would be harnessed for hydroelectricity, not only to empower the radio transmitters and light the homes of missionary radio staff, but also to provide electricity supplies to the host city itself. And far greater unexpected benefits were also to flow from the unsurpassed transmission conditions from the top of that great mountain range on the very line of the equator.

After enormous effort, the new radio station, Voice of the Andes, made its first broadcast on Christmas Day 1931, in both the English and Spanish languages. Code-named HCJB (*Hoy Cristo Jesus Bendice: Heralding Christ Jesus' Blessings*), this was a truly historic, epoch-making event in the annals of Christian missionary endeavor. The first program opened with the hymn *Great is Thy Faithfulness*. This was to prove a more appropriate choice than Clarence Jones or Reuben Larson could have known at the time — for today, well over half a century later, HCJB is still very much on the air, a veritable cornerstone of global Christian communication and a major witness to the unfaltering faithfulness of God. From HCJB, the first Russian-language Gospel broadcasts in the world were made by Peter Deyneka Sr. in 1941, long before missionary organizations generally came to recognize the huge potential of radio as a ministry tool.

But how did Peter Deyneka Sr. come to make that first Russian broadcast? And how was his oldest child, Ruth, to become involved in Russian Christian radio at its very inception?

Before leaving the United States for his trip to South America in 1940, Peter received an invitation from Clarence Jones to visit him in Quito on the way home. Peter's return journey took him to Chile on the west coast of the continent, then northward through the Andes, eventually to the equator and up to Quito itself, nearly 10,000 feet high in the mountains.

The moment Peter arrived, Dr. Jones gave him the opportunity to preach in English via HCJB in a program directed toward the United States. After it, Clarence asked him: "Next time, why don't you preach in RUSSIAN?" Peter was perplexed: "But who would be listening?" Always a great missionary experimenter, Clarence responded, "Speak, and *we'll find out!*"

As the transmission date for the first Russian program approached in March 1941, announcements of it were made in English-language broadcasts to North America. These included an unusual message of a quite personal nature: would listeners in the Chicago area please call Mrs. Peter Deyneka (and Vera's phone number was given) to make sure she would be listening to HCJB the next day? Her husband would be preaching on it in her native language, Russian!

Now Vera had still learned very little English. Whenever the phone rang, Ruth (being the eldest of the children) was always sent to answer it. So when the phone rang (not once but many times!) in response to that message on the radio, 13-year-old Ruth was the first to learn that her father would be speaking on the radio . . . that this would be an *important event* . . . and that the *WHOLE FAMILY should listen!*

Ruth recalls switching on their big, old-fashioned, shortwave radio set, searching for the right wave band, and leaving the dials set to HCJB in readiness for the time when they could hear their father again. They were eager to do this, for by then he had already been away for several months.

At the advertised hour, the whole family gathered around the set and began eagerly listening, hoping to hear Peter's voice. They were not disappointed! Ruth puts it very aptly: "Soon my father's voice came booming over the airwaves. As we were sitting and listening to him preaching from

South America, the phone kept ringing as, one after another, friends exclaimed excitedly: 'We can hear your Dad! Are you listening? Can you hear him?' And I was able to reply, again and again, 'Yes, yes, thank you, we are listening to his voice!'"

Only the Lord could have known what an important occasion that broadcast would prove to be — important not just for the Russian people and for SGA, but also for the future life and ministry of Ruth Deyneka, that young teen-ager who had already developed both a deep concern of her own for unsaved Russians, and a clear picture of the benefits and blessings that can spring from missionary life.

Ruth explains: "As I listened to my father preach in the Russian language that day, I was *excited*, I was THRILLED. And somehow, some little seed fell into my heart and soul. Even so, as I sat there listening, just a young teen-age girl, I never dreamed that one day God would send ME to that station to serve Him!'"

Of course, many things were yet to happen before Ruth eventually arrived in Quito, Ecuador, as a full-time missionary with SGA. First, there were several more years of education, then much travel, early ministry experiences, falling in love, and marriage. Just as importantly, she would first have to learn much more about herself, the needs of others, and about her Lord.

Ruth soon took major steps forward in all these respects. Her father, on his return to Chicago from South America, was invited by the Russian Evangelical Church on Crystal Street in central Chicago to speak about his recent experiences. Preaching with characteristic vigor, Peter Sr. particularly spoke about the young people and children he had met. In the traditional Russian culture of that time, due respect was generally accorded neither to the intelligence of younger people nor to their ability to understand their need of salvation. Peter, being unaware or deliberately unappreciative of this, had called even children among the immigrant populations of South America to repent of their sins and make decisions to follow Jesus Christ. He was able to describe how hundreds upon hundreds of them had gone forward after his messages, and clearly and definitely accepted Jesus Christ as their personal Savior. Ruth reports that "as my Papa was preaching and telling of all these events, I remember my heart was very touched."

At the end of his message, her father made a fresh appeal to the Crystal Street congregation: if there were young people who would be willing to give their lives in service for Jesus Christ, would they step forward as an outward sign of their dedication to Him and their readiness to be obedient to His call?

Ruth went forward.

Recalling that defining moment, she says: "Very vividly I remember going down the central aisle of the church to the front and getting down on my knees. With deep emotion and many tears, I committed my life to serving Him among my Russian people. From that moment on, if people asked about my future I would still answer yes, I was going to be a Russian missionary — but not any longer just because it seemed the right thing for me to say, but because *God had called me to this* and I had made my personal commitment to Him. Now I was sure of my future. Now I had a *real aim* in life, and even at 13 I set

Ruth at age 13, the time when she committed herself to work for the Lord among the Russian people.

my sights upon it. At this age, it was of no significance to me that Russia was virtually closed to the Gospel. If there were atheists in power in the Soviet Union, they did not worry me. Had not my father just returned from a ministry trip among Russians in South America? I knew that the Lord would lead and guide me, and in due time would show me exactly where I should serve Him, whether in Europe or elsewhere. At that decisive point in time, the necessity was simply to *be willing to obey Him, and HAVE A COMMITMENT TO THAT END.*"

Thus Ruth came to make another life-changing decision, prepared to proceed further down the path of total trust in Jesus Christ. For her it was natural, not an act of heroism. Did she not deeply appreciate the family, church and mission atmosphere in which her parents lived out Scriptural principles of faith in God? Moreover, Ruth had had a basically Russian upbringing. To become a missionary to Russians herself was very logical. And time was to confirm that 13 was not too young of an age to make a true and right response to the call of Christ.

More recently, the trend in both Christian circles and Western societies as a whole has been toward delaying decisions about the career, or even the type of career, which a young person may enter. But Christ can still call people of almost any age to serve Him, for the first time, or afresh in some new sphere. And it can be easier to develop single-mindedness of purpose if we are called when young. This can have significant advantages over "keeping options open as long as possible."

Once Ruth had so publicly responded to the call of Christ, the pace of her preparation for missionary service quickened — at home, at school, and in church.

At home she learned much about SGA through helping her father with his correspondence. As she grew older, when Peter Sr. needed something written, many times Ruth would be the one to write it. Just as it became normal for her to handle phone calls professionally, so she became adept at letter writing. She sees herself today as a natural correspondent, and is sure this stems from the office work she began to do in the mission office in her own home when she was still in her early teens.

It was also in her own home that she first learned to testify to others concerning faith in the Lord. Often, people previously unknown to her would be brought home by her father. There, Peter Sr. would share the Gospel with them verbally, while Vera — through the warmth of her care for everyone — would demonstrate the love of the Lord practically. From early childhood, Ruth had become increasingly impressed not only by the naturalness of both these types of witness, but also by the noticeable impact they had.

Ruth saw the necessity and the value of pointing others to the Lord Jesus Christ, and increasingly became involved in the task of trying to bring others to Him. The ability to witness effectively and unselfconsciously to unbelievers comes more naturally to some Christians than to others. A natural ability to do so at the outset of full-time service is a true gift from God.

Meanwhile at school, Ruth's academic career continued to advance. Of that time, Ruth says: "I wasn't an overly brilliant student, but if I put my mind to my studies, I enjoyed them and I progressed quite steadily through high school."

Not long after the commencement of Ruth's education at Carl Schurz High School in Chicago, the United States became actively involved in World

War II. As Ruth progressed through the school years, she and her fellow students grew increasingly aware of departures of young men to the military, and in many cases overseas, to battle zones and front lines. This awareness, frequently reinforced by tragic war news from far and near, engendered in her generation an underlying seriousness which is rarely if ever matched in periods of peace. And Ruth knew that just as many of her peer group had to prepare themselves for possible foreign military service, so she had to consciously prepare herself for whatever Christian service the Lord had planned for her, whether at home or abroad.

During her teens, times in church also helped prepare Ruth for the future. Being a member of a large church had many obvious advantages. However, being a member of a *Russian* church in a predominantly English-speaking city and country also had some disadvantages. Although Sunday services for the whole Crystal Street congregation were held entirely in the Russian language, church activities for her age group were mainly in English. Prayer, however, remained almost entirely in Russian. This, combined with the exclusive use of the Russian language by the Deynekas at home including family prayer times, was to later cause unexpected problems and personal embarrassment for Ruth.

In the meantime, though, in at least one significant area of church life, Ruth was able to begin using skills she had been developing. As she entered high school, memories of Vera's strap beside her piano stool dimmed, for piano playing became a source of real enjoyment. In no small measure, this was the result of lessons she had begun to receive from a leading Christian hymnwriter, Merrill Dunlop, the originator of a large number of well-known Gospel songs. Of these, many have been published in editions of *Gospel Songs*, *Singspiration* and *Youth Favorites*.

Ruth describes Mr. Dunlop as "a wonderful teacher, a great encourager and a real inspiration to me." With his help, she developed a talent for what was known in those days as "evangelistic playing" — in other words, being able to play for services at church. When the pianist at Ruth's church married, opportunities arose for Ruth to play in the services. These occasions further deepened her desire to play better still. They also made her all the more thankful that her parents had made her persist with the piano when a child. So she completed the foundations for the piano-playing skills she has subsequently used throughout her missionary life, even to the present day.

While Ruth was in her teens, young people from Christian homes generally lived much more protected, sheltered lives than their present counterparts. Thus, most of Ruth's social contacts were within her church and it was natural that her best friends should have come from that circle. First and foremost among them was Pauline Mazur. Now Mrs. Andrew Semenchuk, Pauline is still one of Ruth's best friends.

Pauline's own story is both fascinating and inspiring. She became a born-again believer after her mother had trusted Jesus Christ and witnessed to her daughter about Him. Being the family of a Russian Orthodox lay priest, Pauline and her mother felt they should attend his Orthodox church even after their conversions, but also went to the Russian Evangelical Church on Crystal Street now and again for special events. Then, when Father Mazur fell gravely ill, Pauline, along with her mother and other members of the Evangelical Church, shared with him the need for a personal knowledge of God through faith in Jesus Christ. A week before he died, this religious Orthodox priest accepted Christ as his own personal Savior — an enormous comfort to Pauline and her mother.

As close friends, Ruth and Pauline were a real help and encouragement to each other. Pauline remembers the many times they traveled across Chicago to various church youth functions and the joy they felt at the great Christian festivals. Especially memorable were celebrations of the risen Christ each Easter morning at the vast Soldier Field stadium near Chicago's Michigan lakefront. Pauline recalls with pleasure the duets she sang with Ruth at Christian meetings . . . and the fun they enjoyed on the beach.

"Liberties were much fewer in Christian circles in those days," Pauline recently reflected. "Young people today have much more freedom than we had or wanted! But we did not feel at all deprived, for there were many things to do at church. We were less exposed to temptations outside the church. And in those days before television, we were also much less exposed to temptations which now invade the home."

Ruth's friendship with Pauline stepped onto a more distant footing after high school graduation in 1945. Pauline, who had been working as Peter Deyneka Sr.'s secretary, left Chicago for SGA's Russian Bible Institute in Toronto, while Ruth found herself heading in the opposite direction for an already well-known Christian training college in the small town of Cleveland, Tennessee. Founded by Dr. Bob Jones Sr., a noted Methodist preacher and friend of Peter Deyneka Sr., this college has since become the great Bob Jones University. However, even in 1945 it was to not-quite-18 Ruth Deyneka a completely different and exciting type of place and experience.

Ruth was glad to have a companion, Jeanette Porter, for her first long train journey from Chicago to Cleveland. Jeanette's father, Dr. Charles

Porter, a former pastor of Moody Memorial Church in Chicago, was a committee member of SGA. Jeanette helped to get Ruth settled into the new area, new culture, and new era of her life.

The Deynekas in 1947, during Ruth's college years (Lydia, Peter and Ruth in back).

Though discipline at the college was much stricter than today, Ruth appreciated it, for she had been well-disciplined at home. The students were even told what time they should be in bed and what time they should rise. Rules and regulations affected most areas of their lives — for example, the insistence that electric lights should always be turned off by the last person leaving a room. Far from finding such rules annoying, Ruth affirms that she appreciated the need for them and kept to many of them even after leaving college.

She also began to appreciate the different food. Whereas at home she had only had Russian-style meals, there in the southern United States she was confronted with such regional specialties as buttermilk biscuits, grits (a form of cereal), gravy and cornbread. Even more truly American students from the northern states found the cooking strange, and many had difficulty adjusting to the local diet. Ruth, however, took it in stride. She knew that if the Lord was going to call her to travel as a missionary, she would have to be flexible. For her, even mealtimes were missionary training! Looking back, she thanks God for helping her develop such an attitude so soon, for it would be put to quite strenuous tests in Europe, the Caribbean and South America. Today, she says she enjoys all kinds of food and cooking — a real blessing, for her recent travels have been even wider than before.

Not only did Ruth encounter types of food at college she had not previously tasted, she also met many new people, attitudes and ideas. Back home in the Midwest, her denominational experiences had been restricted to the Russian Evangelical and closely related Russian Baptist Churches. Happily, in her new situation where she mingled with young people from many different denominations, Ruth's personal faith and understanding of the Scriptures were strong enough to give her more pleasure than problems in learning of the wider Christian family.

However, her early days at college were not entirely problem-free. And her most significant source of difficulty was perhaps in the least expected area — prayer. Prayer had always featured prominently in Ruth's life. Her father and mother were prodigious prayer warriors. At home, nothing had been done without prayer, from shoe shopping all the way to the making of their mission, SGA. Through her whole life, Ruth had come to realize that all she had and had become had been brought about by prayer. Prayer was therefore a spiritual activity she had long appreciated and enjoyed.

At Bob Jones, there were evening prayer times when prayer requests were made in small groups and prayers were offered up to God sometimes voluntarily and at other times by one group member after another around the little circle. Unexpectedly though, Ruth at first found participation in prayer at college "very, very difficult!" She goes on to explain: "My prayers were short and hesitant, unlike my prayers at home. For some reason I felt *uncomfortable* praying out loud. Then suddenly, the reason for this dawned on me: until that time, through my entire life to that point, MY PRAYER LIFE HAD BEEN IN THE *RUSSIAN* LANGUAGE! Here, in this new place with new Christian friends, I was expected to pray in *English!* And when I did, at first it was as if I was just reciting something, whereas before my prayers would flow."

Thus, yet again Ruth had to train herself so that new dimensions of life and faith could be added to her rich Russian cultural and spiritual heritage. This was absolutely vital for someone who did not yet know where or what her ministry to her beloved Russian people might be.

And of course, others trained her too. At Bob Jones, the teaching, like the whole college atmosphere, was firmly Christian. Ruth particularly appreciated the classical music, drama and fine arts classes. Music was one of her greatest loves, but early on at college she became certain that, for her, "church" music would be much more important than "concert" music. She considered that using music to serve Christ was much more important than being able to use it merely to satisfy herself or others. So after the first semester, she switched from a music major to Christian education. She was to find this a much broader and more rounding course. It was one which she increasingly considered very valuable with her future career as a missionary in mind.

Among the other courses she took, speech was compulsory and drama was optional. Both, however, were to prove to be God's choices for her. Features of the speech course were preparing scripts and performing them, either solo or in speech choirs, good training for any would-be public speaker. Drama seemed less likely to be of practical use to the would-be missionary. But within a few years, Ruth was to find herself drawing very actively on even that training as she and her husband later came to present a regular evangelistic TV program! So although she had been unsure at first in which direction her studies should be directed, and was too far away from home to be able to discuss them in detail with her parents, she became increasingly confident that she was receiving and following guidance from above.

In her third year of study at Bob Jones, a fresh and completely unexpected opportunity arose, one with which Ruth was really thrilled — the chance to formally study the Russian language! This was something Peter and Vera Deyneka had required of all their children at a basic level when they were small, but neither Ruth, Peter Jr. nor Lydia had found joy in it then, perhaps because their lessons had occupied most Saturday mornings! Today, Ruth and Peter recognize the irony that, although they had mainly submitted to those lessons out of obedience rather than willingness, as missionaries to Russian people they have had much cause to be very grateful to their parents for them. Indeed, even by the time Ruth was only 20 years old she had come to see that a good knowledge of the Russian language could be used to honor and glorify her Lord. Therefore, as the college authorities began to broaden their curriculum and brought in a husband-and-wife team to teach Russian, Ruth jumped at the opportunity to study this again in a more advanced way than before.

Ruth also learned much at Bob Jones from activities organized by the students themselves. Its student societies, like those everywhere in the United States, were run by committees of elected officers. Although it did not occur to Ruth at the time that being involved in free-time activities was also part of her training for future missionary service, looking back she recognizes how valuable they were in such respects. "By being an officer," she says, "and even president of a literary society for a while, I had to learn how to keep records, how to file things, how to write letters when we needed things, and of course how to run business meetings in an orderly and efficient way. So I have come to thank God for *all* the different opportunities I had at Bob Jones — educational, spiritual and practical."

Perhaps even more than most higher-level education students, Ruth found it a struggle to make ends meet. It was even more so for her parents. There were tuition fees, board and lodging, travel, and everyday expenses to be met. Because family funds were always tight, from the very beginning of her college courses Ruth signed up for a paid work program. During her first three years at college, she waited on tables, cleared and cleaned the tables late into each evening, then got up at 5 a.m. the next morning to set the tables for breakfast. In her fourth and final year at Bob Jones — by now a university — she was appointed a dormitory assistant. She reveled in this new responsibility, for it more directly involved dealing with other people — even if most of the time it meant ensuring that the younger girls were in or out of bed punctually and that their beds and possessions were kept tidy! And by no means were all of those girls as disciplined or as comfortable with discipline as Ruth herself! Ruth's own mature approach to these duties, coupled with her sympathetic and caring nature, led the university authorities to invite her, when she was about to graduate, to join the staff as an assistant in the girl's residence. But she declined — by then she knew she would soon be heading for the foreign mission field.

Thus, Ruth's life as an undergraduate was very full and busy. Strongly motivated to learn all she could as a preparation for her future ministry, she was also constantly challenged and encouraged by student colleagues. Many of them had already committed their lives to Christian service too, and were preparing for missionary work abroad. Two of those friends deserve special mention. The first was Pat Auten, one of her prayer partners throughout the four-year college course — and thereafter for many more years until Pat developed cancer and was called home to Heaven not long ago. After they left Bob Jones University, Ruth and Pat never met again because they became too far apart. Pat and her husband went to Alaska as "tent makers" — working as teachers, but witnessing and working constantly for the Lord — whereas Ruth's extensive travels took her in virtually the opposite direction.

Academics have long held a concept of "invisible colleges" — groups who share similar attitudes and approaches to research problems despite being scattered in different cities, countries or even continents. Now, many other types of affinity groups have been spawned by the Internet, enabling those who mutually enjoy computer-age opportunities to share thoughts and experiences over distances of many thousands of miles. But long before any of these networks became popular or even possible, Christians in different places have regularly united their hearts, minds and souls in a global prayer net, and still do. Regarding her personal prayer fellowship with Pat Auten, Ruth calls it precious and says, "We prayed for each other and wrote, especially at Christmas time, for over 40 years. In these ways, we shared many joys and burdens together, though never seeing each other after leaving college. Since Pat has gone to be with the Lord, I miss her prayers even today."

Ruth's second great friend at Bob Jones was a close relative, Nick Leonovich. He, too, already felt called to Russian missionary work, though neither Nick nor Ruth knew then that in the far-off 1980s they would find themselves both working for the Lord in the same building — SGA's U.S. office in Wheaton, Illinois — both having gained long experience in the same ministry medium of radio! At Bob Jones University, Ruth found it comforting to have a relative in the same college, someone with whom she could share a familial feeling of home.

One friendship, however, was to become a source of great difficulty and raise deep points of principle. In Ruth's fourth and final year of college, she became more and more active in student missionary circles and was elected vice president of the Women's Missionary Prayer Band. Having to work closely with its counterpart society for men, Ruth naturally became acquainted with her equivalent male officer. Sharing common interests, as well as similar responsibilities, Ruth and this gentlemen often met on committees and in prayer and missionary meetings. Soon, a more personal interest in each another arose and began to develop. After a while, Ruth even found herself wondering about the possibility of life together with him in the future.

There was, though, a major problem. Ruth puts it this way: "He was a wonderful person, he loved the Lord, and his heart's desire, like mine, was just to serve Christ. But as we shared our requests together in prayer, I had to say that I had long felt called by God to RUSSIAN ministries. *But he did not!* He said he was leaning more toward China, should God open that door for him. But if He didn't, my friend had absolutely no burden whatsoever for, nor interest in, the Russian-speaking people!"

So as their friendship continued to develop in what Ruth describes as "a very nice and spiritual way," her dilemma only deepened. Would it be acceptable to God if she were willing to serve Him anywhere her friend might lead — even though her own call and subsequent commitment had been so unequivocally to the Russians?

Ruth continues: "I began to reason within myself and argue that there was nothing wrong with our relationship because we were both asking God to take our lives and use us for His glory. No matter what had gone before, I was inclined to marry that young man, whose company I was enjoying so much! But as I leaned in that direction, knowing he would not be taking me to the right mission field, my prayers became very clouded."

At home that Christmas time, Ruth decided to discuss the matter with her parents. She explained how the relationship was very honest and pure before God, and how she and her friend were in full agreement as far as serving Him on the mission field was concerned.

Fortunately, or unfortunately, at that point her father popped Ruth the awkward question: "Has your friend a burden for the Russian people?" She had to reply honestly, "No, *none at all!*"

Her parents were kind and sympathetic, but Peter Sr. immediately said, "Well, we are going to pray and pray heartily about this, because we feel you are so well prepared to serve God among the Russian people. You speak Russian, you know the culture, you believed God had called you to minister to them. We are going to pray that God will clearly show you His will!"

And soon God did — though neither in the way Ruth expected nor imagined! She confesses she was able to say "Fine!" to the purpose of her parents' prayer — but at the same time, she was stubbornly praying that it would be God's will for her to marry her friend after finishing her education the next summer! As Ruth bade farewell to her mother and father at the end of that Christmas vacation, she recalls her father asking her once more how serious she was about that relationship. Very sweetly, Ruth replied, "Papa, I really feel it will probably be right for me to marry this gentlemen, for he is a man of God and we both wish to serve Him."

Soon after her arrival back at school, Ruth was called to the office of the university president. He told her he had received a letter from her father, stating that he was very disturbed by her relationship with a fellow student.

"Ruth," said the president, "this is a family situation! But you are underage. I have to tell you that your parents are asking that you go home for a year, at the end of this term."

To say Ruth was shocked and upset is an understatement! Not only was that bombshell imbued with immediate implications for her personal life, but for her studies too. She had only one more semester to complete before graduation — now this would be delayed! But she instantly realized that she had no choice but to comply with the clear wishes of her parents. They were paying most of the costs of her education. Furthermore, she had always tried to be an obedient daughter. However much she disagreed with their decision, to her credit her instinct was to act as they wished.

So not long afterward, she packed up and went back to Chicago. On the journey home, her mind was in turmoil. She was upset and disturbed emotionally. Yet through it all, she had the grace to know that her mother and father were doing what they thought was right in the eyes of the Lord. She respected them for that. Therefore, the prayer she kept praying with complete honesty was: "Lord, you will have to *show me very definitely* that this is Your will, for at the moment I don't feel that way!" On arriving home she kept in close touch with her friend, by letters and phone calls.

While she had been studying at Bob Jones, SGA had continued to grow, and with it the volume of work in the mission office. Having time to fill, Ruth was now able to help with the office work. Despite her inner struggle, she enjoyed her tasks. After a few months, another of her close relatives, Alex Leonovich — Nick's older brother — came to visit.

The Leonovich family roots were in the same district of White Russia as those of the Deynekas and Demidovichs. In the purposes of the Lord, these families had always been great friends, and several members of them have long since worked together in Russian and Slavic missionary circles. Natasha, the much-loved mother of Alex and Nick Leonovich, was an aunt of Vera Deyneka. Thus Alex and Nick, along with their brother Peter and sister Betty, were first cousins of Vera, though of a different generation. Meanwhile, because of the relative closeness of their ages, Ruth considers Alex, Nick, Peter and Betty cousins of her own. Today, although past normal retirement age, both Alex and Nick continue very actively to serve the Lord — Rev. Nick Leonovich in radio and preaching ministries for Russian Ministries, and Dr. Alex Leonovich in the honored positions of president of the Russian-Ukrainian Evangelical Baptist Union (RUEBU) of the United States, and director of Slavic Missionary Society (SMS). Ruth has also since come to greatly value the loving support and friendship of Babs Leonovich, who became Alex's wife.

Genealogical details apart, Ruth had always particularly loved and respected Alex. And in turn Alex, a flower boy at Peter and Vera's wedding, had long had a soft spot for "little Ruthie." Hearing of her present predicament, he had readily agreed to her parents' request to come to Chicago and have a kind of big brotherly talk with her about her life and future. Their discussion lasted well into the small hours of the morning as Ruth and

Alex talked, read God's Word, and prayed together until about 3 a.m. Alex's wise counsel was this: Ruth had truly committed herself to God for Russian ministries because He had made His will so clear to her on this. Therefore, she should remain open to His further leading in this regard because He would go on leading just as clearly as before, beyond all question and all doubt. Concerning her friend, if he were truly God's man for her, God would keep him for her so they could be together. But for the time being at least, in view of the doubt she and others felt about him, she should let him go.

After listening to Alex's wise and loving remarks, Ruth's response was: "Lord, I truly only want Your will in my life. If this man is not the one I am to marry, then I am willing to give him up."

God responded swiftly to that act of faith. Ruth wrote to her friend, explaining the conclusions she and Alex had reached. His reply was quick and clear: he understood, and was sure he would find someone else to accompany him to the mission field. According to another friend, writing merely two weeks later, that was exactly what he had already done!

Thinking back to that relatively short, yet painful and pivotal episode of her young life, Ruth recognizes she made two key mistakes. One was *trying to get God to approve of HER choice* of future partner. The other was *being prepared to ignore HIS choice* of where her ministry should be focused.

Ruth concludes: "Motivated by thoughts of marriage, I lost sight of the complete picture God had for my life of service. I made the excuse that my friend was a wonderful Christian, who wanted to serve God as a missionary, who wanted most of the things I was longing to be and do — except be a missionary to the Russian people! I was forgetting that I needed to put *everything* into the hands of God. Today, I am so thankful that He did not answer all my prayers for guidance in the way I wanted at the time. After I made the break from that young man, both in my heart and in my thoughts, I sincerely began to ask God what He had for me next and how He wanted to use my life. He SOON showed me! Later, in His own time, He sent me the man of His choice, with whom to serve in Russian ministries.

"Meanwhile, I am glad to say, my former friend has had a fruitful ministry over many years in Columbia and God has greatly blessed him too."

CHAPTER 4

ℋis 𝒲ill, ℋis 𝒲onders
1950 - 1953

Once Ruth had renewed her commitment to missionary work among the Russian people, she began to seek from God the correct place for it. During her unplanned year away from college in 1949, she continued to help in the SGA offices which were now on North Kedzie Boulevard in Chicago. One day she heard there was a visitor, Dr. Robert C. Cook. At that time with Youth for Christ International, he was preparing for a large congress to be held in Europe. He had come to SGA to discuss arrangements for the congress prayer meetings which Peter Sr. had been asked to lead. Passing through the typing area, Dr. Cook saw Ruth, stopped, and said, "Ruth, why don't you come to Europe too? There will be many Russian refugees to whom you can witness in your own language. I will pray about this! Why not do the same?"

A few years earlier, during World War II, Germany had invaded countries to its east, including present-day Poland, Belarus, parts of Russia, and Ukraine. As it did so, it began to remove people from their homes and home countries to work in German factories and on farms. Sometimes entire families were taken; on other occasions, only older children or men.

So it was that by the end of the war, literally millions of displaced persons (DPs) were left stranded in strange and difficult circumstances. Most of the DPs could no longer be required to continue the enforced work they had been doing, but none were at liberty to go back home until their return had been reasonably organized. Furthermore, many of these unfortunate people had come to fear the new governments in their native countries and no longer wanted to return. Before resettling elsewhere, these people had to await agreements with potentially receptive nations, most of which were now in the New World continents of North America and Australia.

In the meantime, all the DPs had to be fed, clothed and accommodated. Living quarters were often organized in former army barracks — needed no more for such purposes since fighting forces had been scaled down and whole regiments of soldiers had been demobilized. Other housing was provided in low-quality, temporary, wooden or prefabricated huts. Overcrowding was the norm, with very little personal privacy. Meals were mostly prepared in communal kitchens.

Although conditions in DP camps in Western Europe were poor, further east — in the Soviet-occupied area of Germany, for example — they were usually much worse. Many displaced Russians in Central Europe were forcibly repatriated, while others were shot as traitors on the often wrong pretext that they had "allowed" themselves to be taken to work for the Germans. Other Russians from Central and Eastern Europe were managing to escape to the West, where they arrived as sad, frightened political refugees. They, too, needed temporary accommodations until they could move on to more permanent homes in the Free World.

Dr. Cook's unexpected and challenging thoughts rang through Ruth's mind all day long. So when work ended, she hurried to her little bedroom on the second floor of the SGA building and spent much time on her knees. "Now Lord," she pled, "I really want to be *sure* of Your will. I nearly made *one* mistake! Please make it clear what you want me to do about this ministry in Europe."

The first person to whom she spoke about the possibility of working in Europe was her father. He was thrilled: "That would be *wonderful!*" he said. "There is such an open door among DPs. We are planning a whole summer of ministry among them in various camps. A lady has donated a station wagon for us to use, so we will be taking a whole team. You can be a member of it!"

Shortly afterward, the Chevrolet station wagon was ready for collection — some 1,500 miles away in Dallas, Texas. Ruth went with her father to collect it, and give secretarial help with letters and other items on the long journey. They had a great time together. Ruth particularly appreciated the fact that neither then nor at any other time did her father or mother talk negatively about what Ruth has called her "little romantic episode." When her parents had prayed together about it, they had been sharing the matter with God. Once He had set Ruth's heart at rest, that was the end of the problem for her parents.

The donated Chevrolet station wagon was a beneficial ministry resource for years to come.

After their return from Texas, there was still a little time left before Ruth's scheduled return to college to finish her studies. It was suggested that she go to the Russian Bible Institute in Toronto, to take some courses in the Russian language. The Toronto RBI had been founded by SGA six years earlier to meet the growing need for well-trained, Russian-speaking Christians to work in Russian communities. Facilities at The People's Church in Toronto, whose pastor was the renowned Oswald J. Smith, had been provided for that purpose. Under Dr. Smith's inspirational leadership, The People's Church had become very missionary-minded and most supportive of Slavic ministries, largely because of the fast-growing numbers of immigrants from Central and Eastern Europe who were settling in Canada after World War II and the clear challenges they represented for pastoral and evangelistic work.

Ruth arrived in Toronto and immediately began to enjoy fellowship with the other students. They were all dedicated young Russian Christians like herself. All became good friends. One of them was Jack Shalanko from Niagara Falls, Ontario. She was destined to meet him again three years later, far away on the border between Italy and Yugoslavia. Meanwhile, in the Russian church in Toronto, Ruth began to find outlets for several of her talents, especially helping with the music and singing in the choir.

Thus, what could have been a most unhappy period in her life began to develop into what she describes as a "very, very happy and blessed time." Ruth and her father were booked to sail from New York to Europe on the *Queen Mary* ocean liner on July 7, 1950. So when Ruth returned at last to Bob Jones University to complete her final six months of undergraduate studies, she now had her first missionary assignment firmly fixed on the horizon — a clear aim with a firm objective.

Reviewing that sensitive period of her life, Ruth remarks: "At age 13, I had committed myself to serve the Lord, but in growing up there had been both forward paces and backward paces. Finally, during my last semester at Bob Jones University, I was able to put the recent past fully behind me. I was set to read several chapters of 1 Corinthians as a lesson assignment for my Bible course. I vividly remember lying on my top bunk, just reading along in the King James version. Suddenly, it almost seemed as if these words jumped out at me: *'Awake to righteousness, and sin not; for some have not the knowledge of God. I speak this to your shame.'* But it was as if my eyes and heart were made to read it in this way: *'Awaken, RUTH, and sin not, for some RUSSIANS have not the knowledge of God. I speak this to your shame.'*

"This was a startling confirmation to me that it was time to finish my schooling. It was time to put my call into action and go out to my people with the news of God's love for them all." Thus, encouraged in her spirit and with her heart and mind at rest, she enjoyed that last semester at Bob Jones. She successfully finished her studies, received her bachelor of arts degree, and prepared for her departure for Europe.

Ruth and her Papa share the platform at the Youth for Christ convention in Winona Lake, Indiana, just prior to their departure for Europe in 1950.

In SGA's *Slavic Gospel News* magazine for June 1950, this rather terse announcement appeared, completely concealing the mélange of emotions it must have invoked in the Deyneka family:

PETER DEYNEKA AND HIS DAUGHTER RUTH TO EUROPE
The Lord willing, Peter Deyneka and his daughter Ruth are sailing the first week in July to Europe where missionary conferences and evangelistic meetings will be held among the Russians, Ukrainians, Polish, Czechs and others in the following countries:

> Wales, Scotland, Ireland, England, France, Italy, Switzerland, Belgium, Germany and others. Brother Deyneka will be gone for about three months, returning some time in October. Miss Ruth Deyneka will remain for a year or longer, working among the Russian children, youth and women.

Vera bade the team farewell. She said much to Ruth, as any loving mother would have done to a much-loved daughter at the outset of such an open-ended journey to a distant continent. Yet despite the sorrow and anxiety Vera must have felt at Ruth's departure, she was much more concerned about her daughter's happiness than her own. "Ruthie," she concluded tenderly, "maybe God has the man that will be your husband waiting for you there in Europe. I shall be praying that you will know God's will in this and that He will bless and use you no matter where you go!"

Ruth laughed at the thought of a future husband awaiting her somewhere in Europe. "Oh, Mama," she replied, "I don't think so! But thank you for your prayers!" At that precise moment, romance could not have been further from her mind. Instead, she was totally taken up with the thrilling thought that she was at long last beginning to satisfy God's will as a missionary to the Russian people.

The journey across the North Atlantic passed smoothly and quickly, and Ruth and her father were soon enjoying the Youth for Christ congress in Brussels, Belgium, along with fellow Christians from many other countries of the world. But even the excitement of that great gathering was soon to be surpassed by an even more highly memorable day for Ruth.

As the congress was ending, Ruth received an invitation to join some veteran missionaries, Mr. and Mrs. George Grikman, as they went to conduct a Gospel service among Russian immigrant coal miners in a town not far from Brussels. That Sunday afternoon, Ruth and others traveled out from the Belgian capital by car to the home where the meeting was to be held. Many people gathered for it, glad of any excuse to leave their makeshift homes in old barracks for a while. Ruth was asked to give her testimony. She did so, delighted by that first public opportunity in Europe to witness for the Lord in the Russian language. Days before, when she had been invited to that meeting, she had gone to her room, gotten down on her knees, and thanked God that after such a short time in this new country and continent she would be able to personally witness for Him.

The typically Russian service lasted about two hours and included singing, poetry and sermons. At its end, the locals and visitors greeted and talked with each other before the Brussels group had to return to their car parked some distance away. As Ruth walked toward it, she became aware of a teen-age girl hovering nearby. When Ruth addressed her in Russian she responded, and a conversation developed as they walked along together. The more they talked, the more Ruth sensed that Georgina wanted to say something very important — but could not guess what it was.

"Finally," says Ruth, "I just decided to ask Georgina when she had accepted the Lord Jesus Christ as her Savior. She looked at me with the widest eyes and said, 'I *haven't!* That's why I am walking here with you. I wanted to ask you if, even at my young age, I could really know that Jesus Christ had washed my sins away? Can I really trust Him and know He will accept me to be His child? I always thought salvation was only for old people and not for young people, but you are young and look so happy that I want to accept Christ myself!'

"And so Georgina and I stopped just where we were and I responded to her questions. Then, in my eagerness, I said we should pray. She should ask God to save her, and then I would pray for her too. She heartily agreed! So we both prayed, and we both cried.

"And I thought, 'Oh Lord, I've only been on the mission field a *few days*, and *You've given me my FIRST SOUL!'*"

And so He had — a teen-age Russian girl from a family of displaced persons close to Brussels, a much treasured trophy of God's grace. What a reward for Ruth's faith and readiness to witness! What a confirmation of her commitment to the cause of Jesus Christ and her love and concern for her fellow Russians!

Sadly, Georgina's parents — although she was probably right to describe them as Christians — did not join in the joy of Ruth and their daughter as the girls ran up to them and exclaimed, "We've some very happy news to share. Georgina has just asked the Lord to be her Savior!" With deadpan expressions, the girl's parents — typically Russian in their attitude to young people who embrace the Gospel — replied: "Yes, well, when she grows up she will be able to understand what she has done!" Ruth was convinced that it was Georgina, not her parents, who already understood the Gospel most! And time itself was to confirm this. Exchanging addresses, Ruth and Georgina corresponded over the years and even met later in the United States. And Georgina has kept on living for the Lord.

Many more blessings on Ruth's ministry were soon to follow, though the conditions in which she and others witnessed were often tough, particularly for young women missionaries.

By 1950, already five years after the war had ended, large numbers of DPs and political refugees still languished in the camps of Central and Western Europe. By this time the numbers of those seeking political asylum were actually growing, as one by one the countries of Eastern Europe began to suffer under the control of new, hard-line communist governments. Bulgaria, Czechoslovakia, East Germany, Hungary, Poland, Romania, Yugoslavia, and even remote little Albania all became affected in this way. Stalin-inspired, Soviet-style control of both nations and individuals spread like wildfire. Such control involved not only *relatively impersonal* things like the means of industrial production and distribution, but also *more personal* things including social welfare and education. It even spread to *intensely personal* things, down to and including each individual person's mindset and religious beliefs. In all those countries, once communist governments had been installed, atheism was quickly pronounced the state religion. Individuality and self expression were often brutally suppressed. Small wonder that large numbers risked their lives attempting to leave the countries of their birth, desperately hoping that they would be able to begin new and better lives elsewhere.

It is completely understandable, therefore, that among DPs and political refugees alike there were deep needs and great opportunities for Christian witness and service. Unfortunately, most of these enforced immigrants were not allowed to work. As a result, time weighed heavily on their hands. Fortunately, camp authorities were usually more than willing to allow outsiders in to organize events — cultural, educational and religious — to occupy the inmates. And it was into situations such as these that SGA was sending more and more missionaries, seeking to encourage Christian refugees and to share the Gospel with the many who had not heard it before or had not yet responded to it. Most people living in the 20th century have too little time to think about eternity. Time was the one commodity the DPs had in rare abundance!

When Peter Deyneka Sr. reboarded the *Queen Mary* in the fall of 1950 in Southampton, England, to return as planned to the United States, Ruth went with him to the ship — but only to help him settle in his cabin.

"Are you *sure* you want to stay in Europe, Ruth?" he asked tenderly.

"Yes, Papa, I'm sure!"

"Do you need some money?" he inquired.

Ruth shook her head. "Why do I need money? I have $10 in my pocketbook and friends back home who care about my ministry. I have a ticket to Germany. If Mama sends me care packages of food, I'll be all right!"

Her father wept as he hugged her and said goodbye. Kneeling down together, they committed each other to the Lord. He said later: "Her courage TOUCHED MY HEART!"

Ruth was to spend most of the next two years working in DP and refugee camps, usually among the women and children. Her main colleague and companion was Frozina Kucher. Frozina was a girl of Russian heritage from a Slavic community in Western Canada. Blonde, blue-eyed and creamy-skinned, Roz (as most of her friends still call her) did not look tough enough to work in such arduous situations. But revealing a resilience which belied her looks, she had already done so most successfully for more than a year. Indeed, her quiet, sympathetic manner, firm faith in the Lord, and love of His Word have helped ensure that her ministries then and long into the future were greatly blessed.

Ruth and Roz worked together well, and the Lord began to use them mightily. Roz vividly recalls one meeting in particular which she and Ruth led at a camp in West Germany:

"I stood on the platform — one young, rather tremulous girl, facing rows of haggard, sad, Slavic people. I had just finished speaking from the Bible and praying. I asked all who wanted to accept Christ as Savior to stand. In response, *the entire audience rose!* I began to weep at their evident heart hunger, feeling helpless to counsel so many. I had studied personal evangelism in the Toronto Russian Bible Institute, but I had never expected anything like this.

"My co-laborer, Ruth, was also choked with emotion. 'Pray, Roz, pray!' she whispered. 'Tell the people to repeat the prayer after you.'

"As I prayed each phrase, a roar of response resounded from the audience. Hearts were eagerly opened to receive the Lord!"

Commenting on this and other memorable events from that period, Norman B. Rohrer and Peter Deyneka Jr. wrote in *Peter Dynamite*: "The fruit was ripe. Happy were the reapers to whom God gave the harvest!"

Roz and Ruth were truly happy as they witnessed the wonders of God's grace. And they worked together most harmoniously — in more senses than one. Not only did they enjoy each other's company and were at one with each other in the Lord, but they were also musical in different and complementary ways. In meetings, Ruth often played the piano or the new accordion which Peter Sr. had bought for her in Italy before his return voyage home. Meanwhile, Roz sang solos to Ruth's accompaniments, and sometimes the girls sang duets. And their music was also instrumental in winning souls for the kingdom of Heaven.

One such unforgettable day was in early 1951. Ruth and Roz were leading a service for refugees in a village in eastern France. Meeting in an apartment room, Ruth and Roz sang a duet of the enduring hymn by Joseph M. Scrivens, *What a Friend We Have in Jesus*.

They were just ending this when a commotion began in the nearby hallway, prominently involving the deep, raucous voice of a man who had had too much to drink! As the swearing, yelling and hollering continued, the owner of the apartment ran out to see who was making all that noise. On returning, she whispered to the girls, "Oh dear, that's Mr. Volkov. He's drunk again, and I guess he's looking for his wife. When he drinks too much he likes to beat her up!"

Roz suggested that Ruth should continue playing her accordion so they could keep singing one hymn after another. After a while they stopped and heard a very different sound — Mr. Volkov crying! They brought him into the room where, still weeping, he began to tell his story. When he had heard the singing of the Gospel hymns, especially *What a Friend We Have in Jesus*, even through his alcoholic stupor his mind had flashed back to his childhood years in the U.S.S.R. In particular, he had remembered similar types of meetings in his own home when he was nine years old. Once, his parents had invited friends and neighbors in and they had sung that very hymn. A few days later, in the middle of another meeting, there had been a hammering on the door. It was the police. Mr. Volkov recalled how everyone had tried to escape or hide. He had done so successfully. But his parents had been caught, arrested and taken away. From that night on, he had never seen them again.

Between sobs, Mr. Volkov continued his story. After that traumatic night, he had not continued to live the way his Christian parents had taught him — indeed, far from it! He and his brother had survived just how they could, sifting through garbage heaps in the nearby city of Riga, Latvia, in search of food, and joining with gangs of youths to intimidate and rob others. His whole life had degraded into one of sin and vice.

But, he concluded, chancing to hear Ruth and Roz singing that particular hymn with all its personal associations had broken through his tough facade, and he had begun to reflect on his wicked life.

Later that same day as he listened to the Gospel, he was convicted even more. Finally, he asked God to cleanse and restore his life, gaining His forgiveness by accepting Jesus Christ as his personal Savior.

The Lord also moved in powerful ways in the lives of the DP camp children. Undoubtedly, the youthfulness and enthusiasm of junior missionaries like Ruth and Roz were especially used of the Lord in children's ministries. In Austria, Ruth found herself addressing Russian children who had never before heard Bible stories. This was a result of the laws enforced in the U.S.S.R. over many years which forbade young people under the age of 18 from attending church, and made even Christian teaching by parents in their homes a punishable offense. Freed at last from such severe restrictions, many DP children were anxious to learn what the Bible said. For Ruth and Roz, it was a joy to teach them and to relate the famous stories of the Bible to everyday life in the middle of the 20th century. And it was wonderful for all concerned whenever some of those children or young people — whose early years had been so unhappy and insecure — came to plant their spiritual feet on the solid rock of personal faith in the Lord Jesus Christ.

Men, women, teen-agers, boys and girls were won for the Lord through Ruth's work and witness in Europe. By the late spring of 1951, she was full of thanks to God for the many blessings she had seen and received through the previous winter. Writing home, and so characteristically emphasizing blessings rather than personal hardships, she exclaimed, "I have never been so happy in all my life as I have been in the last six months in Germany and France. My heart is greatly stirred and moved with compassion for the DPs and refugees. Many have accepted the Lord as Savior, and believers have been encouraged."

It was an older SGA mission associate, Gospel singer Winifred Larson, who rightly stressed other aspects of that work in her article for the *Slavic Gospel News* magazine for the fourth quarter of 1952. Winifred had been one of the very first helpers at the SGA office soon after its inauguration in 1934, and had first met Ruth when the little Deyneka girl was only seven years old. Fifteen years later, Winifred had accompanied Peter Sr. and Ruth to collect that Chevrolet donated by a friend in Texas. In early 1952, she had been joined by Ruth on a speaking and singing tour of Great Britain.

Winifred wrote of those times as follows, referring first to Saturdays in the mid-1930s when Vera had often taken her elder daughter down to the SGA office to help with the cleaning:

> Without a doubt, little Ruthie engaged herself in a great deal of childish bits of daydreaming as she faithfully assisted us in the office with that which her little hands were capable of doing. I'm sure (though) that neither of us ever entertained a thought that that was our "boot camp training" and that our hands and hearts

might serve together in years to come, and in Europe of all places. Truly, God moves in a mysterious way His wonders to perform.

For 14 years, those pictures remained in God's camera shop until He felt that they were ready for gradual developing.

Winifred continued the same article, recalling that long journey they had made together from Chicago to Texas and back with the Chevrolet — and then turned to the hardships Ruth had subsequently endured during her DP work:

> Three years ago the first film developed. Ruth and I, together with her father, made an extensive missionary trip of several thousand miles, right in the midst of the time when Ruth was confirming her choice for life! I need not further elaborate how God has answered her mother and father's prayers, but the following year we were together on a similar journey in Europe, yet how different.
>
> Ruth has performed a most effective, faithful, fruitful and sacrificial work in the DP camps. It isn't so glamorous to leave American comforts and live in basement temperatures, atmospheres, and inconveniences and sometimes at the end of the month wonder if the salami sausage Mom and Dad sent would hold out. That which she has been able to harvest for eternity has repaid (her efforts) a hundredfold. God has placed His seal of approval upon it all by preserving her from sickness and dangers which are otherwise unavoidable because of the prevalent conditions.

The lives of itinerant missionaries frequently involve *arriving* in places, and frequently *leaving* them. Such was Ruth's experience in Europe from 1950 until she was due to return to the United States for her first furlough in 1953. It was the experience of most of her colleagues, too.

While Ruth and Roz Kucher had been working together in Germany, Roz had met a new arrival, Ruth's cousin Nick Leonovich. Like Ruth, he had traveled to Europe for SGA after completing his studies at Bob Jones University. Soon after their first meeting, Nick and Roz fell in love, married, and left the DP work to develop their ministry elsewhere. Ruth was delighted that Roz was now not only a friend, but also a relative — though saddened that their period of ministry together had come to an end. None of them knew at the time that in the early 1980s Ruth, Nick and Roz would all find themselves working together for the Lord with SGA in one place again. But that is a much later part of Ruth's story.

More immediately, it was decided that Ruth should relocate to Nice in southern France. This was to help an older SGA missionary couple, Paul and Nadine Naidenko, whose task was to share the Gospel with the thousands of Slavic immigrants living in that area. Most notable were families of the Russian nobility who had fled the U.S.S.R. at the time of the Bolshevik Revolution — while many members of the wider family of the Tsar were being cruelly hunted down and murdered.

As before, it was the combination of Ruth's youth and transparent happiness in the Lord which impressed others most, young and old alike. One of her hostesses wrote to SGA to say: "Only the Lord knows how much joy my grandchildren and I experienced during Ruth's visit here. I was walking around whispering: 'Mrs. Deyneka is indeed blessed of God by having a daughter like this!' I am 50 years old, but this is the first time that I have met a girl who is *so consecrated to the Lord!*"

This same correspondent continued by saying that ever since she had read in *Slavic Gospel News* that Ruth was on her way to Europe, she had prayed that God would send her to their village in France. Finally, "the happy time came, and at last my grandchildren and I were at the station to meet her. The children were biting their nails with excitement as the train was pulling into the station! Ruth and Mr. and Mrs. Naidenko got off. I had gone to the station on a bike and brought a wheelbarrow along. We put Ruth's piano accordion and suitcases into the wheelbarrow, and started for home.

"The children loved Ruth very much. She led them both to the Lord. She told them how she was saved as a little girl and asked if they would like to give their hearts to Jesus too. They said 'YES,' knelt down and prayed. Oh, what joy! *Praise the Lord!* We are going to keep on praying for Ruthie and for the other young missionaries who are carrying Christ's light to this dark world."

France in the 1950s was certainly not a country much illuminated by the clear light of the Gospel of Jesus Christ. In most cities, towns and villages there was — and still is today — much ritualistic religion, but little true personal knowledge of the Lord. And born-again Christian believers among the immigrant populations were proportionately almost as rare as true believers among the French themselves. Thus, there was great contrast between the scenic beauty and spiritual gloom of this sub-Alpine region. In her report to *Slavic Gospel News* in the summer of 1951, Ruth wrote as follows of a visit to the provincial capital, Grenoble:

> Mr. and Mrs. Naidenko and I were met at the railway station by a sister in the Lord, accompanied by her daughter. She is almost the only Russian witness there among hundreds of Slavic people in the city. A service was held in her home, and many attended. Tears came quickly as the hymns were sung and the Word was given. Literature was heartily accepted. Then this dear sister took us to another town about 60 miles away where we had another blessed service. Here there is a group of believers, but without a pastor or leader.

As so often in Russian communities, Ruth discovered that out of the many young people — even of Christian parents — very few knew the Lord. Most of the others considered that spiritual things were only for old folk and consciously ignored them. Meanwhile, somewhat paradoxically, the parents did not think their own children were old enough to be able to understand such issues. In one city, Ruth was able to witness tellingly to many of the teen-agers and others in their twenties in an impromptu session before some had to leave to join the afternoon shift at a local factory. Several of the boys were late for work because they could not bring themselves to leave the meeting.

Later, Ruth heard that those young people had been surprised — even astonished — by their encounter with her. They had never thought that anyone of their age could talk so freely about God and be so happy and satisfied with life! Several told their parents that they would gladly accept this young person's God if only they could hear more about Him and learn how to follow Him themselves. Ruth continued her 1951 *Slavic Gospel News* magazine report as follows:

> You can imagine how the parents begged us to come back. I have such a burden for these lost young people. Please join me in prayer that the Lord will send a (permanent) worker there soon.
>
> I cannot help thinking of the young people back home, so placid and content with everyday living while here so many are waiting for someone to come and tell them of the love of God. Young people of America, can't *you* hear the people of Europe calling you, "COME OVER AND HELP US!"

It was during Ruth's second summer in Europe that she spent time in Great Britain and Northern Ireland with Winifred Larson, mainly seeking to raise the interest of British Christians in the DP and refugee work on the European continent. A British office of SGA had been opened in 1950, following an inaugural British committee meeting which she had attended along with her father. By 1951, the new British section of SGA was already committing both personnel and funds to the work in Europe. Strategically located for this, it still exercises today its primary responsibility for selected countries in Eastern and Central Europe. On their United Kingdom journey in 1952, Winifred and Ruth spoke mostly to Christians about the needs and opportunities of the Slavic work. However, Winifred was glad to be able to report afterward not only that "Christians were revived, and young people felt the challenge and caught the vision," but also that "sinners were saved" during that itinerary.

Crossing over to Ireland, primarily for a Youth for Christ convention in Belfast, Ruth joined up once more with her father who had come back across the North Atlantic for a series of evangelistic meetings and to again lead the YFC prayer sessions. One of the young pastors attending the convention felt strongly that the Lord was leading him to visit some of the DP camps on the continent of Europe. At Mr. Deyneka's suggestion, a small team of four was formed to visit a very large camp near Trieste, then a "free port" between Italy and Yugoslavia. This teeming camp, the temporary home for some 10,000 refugees, had been visited a little earlier by SGA missionary Andrew Daneliuk. Andrew was appointed team leader for the new visit, with Ruth, Ethel Lutkie — another young SGA missionary — and the young pastor in support. Unknown to Ruth, the Lord was to use that expedition to bless her in an unexpected and enduring way.

In advance of the team's arrival in Trieste, Ruth had written to American soldiers responsible for the regular English-speaking youth rallies every Saturday, requesting that they reserve rooms for the visiting team. She also asked if the team could be met at the train station and helped to the home where they would be staying. As they were walking from the station to their *pensione*, a couple of the Christian soldiers who had come to assist them remarked that a new missionary who spoke Russian had just arrived to work in the camp. Ruth considered that there were so few young Russian-speaking missionaries that, whoever he was, she must know him. When asked the missionary's name, the soldiers could only suggest that his first name might be Jack. The only "Jack" Ruth could think of was Jack Shalanko, whom she had met during her brief period at the Russian Bible

Institute in Toronto. He had spoken Russian — but had been some way from completing his training.

The next evening, however, there was an English-language Youth for Christ rally in Trieste itself — and surely, whom should Ruth meet there for the first time in over three years but *Jack Shalanko!* Ruth confesses how surprised she was to see him again. He explained that after finishing his studies he had come to the mission field — having received a call from the Lord to DP camp ministries, very much like Ruth's own.

During the week that followed, Ruth and Jack took turns to interpret for the visiting British pastor as he spoke in the DP camp meetings. Then each day in a nearby park, the team plus Jack lunched together on meat, sliced tomatoes and bread, read God's Word, and prayed. Later, Ruth described the time as "a very wonderful week of fellowship and friendship, and joy in serving the Lord."

The week ended with their last services together on the Sunday morning and afternoon. Afterward, a few of the missionaries and camp leaders set off on a winding-down walk in the park. Ruth muses, "It was at that time that Jack showed interest in me personally, and I must say I did not expect it and was startled! But as I looked at him, I wondered what God had for us. Certainly, Jack had a burning desire to serve the Lord among the Russian people, and his message was a very deep, spiritual one as he preached. We said goodbye that Sunday night after spending quite some time together and talking about things of the Lord."

Returning to France, Ruth began to write to Jack. Sharing many things with each other through correspondence, their friendship deepened. However, Ruth confesses that she was still *"very surprised* when Jack wrote announcing his love for me, and proposing that we should get married! I confided in Brother and Sister Naidenko about our friendship, and together on our knees before God we asked Him to show me His will for Jack and myself, as to what God had in store for our lives."

Feeling peace about this relationship in a way she had never experienced over her earlier romantic friendship at Bob Jones University, Ruth was thrilled to be able to write home with the news of her engagement to Jack. Her mother had never met him, but Peter Sr. had heard Jack speak, albeit briefly, at his graduation from RBI and had been impressed. Thus, Peter Sr. and Vera heartily approved, and the wedding was arranged to take place during Ruth's planned furlough home at the end of 1953. In the meantime, Ruth and Jack were glad for one special opportunity for time together and to better prepare for their marriage than through let-

ters alone — Jack visited Nice for Christmas 1952. There, he too was able
to help in the ministry organized by the Naidenkos. So the faith of Ruth's parents, plus her own willingness to be obedient both to them and to the Lord,
began to reap the rewards they deserved.

In January 1953, Ruth sailed back across the rough North Atlantic to the
United States for her furlough while Jack returned to Trieste. They had enjoyed working together and had prayed much that the Lord would clearly
show them where their first ministry as a married couple should be. Because
"His ways are not our ways" (Isaiah 55:8), the door He was about to
open for them was altogether unexpected — it was not even one they had
ever imagined!

Twelve years previously, as a 13-year-old girl, Ruth had tuned her parents' shortwave radio set to HCJB's Voice of the Andes in Quito, Ecuador,
so that her mother and the rest of the family could hear Peter Sr.'s pioneering, Russian-language Gospel broadcast to North America. After it,
her mother had been overjoyed to be able to cable back immediately to
her father: *"Glad to hear your voice and message — came over very
clear!"* Peter Sr. had gone on to broadcast 16 daily messages before returning to Chicago. By then, he too had become convinced that radio was
a highly strategic new missionary tool. Clearly, it had great potential for
reaching Russians in North and South America — but even more for reaching them in the U.S.S.R. and other Slavic countries.

War and communism had virtually closed huge areas of the world to
traditional missionary work. But as Rev. Joseph Steiner — for many years
head of the Hungarian-language branch of Trans World Radio in Monte
Carlo, Monaco — has often strikingly observed, although *doors* into Eastern Europe might have been largely closed during that period of history, *the
roofs were open!*

Realizing this, immediately upon his return to Chicago, Peter Sr. had
energetically sought to enlist preachers to establish a permanent, SGA-
supported, Russian radio ministry from Quito. His first recruit for this had
been the Russian Chicagoan, Constantine Lewshenia, who had begun to
regularly broadcast in the Russian language via HCJB in 1942. It had been
intended that Const's assignment to Quito would be temporary since he
had been chosen to inaugurate a second Russian Bible Institute, this one
in Buenos Aires, Argentina. The primary purpose of this new school would
be to train pastors and teachers for the new churches springing up so fast
among Slavic immigrant communities in southern South America, the region which Peter Sr. had recently come to know so well.

Today, Constantine — living in Wheaton, Illinois — is by his own admission "almost completely retired." He grins as he recalls the early 1940s and his longer-than-expected first term at HCJB: "I had to stay in Quito until they found someone to replace me more permanently," he explains. "And Elizabeth Zernov was the one sent to do that." Elizabeth was one of a family of four very talented daughters, born in Russia, but taken by their parents to the United States when the girls were all still small.

Why Const's grin? During the overlap month in which Elizabeth and Constantine worked side by side at HCJB in 1943, they got engaged!

Subsequently, apart from a few years in the mid-1940s with Alex Leonovich holding the fort at HCJB, Const and Elizabeth helped set the RBI in Buenos Aires on its road to success. They then continued to work together in SGA radio ministries in Quito and elsewhere, having done so faithfully and effectively virtually to the present day. In 1994, Constantine's consecrated work for the Lord over more than 50 years was recognized by Chicago's Moody Bible Institute when it honored him as its Alumnus of the Year — an award richly merited. Meanwhile, the inspired and committed service of his wife, Elizabeth — over much the same length of time — has similarly been of the highest caliber. In reporting Moody Bible Institute's award to Const, a 1994 SGA press release read as follows:

> For 52 years, Const and his wife, Elizabeth, faithfully served SGA with the greatest distinction. Even after their official retirement from the mission, Const and Elizabeth still logged daily hours at SGA headquarters, helping whenever and wherever they were needed. Even now, their love and commitment to the people of the Commonwealth of Independent States (CIS) continues unabated, as does their service for the Master.

And what were the consequences for Ruth and Jack of the growing SGA involvement in South America? By 1953, advances in radio technology meant that programs could be produced more quickly and easily than before, and shortwave signals could be powerfully and effectively transmitted to virtually anywhere on Earth from a single station. The church in the U.S.S.R. was badly suffering from state-perpetrated persecution and was in deep need of encouragement from elsewhere. However, the Cold War between East and West was tightening its grip, so help for that church could not be given in time-honored ways. Seeing the potential of Ruth and Jack to become another very gifted husband-and-wife radio ministry team, Peter

Sr. proposed that they should relocate to Quito and join its SGA staff in radio ministries to the Russian people.

Jack had not been in Europe long and was enjoying his work there. Thus, he was at first unsure what his response to that new call should be. God soon gave him the answer, unexpectedly, yet clearly and conclusively. One morning he read in a local newspaper that the status of the city of Trieste — which since the end of World War II had been declared a free territory — was about to be changed: the United Nations had decided to unify it with Italy. In preparation for this, *all foreigners had to leave!* Jack recognized that, as a Canadian, he had no choice in the matter. God had spoken! Jack immediately wrote to Ruth and her father. He felt it would be right for him and his new bride to accept the invitation to move to HCJB as soon as possible.

So in a white wedding on the bright sunny day of November 21, 1953, Ruth became Mrs. Jack Shalanko, knowing that she would be setting up home somewhere she would never have thought of herself — in Ecuador, South America. Jack and Ruth's marriage service was held in Chicago at the Midwest Bible Church, where Ruth was to become a member in 1957. Her Papa officiated.

Ruth and Jack Shalanko on their wedding day, November 21, 1953.

However, the happy young couple knew it would be some months before they would reach Quito, for the board of HCJB stipulated that all new missionaries to be stationed in Ecuador should first acquire some knowledge of Spanish, its principal language. The school HCJB recommended was the Institute of Spanish Language Studies in Costa Rica, a small Central American republic just west of Panama. This school provided a special Spanish course run by Christian teachers who emphasized the use of that language in Bible study, and also organized practice for praying and preaching in it.

It was just as well, though, that Ruth and Jack did not know it would be over a year before they would reach Quito. They could not know either that only two years into the future Ruth would have to face the very real possibility of losing her new husband forever!

CHAPTER 5

Maqueños, Mules and Microphones

1953 - 1980

From the outset, Ruth and Jack were clearly destined to lead a most eventful married life. Even their first long journey together, one month after their wedding, quickly became more interesting than expected! Taking the train from Chicago to southern Florida, at Miami Airport they joined up with other missionaries also bound for the Spanish language school in San Jose, Costa Rica.

The second leg of their journey was by air to Havana, Cuba, where the Lineas Aereas Costarricenses aircraft landed for refueling. In the poky, smoky airport terminal at Havana, the whole group of missionaries in transit excitedly exchanged notes and tried to anticipate the Spanish-language training they would soon begin in preparation for a wide range of ministries throughout South and Central America.

Suddenly, out of the blue an announcement over the public address system attracted their attention: a small technical fault had been discovered on their aircraft. This would have to be repaired before it could continue to Costa Rica. But no spare was available in Cuba, and being New Year's Eve, one could not be flown in from Miami until the next day. The passengers had no choice — they would be staying overnight in a local hotel at the airline's expense. Hence, it was in Havana that Ruth and Jack spent their first night in Latin America and enjoyed their first encounter with true Latin American food. In particular, the mixture of rice and beans followed by papaya provided tantalizing tastes of things to come. However, all were glad when the piston-engined LACSA plane was ready the next afternoon to resume its plodding way to Costa Rica. At San Jose Airport, the flight was met by American missionaries Russell and Patricia Camp. Happy and smiling, they greeted Ruth and Jack: "We signed up to be your big brother and sister in San Jose and to help you settle in!"

Ruth and Jack were glad of this, for neither of them spoke a word of Spanish yet. And so much in the little republic of Costa Rica, near the eastern end of the Central American isthmus, seemed very foreign. They could not know then that their friendship with Russ and Pat, begun on New Year's Day 1954, was to deepen down the years, aided by the long period in which the Camps were to work in Ecuador for the Mission Covenant Church.

Help was needed with finding an apartment in the Costa Rican capital, as well as with renting dishes and linen, stocking the larder, and a host of other practical aspects of setting up home for an extended period in a strange place. Help was also needed with college orientation. In these and many other ways, Russ and Pat nobly assisted the new arrivals.

But it was still a difficult time for the Shalankos. Both were especially burdened for Russian people and had already worked as missionaries among Russians in Europe. Now, against their own instincts, Ruth and Jack were required to take many months out to study a language which seemed unnecessary for their future radio missionary service. As they discussed this, they despaired: "We'll *never* use Spanish in our ministry! Our hearts are burning for the RUSSIAN people!"

Thus, it initially seemed as if their enforced stay in Costa Rica might be a waste of time. When classes began, their doubts quickly deepened to despondency — their teachers only spoke Spanish, and it was hard to even gather what assignments were being given! For a while, Ruth and Jack had to rely on others in the class who already knew their Spanish numbers just to discover which pages and which exercises had to be completed!

The turning point came one evening. Depressed and almost desperate, Ruth and Jack agonized over their predicament. Finally, Ruth was led to pray: "Lord, for some reason You have brought us here to learn Spanish, but I'm not catching on to this language. It's very difficult for me to understand. I really want to do my best, so I need Your peace and help as we study here in Costa Rica."

Jack took up the theme: "Yes, Lord, if we are to spend time learning Spanish, please help me learn it to the best of my ability for Your honor and glory!"

God heard and was to answer both those prayers. Looking back now, Ruth smiles: "As usual, God knew many things we did NOT know!"

Not long afterward, Ruth and Jack learned of a Russian man living in Costa Rica, married to a local woman. They were taken to his small, simple home. When they began conversing with him in Russian, he was curious to know why they were in Costa Rica. When he heard they were there to learn Spanish before becoming radio missionaries at a station in Ecuador, his eyes lit up: "Do you mean at Voice of the Andes?"

When they said yes, their host ushered them into another room. In the corner stood a large shortwave radio set. He smiled and said, "This is my Russian friend. Every day I listen to the Russian programs from HCJB!"

From the way the man answered their questions, they realized he was not yet a believer. However, he affirmed that unless it was completely unavoidable he would never miss a Russian program from HCJB. At all other times, at work, or at home with his wife and family, he had to use Spanish. So it was a special thrill for him, so far from Mother Russia, to be able to listen to radio programs in his native language.

Ruth comments: "Meeting this man was a *real encouragement* to us and helped us feel happier about our time in Costa Rica."

Further encouragement came soon after this when they were introduced to a local Christian radio station in San Jose, call-signed TIFC. Jack was delighted when Bob Remington, one of the station managers, asked him to begin using the TIFC facilities to tape Russian-language sermons which could then be mailed to HCJB. In this way, Jack's missionary radio ministry could begin even before he and Ruth reached Quito! He certainly *did* wish that and began sending tapes to Quito quite regularly.

Together, these developments helped give Ruth and Jack the peace about their stay in San Jose for which Ruth had prayed. But Jack had also prayed that if he had to learn the Spanish language God would help him excel at it. God was to answer this prayer too — largely because Jack was particularly diligent with his studies. Ruth recalls how thrilled Jack was one Sunday morning after worshiping in a Spanish-speaking church: for the first time, *he had been able to follow the gist of the sermon!* In fact, Jack made rapid strides with his Spanish and in time came to speak it very fluently. He also developed a good accent because he recognized that many Spanish sounds are similar to those in Russian. Thus, Jack would be able to engage in Spanish ministries in Ecuador almost as soon as he and Ruth eventually arrived in South America — just one of the many things God had been able to foresee, but which they themselves could not.

In the meantime, though, Ruth and Jack began to learn some of the more frustrating aspects of life in Latin America, where delays of one kind or another are commonplace. The Shalankos had expected to spend two study terms, each four months long, in San Jose. Toward the end of them, jolting news came from Quito: securing additional Protestant missionary visas for Ecuador was proving difficult for anyone. HCJB hoped to be successful soon, but in the meantime, Ruth, Jack and others could only remain in Costa Rica and await better news! As we can imagine, the regular prayer meetings held by the whole group of Ecuadorian missionaries-in-waiting grew increasingly earnest! Yet those times of entreaty also helped forge friendships for life, several of which Ruth enjoys to the present day, especially with Pat and Russ Camp, Gloria Giesler and John Mosiman, Helen Broach and Nancy Woolnough.

By now, though, Ruth and Jack had the assurance that the Lord had some special plan for their growing, Spanish-language skills. Thus, the new delay troubled them far less than it would have if they had known of it from the outset. Furthermore, they had become aware that a new little Shalanko was on the way. Their son John, originally expected to greet the world in Quito, was born in Clinica Biblica in San Jose on November 26, 1954. Four weeks later, about the earliest that baby John could readily have traveled so far, HCJB signaled that the door into Ecuador had reopened, albeit only with tourist visas. Thus, rejoicing in the Lord's timing and after a scheduled overnight stop in Panama City, Panama, the Shalanko family finally arrived in Quito that Christmas Eve. They were glad to have completed their extended and testing trek to HCJB at last.

Hard as we may try, it is impossible for us to imagine the excitement and quickened heartbeats with which Ruth and Jack stepped off the plane in Quito. There had been so many months of planning and preparation, and so much study and prayer! Quito, nearly 10,000 feet up in the Andes, also left them breathless and panting on account of the high mountain air, merely two-thirds as dense as at sea level. Meanwhile, the colorful costumes of the nationals, the cobblestone streets, and the mélange of great public buildings and little mud-brick adobe homes — brown-walled with thatched roofs, or whitewashed and red-tiled — were as exotic to them as the grasses, flowers and cacti of the hillsides sweeping up to high, snow-capped peaks.

The Shalankos were soon glad they were already reasonably familiar with Spanish, for in Ecuador in the early 1950s little English was spoken. It was now easy to see how wise HCJB's language policy had been! Also, the local diet was much less of a surprise than it would have been without the stay in San Jose — though Ruth and Jack had not previously savored the delights of many local specialties, including field corn, *yucca* (manioc), *ahi* (a hot red pepper sauce), or *maqueño* (a fried banana dish).

What did they find on their arrival at HCJB itself? A thriving, cosmopolitan center of up-to-the-minute Christian missionary endeavor! The radio ministries of HCJB were already 23 years old. The first regular, SGA-prepared, programs to the U.S.S.R. had been broadcast in 1942. Although HCJB's staff levels had dipped during World War II, they had risen rapidly following the end of hostilities — from no more than 15 in 1945, to 87 in 1953, supported by over 100 Ecuadorian nationals. Christian transmissions in new languages and to new areas of the globe were being added at a steady rate.

But how and why is shortwave radio such an effective means of spreading the Gospel almost anywhere around the globe? Shortwave radio signals, like all electromagnetic rays, travel outward from transmitters in straight lines. They are then returned earthward by the ionosphere — a natural, invisible sounding board high above the planet's surface. Without the ionosphere, radio waves would go on spreading outward, ever deeper into space. But between the surface of Earth and the ionosphere, they bounce back and forth as they spread further and further round the globe. Therefore, usable "reception footprints" are found under the first, second, and sometimes even the third of those bounces! By careful engineering and good management of radio wavelength or frequency, signal strength and direction, and angle of elevation of the transmitted beam, it is possible to ensure reception areas in almost any selected areas of the world. Thus, through understanding and intelligent use of these divinely created features of the universe, by the mid-20th century radio missionary work had become possible literally *from one side of Earth to the other!* Better still, very wide-area coverage could be achieved from a mere handful of transmitters.

Soon after HCJB had made its own first broadcast on Christmas Day 1931, it had become clear that inspiration by the Holy Spirit had played a vital part in the choice of Quito as its site, although this had flown in the face of expert advice at the time. Today's broadcasts from HCJB benefit from an awesome one million watts of transmitter power. In the 1940s and early 1950s, broadcasts from Voice of the Andes relied on a mere one percent of that. Yet as Lois Neely affirms in her book about HCJB, *Come Up to This Mountain*, even in those years: "From Sumatra, from Sweden, from the high Arctic of Alaska, Canada and Russia, Christians were being encouraged and souls saved."

Normally a 10,000-watt transmitter, like that which had been installed at HCJB by amateur radio technician Clarence Moore at the end of 1939 and the beginning of 1940, would not be expected to successfully broadcast over such long distances. Dr. Clarence Jones, founder of HCJB, has gleefully explained its instant success and the general benefits of the station's special location in his own book *Radio: the New Missionary*:

> At a gathering of the top-flight radio technicians of the United States in New York in 1943, Mr. Moore was invited to be present. On his convention badge, there had been printed as identification: MOORE — HCJB — QUITO.
>
> More than one man came up to him with a warm greeting saying, "Hello, HCJB! We know you. We've been listening to your station for years. My! What a whale of a signal you put out up there — 3,000 miles away." Another person in the group that had gathered around chimed in, "Yep, same with me. I hear you beautifully. Say, you fellows must have had a smart bunch of technicians when you started out, to go way up on top of those mountains and locate your station there!"
>
> Pressing for details as to the reason for their statements, Mr. Moore said, "What makes you say that?"
>
> "Look here, fellow," the radio engineer replied, thrusting a radio textbook under his nose. "You know that ordinarily speaking and for some frequencies, *the higher above sea level you get your antenna tower, the farther out your signal will go!*"
>
> HCJB is nearly 10,000 feet above sea level, so with only a 100-foot antenna tower its signal is heard worldwide. God had said in the beginning of HCJB, "Come up to the top of the mount."
>
> "Furthermore," another radio man broke in enthusiastically, "we have found that one of the finest places in the world to broadcast a radio signal north and south is the *line of the equator.*"
>
> Thus it was, that some 14 years *after* God had called the non-technically minded founders of HCJB to the top of the mountains of Ecuador, close to the equator, He revealed the reasons for this step which He alone knew. Having seen the faithful guidance of the Spirit of God in this and a hundred other similar instances, the staff of HCJB can only cry out with joy in admiration of His wonder working, and say like Eliezer of old, "*I being in the way, the Lord led me*" (Genesis 24:27 KJV).

Often after that happy revelation, Dr. Jones would recall the much negative advice he had been given in 1930 — and then the total turnaround of the experts — with these ringing words: "*We knew all along* Quito had to be the best, because it was GOD'S CHOICE. It's nice that technology finally caught up!"

For Ruth and Jack, becoming associate members of HCJB was like suddenly becoming part of a completely new and very stimulating family. It was also a very loving one. Looking back, Ruth especially remembers "Mr. D.S. Clark, the field director of Voice of the Andes at that time, and other missionaries who were so kind to Jack, myself and little baby John. Of them, Joe and Betty Springer, beautiful musicians and such beautiful people, are dearest friends even today. Betty so often played the piano for our Russian songs. Ruth and Gene Jordan were also wonderful musicians — Ruth singing and Gene playing the violin and marimba, and directing. In the years that followed, Gene often accompanied the vocalists who recorded Russian hymns. Then there was our most frequent musical accompanist, Lois Hatt, who married Oswaldo Vasconez, and whose friendship I've enjoyed for many years. I see Lois even today in the HCJB compound in Quito, where she is still musical director. A new Canadian SGA missionary, Stella Jarema, joined the Russian staff at HCJB soon after we did, and our friendship began as we started working and recording music together. There was great fellowship with Swedish missionary Sonja Persson, and I could never forget Gloria Giesler and John Mosiman, with whom we had made friends in Costa Rica. They married in Quito — and even lived with us for several months while their apartment was being fixed. That was when our many years of friendship with the Mosimans really began. Their children and ours grew up together as close friends. I thank God for all these and others — for all that they showed us and shared with us as we commenced our radio ministry, which was to continue in Quito for many years."

Ruth and Jack set up home in a five-room apartment on the ground level of a three-story block rented from the Christian Missionary Alliance. Conveniently, it was only six blocks from the offices and recording studios. Although Quito is very close to the equator, and therefore experiences relatively subdued weather changes from one season to another, its high altitude ensures that air temperatures can fall quite low, down to the mid-40s at night. Fortunately, electricity was already available, though none of the apartments or homes had central heating. Body temperatures were regulated mainly by adding or removing clothing as required for personal comfort. A city water supply was on tap, but each jugful had to be boiled before drinking. This is still the case today.

All in all, Ruth did not find her work as a housewife and new mother too difficult or challenging. During the daytime, baby John often lay outside in his old-fashioned pram (one handed down by Mrs. Clarence Jones), protected from Quito's interesting — and interested! — insects by fine netting. At first the Shalankos found their sleep disturbed by the unexpected novelty of donkeys braying and mules making their own distinctive noises in the street outside, but soon grew accustomed to these and all other aspects of their new surroundings.

There was, however, to be one more severe test for Ruth and Jack before their ministry sails could be set for the foreseeable future. This test threatened to bring about an early return to the United States, which would dash all hope for their highly anticipated ministry by radio.

Only five or six days after arriving in Quito, Ruth noticed that little sores were beginning to develop on her baby's face. The first appeared between his eyebrows, then others on his cheeks, first on one, then on the other too. John became bothered by the sores and started to rub them — so much so that Ruth began to find little blood spots on his sheets each morning. Trying to stop the rubbing, Ruth put little mittens on his hands.

Sometimes the sores healed quickly, but other times they would not. Sometimes they were smaller, and sometimes bigger. His parents tried different home remedies. When these did not work, they took John to the mission doctor. The doctor was baffled, only able to diagnose some kind of skin condition. He referred John to a specialist in dermatology who suggested applying certain creams. But the sores continued to spread, even up onto the crown of the baby's head.

At this point, the doctor thought an allergy might be to blame. Despairingly, Ruth tried removing different things from his room — woolen items, rugs, even the curtains from the windows, but all to no avail. Another visit to the doctor led to the dubious suggestion that applying cloths soaked in warm water might help John feel better, for this might remove the scabs. But he then added, chillingly, that if this did not work, it would not seem fair to keep the child in Quito. "I would then recommend you go back to America," were his final words.

Imagine the turmoil in Ruth's mind and soul as she returned home to share those thoughts with Jack!

Ruth recalls sitting in front of the sink that evening and amusing John with things to play with in the water while she repeatedly soaked his little head, just as the doctor had proposed. All the while she was praying, "Lord, *just what does this mean?* We believed it was Your will to come here to Quito. We've spent an entire year learning a language which will not help us in Russian ministries elsewhere. And we've been here only a few months! Is it *really* Your will that we go back home so soon? And if it is, *whatever would we do next?"*

She also clearly recalls the agonizing debate with Jack at supper that evening. Their missionary work in Quito had already become much broader than they had originally expected. Their input to the Russian radio ministries of HCJB and SGA were growing all the time. Jack's Spanish was now so good that he was being asked to preach on weekends in many of the Protestant churches in and around Quito. And Ruth and Jack's musical gifts were also becoming widely recognized through invitations to sing together in English or Spanish, with Jack playing his guitar and Ruth her accordion. They had been praising God for all these different spheres of service. They were happy and fulfilled in their work for Him in Ecuador.

Together they agreed to make John's condition a matter of frequent prayer. But, Ruth says, "What I did not know then was that Jack really made this a matter for *concentrated* prayer! He very seriously told the Lord that he would try to do God's will, *whatever this might be*, and asked the Lord to make it clear. Most specifically, he asked Him for John's healing so that this would be a sign to us that we were truly in Quito by His will."

Two or three days passed. Then Ruth lifted John from his crib — *and realized that all the scabs were gone!* Two days later, all the redness was gone too! "OUR JOHNNY WAS HEALED!" Ruth still marvels over 40 years later. "And he has never had sores like those again. That was a really testing time for us both. But when Jack explained to me how he had prayed, we both knew that *God had healed John.* This was truly His sign to us that we were where God wanted us to be. So we continued there, with *increased determination and even greater joy* in serving Him."

The following summer, the Shalanko family was completed. Ruth has very good cause to remember the circumstances surrounding her second baby's birth. Dr. Ev Fuller of HCJB's medical department had been challenged by the need for a hospital in the region of Shell Mera, originally an oil exploration base some 80 miles by air south-southeast of Quito. There, on the rim of the Amazon basin, most buildings were traditionally made of wood because of its local abundance in the rain forest. However, Dr. Fuller and his colleagues had decided that it would be advantageous if at least the floor of the new operating room in the hospital were concrete. Knowing that Jack had worked in the construction industry before his Bible school training, Dr. Fuller asked him if he would go to Shell Mera to supervise the pouring of the suspended concrete floor they needed.

One day in the dining room of Ruth and Jack's apartment, Dr. Fuller announced the arrival of the building materials. Looking at Jack, he said, "Could you come at the end of April to take care of this job? The Gospel Missionary Union Conference will be held in Shell Mera at that time, so there will be many willing hands to help pour the concrete."

Jack had good cause to turn to Ruth and ask solicitously: "What do you think? Can I go? Will you be all right?"

For Ruth was expecting their new baby to be born on May 7!

As Chapter 6 will elaborate, Ruth had already witnessed ultimate examples of sacrifice by other missionary wives — *THEIR HUSBANDS HAD BEEN MURDERED!* By comparison, what she was being asked was likely to be a very small and temporary sacrifice. And there was always the possibility that the baby might put in its appearance a little later than expected.

So she was happy to say, "Yes, Jack, you can go."

Jack went to Shell Mera. His thoughts, though, were obviously back in the capital. All week, the other men teased him unmercifully about his absent-mindedness!

Meanwhile in Quito, life went on as normal. On Sunday, May 6, 1956, Ruth took 18-month-old son John on the rickety bus to a small service organized by some German missionaries from HCJB. They were trying to plant a new church among the German-speaking community in the city. Ruth had been volunteering to play the piano in their services until they could find someone else to do so more permanently. Not even the advanced stage of her pregnancy deterred her on that day. However, not long after the service ended, Ruth was gripped by her first labor pains.

Calling her friend Gloria Mosiman, who was not only a nurse but also someone with whom little John would stay happily, Ruth made her way to the hospital HCJB had recently opened in Quito. That evening, she gave birth for the second time. It was an easy delivery, the baby weighing in at a comfortable six pounds six ounces. Ruth praised God for so rewarding her readiness to loan Jack to Dr. Fuller at such a key time for the family.

The next morning, Dr. Paul Roberts, who had attended the birth, accessed the missionary radio network (for telephones had not yet reached the jungle areas). It was breakfast time at Shell Mera as he reported to its local missionary radio operator, Marjorie Saint, that he wanted a word with Jack Shalanko.

As the men hastened to pass on this news to Jack in the dining room, they joked: "It's the doctor. The baby must have been born!"

Jack did not think so. "No, it's just an update. This baby won't be born until I'm back."

Within minutes he discovered how misplaced that belief had been! Those around him soundly teased him for that, but warmly congratulated him on the good news of his daughter's safe arrival. Because the bulk of the work on the cement floor had already been completed, Jack was able to start his return journey to Quito immediately — by bus, the only means available. It took all of 10 hours for Jack to cover the distance, greatly stretched by the narrow, winding, landslide-prone roads up into the Andes.

Ruth was dozing when her husband finally arrived at the hospital. She awoke to find him standing by her bed. She smiled and said, "Have you seen her yet?"

Jack answered, "No, I didn't look at the new babies because I would not have known which was ours!"

Ruth could not agree. "It's very simple, Jack. She is the lightest, whitest baby in the nursery. All the others are dark-haired and dark-skinned!" Together, they went to admire their beautiful little blonde baby girl, Lydia Vera Shalanko.

With a home to run and two small children to raise, Ruth now had even more to keep her busy while Jack prepared and recorded his radio programs and extended his local Spanish preaching ministry. However, Ruth was still able to play important roles of her own in both those spheres.

It has long been standard practice for Christian radio studios to ensure that every new program tape is "auditioned" before transmission. This quality-control process is essential since recording sessions rarely run smoothly without interruption. For one thing, sooner or later every radio preacher or script reader stumbles on some words. He or she then backs up to the beginning of the sentence or section to try again. However, the operators do not always remember to remove the offending parts!

To ensure that its own programs were as error-free as possible, HCJB regularly relied on missionary wives and mothers to monitor new program tapes while they were working in their homes.

Ruth was very glad to help with this. "I loved my children," she confesses, "but 'auditioning' was an act of ministry I could do well and came to be one I really enjoyed. I found it a personal blessing too, for I could benefit from literally hundreds of hours of wonderful preaching while doing the housework, especially in the kitchen!"

Meanwhile, Ruth and Jack had discovered a small group of Spanish-speaking believers who were meeting nearby on Sundays. They were just beginning a North American-style, all-age Sunday school and asked Jack to be its superintendent. He accepted. The fellowship prospered. Soon its members constituted themselves as a church. Thus Ruth and Jack became charter members of Iñaquito Evangelical Church — and praised God as they watched it grow from 40 to many hundred members. Today, it is still expanding in very large new premises.

As the children grew a little older, it became possible for Ruth to spend more time in the HCJB offices, assisting with clerical work as well as radio program preparation and recording. When they turned three years old, first John, then Lydia, began to attend the station's own nursery school which was located on the HCJB compound. Ruth recalls that "the smaller children had a very sweet and loving teacher, Helen Howard, who kept them all happy with songs, stories and games outside. They would spend entire mornings at 'Aunt Helen's Nursery School' until collected by their parents at noon."

The Shalanko family (left), the Lewshenia family (center) and Helen Zernov (right) outside the HCJB radio compound in 1957.

Later, as John and Lydia turned school age, they began to attend the Christian Missionary Alliance Academy. This served missionary children from the whole of Ecuador and from Chile, Columbia and Peru. Conveniently, the school campus bordered on HCJB's land. Ruth continues: "So as John and Lydia went to school, I would go to work until I heard the lunch schoolbell. Having fixed lunch in advance, and left it in the oven if need be, I would run home to be there when the children sauntered in! After a quick wash of the dishes, the routine would be repeated in reverse in the afternoon. My next aim was to be home as soon as possible after the last schoolbell rang so I could be there to greet them again when they returned. We were so fortunate to have this school nearby, where the children could do all their formal schooling from grade 1 through grade 12."

Of course, much teaching of children also takes place within the home itself. From the moment John had been born, one particularly important decision had to be made: which languages would the Shalanko children be encouraged to learn? Ruth explains: "Jack and I decided that, just as our parents had taught us to speak Russian, so we would do the same for our children. So at home, we only spoke to each other in Russian and made the rule that John and Lydia would also only speak Russian when they were in the apartment."

Thus, initially, the Shalanko children's first language was Russian. But John and Lydia had no difficulty learning English from their many English-speaking friends. They also picked up Spanish in other ways, for they were living in a Spanish-speaking country and their school curricula included formal teaching of that language. Usefully, their classes covered Spanish grammar, reading and writing in Spanish, and eventually included the history of Ecuador.

Ruth concludes: "So our children became very fluent in three languages — until John was about eight and a half, and Lydia was seven. Then it became an increasing struggle to remind them to speak Russian at home, for they were now speaking English more and more. The time came when Jack and I decided we didn't care to have any more battles over this and dropped our Russian rule. Sad to say, their Russian knowledge then slipped away, for there were really no other Russian-speaking children they knew in Quito. But they have kept their Spanish into adulthood, of course, and speak this as well as they speak English."

Like all wise parents, Ruth and Jack involved their children in their own Christian ministries whenever possible and appropriate. At first, this began as a bit of fun. Ruth taught little John and Lydia some Russian choruses. Soon the youngsters were musical enough to be featured in programs on the radio. As the children grew older, they enjoyed singing with

John and Lydia Shalanko in the HCJB recording studio in 1962.

their parents around the piano or as Jack played his guitar. As young teen-agers, they learned to sing in harmony. Those were happy years! Ruth also recalls that "several times, in different churches, we were able to sing together as a family for the glory of God. And people in Russia today still remember hearing John and Lydia — or as we call them in Russian, *Vanya* and *Lida* — sing on the radio, and they tell me how much they had enjoyed that."

The Shalanko family even released an old-style, 12-inch, 33-rpm stereo record cut in 1972 by the Singcord Corporation. Entitled *Hearthside Melodies*, it featured several of Jack's own compositions in addition to old favorites. Also participating were the HCJB Ensemble, plus Lois Hatt Vasconez on the organ and Gene Jordan on the violin and marimba. John and Lydia joined with their parents in singing

The Shalanko family photo from their Hearthside Melodies *record sleeve.*

two of the songs. Eighteen-year-old John was already as tall as his father and soon to leave for college in the United States. Sixteen-year-old Lydia would have one more year in Quito before following suit.

Son John, now a teacher and coach at a middle school in West Chicago, Illinois, throws some interesting light on Shalanko home life together in Quito: "As a missionary family, we depended very much on the support of other people, and I know raising support is always difficult. But my mother and father always knew they were in God's plans, and very much impressed us that He would provide. Lydia and I were constantly taught that we should not worry about finances and possessions in this life. So we never had an excess of anything, and yet we were happy with what we had. We never went to bed hungry. We were always well-clothed. Somehow the Lord would always provide for His children. We were able to witness to this many times. I am still able to hold to that lesson today — as Mom does, too. With her numerous trips, and for her health and so forth, the Lord has continued to provide for her and enable her to do these different things, because so obviously they have been His will for her.

"My grandfather, Peter Deyneka Sr., wrote the book *Much Prayer, Much Power!* He obviously raised my mom, Uncle Peter and Aunt Lydia to believe this, for every day in our home began with prayer and devotions. Although my parents may have had their own ideas and opinions, they always looked to the Lord to lead and guide. And no matter what, He would show the way.

"And how did they raise us? They made it clear when we were young that God had put them in a leadership role over us and expected us to be submissive: He gives us this commandment in the Bible, in Deuteronomy 5:16 — '*HONOR your father and mother.*' Mom would say, 'When you get to be older, into college years, then you may change your ideas and make different decisions!' In the meantime, we were expected to have faith in what she and Dad decided. I now think this was one important reason why I was able to grow up avoiding many of the pitfalls my friends had problems with. And, of course, we always had some fun diversions to take part in. I especially enjoyed going fishing with my father, and my mom taught me at length to cook. This I enjoyed almost as a hobby. With her musical talent, she helped me with the piano. And although I had piano and violin teachers, she helped me prepare for recitals and practices."

If this sounds as if John is an appreciative son, he is! He concludes: "So Lydia and I were given a lot of opportunities to grow and develop, use our talents, and keep out of trouble. This made us well-rounded persons — and well-traveled ones too. I think of our life in Quito, long furloughs in the United States when I was in the fifth and eighth grades at school, and shorter trips to other parts of Ecuador itself. All these things have been a real benefit in later years."

Meanwhile, as the Shalanko children were growing up, the roles and functions of HCJB continued to grow too, and with them, the types of ministry which Ruth and Jack were able to exercise. In 1955, HCJB opened its hospital in Quito to serve both the mission staff and local people —

the hospital in which Ruth had given birth to Lydia and where Jack had met his beautiful blonde baby daughter. Subsequently, a number of health clinics were also set up by HCJB in neighboring areas. Then in 1959, a national industrial fair was held in Quito at which HCJB was invited to show the potential of television for Ecuador. Jack dressed in his favorite West-

Ruth and Jack in Western gear for one of their HCJB Spanish-language programs.

ern outfit — leather jacket, checked shirt, boots and cowboy hat — and sang to his guitar in both English and Spanish for the closed-circuit TV system in the conference center. This helped lead to the establishment of the first TV station in Ecuador, the first missionary TV station in the world. It was through this that Ruth and Jack came to be involved not only in widely transmitted English as well as Russian-language radio programs from HCJB, but also in their own regularly aired Spanish TV show!

The Shalanko family at an HCJB-TV recording session in the late 1960s.

No wonder they increasingly praised God for what Lois Neely described in her book *Come Up to This Mountain* as both the local *"soft whisper* of the Andes" and its *"MIGHTY SHOUT echoing round the world!"* Likewise, Ralph Freed, in his book *Towers to Eternity* about Trans World Radio, a similar organization to HCJB, refers to the "war of words" that has increasingly epitomized the electronic information age. Its battlefield is the sky, its weaponry radio waves, and its bullets the beliefs of broadcasters. God's Word is a rich repository of eternal truths, a precious store from which priceless messages and pictures of spiritual life and peace have been mined by media missionaries like Ruth and Jack.

Yes, Ruth and Jack's radio and TV programs were in a real sense heavenly treasures to multitudes — true treasures *gleaned from the heavens* — and their life in Quito continued to become more rich, varied, rewarding and blessed by God. But they would never forget exceptional events which happened very soon after their arrival in Ecuador — events which seriously threatened their very life together, their family, and Ruth's future ministries. Indeed, Ruth had to face the distinct possibility of life without her husband.

It had often taken faith for Ruth to pray *"Thy will be done!"* — but never more so than in January 1956.

CHAPTER 6

The Auca Episode
1955 - 1956

Like many countries around the globe, Ecuador became more and more cosmopolitan after the end of World War II. Thus Quito, in the late 1940s and 1950s, was increasingly attracting newcomers of many nationalities. Not only was HCJB itself expanding fast in this capital city, but also foreign embassies, international agencies, and multinational company offices — in step with the rapid growth of aid, trade and communications all around the globe.

During this same period, Quito's importance was also growing as a hub from which workers of many different missionary organizations were reaching out with the Gospel. Ever more remote corners of Ecuador were being targeted, along with more and more of its colorful, indigenous tribes and peoples.

Ruth and Jack had arrived in Ecuador on Christmas Eve 1954. They soon came to make friends with missionaries who felt called to minister directly to various Indian tribes. Within their first two years in Quito, the Shalankos had already stayed with Nate and Marjorie Saint in Shell Mera on the edge of the eastern jungles and vacationed at Dos Rios mission station in their steamy depths.

Then early in 1956, Jack and Ruth had become personally caught up in the awful aftermath of a new missionary venture directed toward a particular, previously unreached Indian tribe. Involving the Saints and several other American missionary families they knew, this venture had gone very wrong. For a time, the whole episode seemed to constitute one of the starkest missionary tragedies of the 20th century. Through this, key aspects of Ruth's own faith and trust in God were to be tested to the utmost.

Ecuador entails not only high Andean mountain ranges, but also much lower-lying tropical jungles which thickly upholster the western rim of the vast Amazon basin. Even by the mid-1950s some of the Amazon region was still uncharted and unexplored, and many of its peoples uncivilized and unevangelized. Little by little, though, the rain forest was being cleared for ranching or agriculture. Oil companies were planting bases deeper and deeper into the Andean foothill jungles to explore new claims. Shell Mera, where Jack had supervised the laying of that hospital concrete floor, had serviced some of those activities. New prospecting camps and outposts further into the jungle, largely or completely inaccessible on the ground, had been supported and supplied via the Shell Mera airfield.

About 10 years earlier, a new type of Christian organization now named Mission Aviation Fellowship had been founded by two ex-U.S. Army Air Corps pilots. The primary aims of MAF are to transport evangelical missionaries, their supplies and their sick to and from remote locations. MAF light aircraft were soon flying over several countries of Central and South America, ferrying workers of other Christian missions to and from stations difficult to reach over land, airlifting much-needed goods and serving as air ambulances for anyone requiring urgent medical attention.

Shell Mera had become a MAF base in 1948 when a little single-engine Piper Family Cruiser had arrived, piloted by ex-U.S. Navy maintenance crew chief, Nate Saint. Nate was a dedicated Christian and a former student of highly reputed Wheaton College in Wheaton, Illinois. He had also become an aircraft engineer of considerable experience and great ingenuity. One of Nate's most astonishing inventions was a method whereby a bucket could be lowered from an aircraft flying tight circles, so that the bucket remained stationary at the bottom point of the inverted cone whose sides were traced by the rope attaching the receptacle to the plane. By this method, objects could be transferred from an aircraft to the ground, or vice versa, without it landing.

Nate, along with Jim Elliot, Pete Fleming and Ed McCully — three missionaries working among the Quechua people of Ecuador, formerly conquered by the Incas — began to believe that the time had come to share the Gospel with other Indians too. They felt particularly led to a notorious tribe known in the Quechua language as the Aucas. The Aucas had developed a well-merited reputation as particularly fierce hunters and killers. They had resisted all previous attempts at friendly contacts, having injured or killed many who had encroached, consciously or not, on their territory — whether white men or neighboring Indians.

Considering it prudent to keep secret their new efforts to befriend the Aucas, those four American missionaries flew numerous and regular sorties over Auca territory in the second half of 1955. They took great care to gradually build up trust with the Aucas, exchanging gifts with them via the bucket suspended from Nate's plane. Encouraged by the response from the Aucas, they began to look for a sandbank in the Curaray River — close to several Auca settlements — to serve as a makeshift landing strip.

Also planned were a temporary camp and lookout treehouse in preparation for possible meetings with Auca Indians. To help construct these, a fifth young American missionary, Roger Youderian, had been brought in by Nate Saint from a station among the Jivaros at Macuma, some 70 miles away to the south. A former paratrooper, Roger had learned how to live and travel like the Indians themselves.

All went so well that by the first few days of 1956, the five men had been able to land and establish a base on a suitable sandbank which they nicknamed Palm Beach. To their delight, on Friday, January 6, two Auca women and one man had ventured out of the jungle to meet them. Personal contact had been established with the Aucas! Suddenly at dusk, after some hours together, the younger Auca woman disappeared into the jungle. She was followed shortly after by the man. The older woman stayed most of the night near the base campfire on the beach, but then left before dawn.

On Monday, January 9, 1956, Ruth and Jack were in their apartment in Quito preparing to begin a new week of ministry when their phone rang. A crisis prayer meeting had been called for that morning at HCJB! Because Ruth had a baby to look after, was pregnant with their second child, and HCJB was several blocks away, they decided Jack should go to that meeting alone. Those who gathered for it listened with astonishment as details of the attempts of the five missionaries to befriend the Aucas were described, culminating with the news that landings had been made on a convenient sandbank . . . and that the missionaries had already met Aucas face to face. Subsequent events have been vividly and poignantly described in the missionary classic *Through Gates of Splendor* by Elisabeth Elliot, wife of one of the five who made the landing on Palm Beach. Chapter 8 of her book is entitled simply *Silence*. It begins as follows:

> At 4:30 sharp Marj Saint eagerly switched on the radio receiver
> in Shell Mera. This was the moment when the big news would

come. Had the men been invited to follow the Aucas to their houses? What further developments would Nate be able to report?

She looked at her watch again. Yes, it was at least 4:30. No sound from Palm Beach. She and Olive Fleming hunched close to the radio. The atmosphere was not giving any interference. Perhaps Nate's watch had run a little slow.

In Arajuno, Marilou McCully and Barbara Youderian had their radio on, too. Silence. They waited a few minutes, then placed a call to Shell Mera.

"Arajuno calling Shell Mera. Arajuno standing by for Shell Mera. Any word from Palm Beach, Marj? Over."

"Shell Mera standing by. No, no word yet. We'll be standing by."

Not a crackle broke the silence.

Were the men so preoccupied with entertaining their visitors that they had forgotten the planned contact? Five minutes . . . 10 minutes . . . No, it was inconceivable that all five would forget. It was the first time since Nate had started jungle flying in 1948 that he and Marj had been out of contact even for an hour.

But perhaps their radio was not functioning. It happened occasionally. The women clung to each little hope, refusing to entertain the thought of anything really having gone wrong. Their suspense was the sharper because most of their missionary friends on the network were unaware that Operation Auca was in progress. In Arajuno, Barbara and little Beth Youderian had primped up a bit, since it had been planned that Rog would come to Arajuno that night while Pete took a turn sleeping in the treehouse. Surely the little plane would come winging over the treetops before sundown. They walked up and down the airstrip, waiting . . .

Just after sundown Art Johnston, one of the doctors with Hospital Vozandes, affiliated with the missionary radio station HCJB in Quito, came into the radio room in Shell Mera. The radio was still on, but Marj sat with her head down on the desk.

"Is something the matter, Marj?"

She told him the situation briefly, but asked that he not divulge it yet. If nothing serious had actually happened, it would be disastrous to publicize what was taking place. There was little sleep that night for any of the wives.

By 7:00 on the morning of Monday, January 9, 1956, Johnny Keenan, Nate's colleague in the MAF, was in the air flying toward the sandstrip which Nate had earlier pointed out to him. As he flew, Marj called me in Shandia: "We haven't heard from the fellows since yesterday noon. Would you stand by for Johnny's report?"

It was the first I knew that anything was amiss. A verse God had impressed on my mind when I first arrived in Ecuador came back suddenly and sharply: "*When thou passest through the waters, I will be with thee, and through the rivers, they shall not overflow thee*..." I went upstairs to continue teaching the Indian girls' literacy class, praying silently, "Lord, let not the waters overflow."

At about 9:30 Johnny's report came through. Marj relayed it to me in Shandia:

"Johnny has found the plane on the beach. All the fabric is stripped off. There is no sign of the fellows."

In Shell Mera, a pilot of the Summer Institute of Linguistics, Larry Montgomery (who is also a reserve officer in the U.S. Air Force), lost no time in contacting Lieutenant General William K. Harrison, commander-in-chief of the Caribbean Command, which included the U.S. Air Rescue Service in Panama. Radio station HCJB was also informed and news flashed around the world: "FIVE MEN MISSING IN AUCA TERRITORY." By noon, all possible forces which might contribute to their rescue, including the prayers of thousands of people in all parts of the world, were set in motion.

Tragically for the wives and children of the five brave, pioneering missionaries, God chose not to answer those prayers. Indeed, by Wednesday, January 11, 1956, it was certain that all five were dead. Later it was found that they had all been run through with spears and subsequently drowned.

Given those tragic events and the little that was understood about them at the time, it is easy to see that any attempt to rescue possible survivors would require a military-style operation — plus great courage from those venturing into the jungle for such purposes. The Aucas had even exceeded their own fearful reputation, if possible, by attacking those five missionaries who had come as friends and with whom they had previously exchanged many gifts. Very soon after the initial alert had been given, it was established that one of the Americans was already dead, but what had befallen the others was still unclear. A search-and-rescue expedition must be mounted — but since the Aucas were renowned for their skill at ambush, it was quite possible that any further visitors from outside would be venturing into a baited trap! Because of the difficult terrain and the position of Nate Saint's stripped and damaged plane on the makeshift Palm Beach airstrip, no aircraft other than a small helicopter would be able to touch down safely. More men would have to reach the site over land.

Ruth takes up once more the story of January 9, 1956, recalling all that Jack had told her as he returned from the crisis prayer meeting at HCJB:

"I remember so well when that meeting was over and Jack came home. It was almost lunchtime, but we sat down and began to talk about those events. The thing that struck us most was that the young men who were missing were *our own age*. We were all in our late 20s or early 30s, eager missionaries who had given our lives to serve the Lord in the various places to which God had called us. Jack and I personally knew all those young men. We had seen their happy smiles. Only five months previously, we had spent time with Nate in his home in Shell Mera. And now we sat and talked about the fact that one of our friends was already in Heaven. His missionary career had already been completed! He had done the job that God had planned for him. And he had gone up to be with Him for his reward.

"I remember very distinctly how, as Jack and I bowed in prayer before eating our meal, we dedicated our lives anew to the Lord and told Him that we wanted to be used in His service *no matter how many days or years we had left.*

"The next morning, Jack and I walked to the HCJB compound to begin our radio recording day. We had just entered the compound when Abe Van Der Puy, one of the directors of HCJB, stopped us. He said to Jack, 'We have decided to join a search party for the missing men. We know that one of them is with the Lord, but perhaps the others have just been wounded and are hiding in the jungle. A search party is being organized to try to find them.' And he asked Jack if he would be willing to be one of the seven missionary men they hoped to assign to it."

In her short married life thus far, Ruth had already come to respect Jack's ability to cope with the natural challenges of untamed country and its populations of wild animals. He had grown up loving outdoor life — hiking, camping, hunting and fishing were pursuits he had enjoyed long before moving to Quito. On Saturdays in Ecuador, whenever there was the time and opportunity, he engaged in such activities as a relaxation after days of study at his desk and tense hours in the recording studios. That was how Jack kept fit. And the game and fish he caught helped to provide variety in the diet of his family. But Ruth had every right to be very fearful of the Aucas. There was no way of knowing what those volatile, unpredictable savages might do next! Would a surface expedition be ambushed?

Would any of its members return alive? Of Jack's possible involvement in it, Ruth says this:

"As Abe asked Jack if he would join the search party, Jack looked at me, hesitating because I was already a mother and expecting our second child. I distinctly remember thinking that if those five wives could so willingly allow their husbands to serve Him among those Indians, *who was I to say no to this special request?* We immediately returned to our apartment so that Jack could pack a small bag with a few changes of clothing to take with him. After he had done this, and just as he was leaving the apartment, we paused and prayed together, committing the whole of the search team into God's hands, that they would have a blessed time together and even find the other men still alive."

The things Jack witnessed and experienced on his trek to the very heart of Auca territory were to affect him most profoundly. On his return, he recounted his experiences in Russian radio programs and often referred to them afterward during his English, Russian and Spanish preaching ministries. He also set them down later in his Russian-language book *How the Gospel Light Pierced the Darkness of the Aucas.* This soon became one of the most sought-after missionary stories in the Russian language. Now 40 years later, Ruth reports that she hopes to reprint it soon, bringing the story up to date through the eyes of Steve Saint and his recent explanation for the killings (outlined in Susan Bergman's *Martyrs: Contemporary Writers on Modern Lives of Faith),* which Steve has elaborated on in personal discussion with his old friend "Aunt Ruth." Meanwhile in the summer of 1956, Jack wrote this for SGA's magazine *Slavic Gospel News:*

I first heard of the attempt to reach the Aucas for Christ on Monday, January 9, at a prayer meeting called at 11:30 a.m. by Abe Van Der Puy. We prayed through tears and with burdened hearts. The next morning, a request was made for volunteers to go on the land party. In a few minutes I was packing my things, getting ready to leave for Shell Mera in three-quarters of an hour. My wife Ruth took it like a good soldier.

We drove to Shell Mera, learning on arrival that pilot John Keenan had flown over the site and had spotted in the river a body with a spear protruding out of the back. Our party consisted of

seven missionaries, supported by a number of Ecuadorian soldiers and Indian carriers. Hours of preparation and gathering of
supplies preceded going to sleep that night. I slept only two hours,
at the most. At 6:30 on Tuesday morning we were flown to Arajuno, where the others were gathering and where Ed McCully had
been stationed. Our missionary crew consisted of the leader, Frank
Drown, Dr. Arthur Johnston, Dee Short, Morris Fuller, Don Johnson, Bud Borman and myself. Drown rounded up the Indians who
were to go, and during this time we had a prayer meeting. It was a
precious time and God gave me Psalm 81. At 10:45 a.m. we were
set to go. We wore tennis shoes. Missionaries have found this is
the best for jungle travel. The Indians of course were barefoot.

The first five or six hours were over land to a point where the
Oglan River flows into the Curaray. It was a rough day. My 14-pound
load felt like a ton. We camped that night as Drown rounded up
canoes from Quechua Indians for the trip down river. We slept little that night.

Thursday morning we started at 7:30, using five dugout canoes. We were wet from morning until night as we waded through
rapids, etc. At 11:15 a.m. we met two canoes of eight Indians who
had been at the site of the massacre. They spoke Quechua, which
had to be translated into Spanish, and as they all wanted to talk at
once it was confusing at first. We headed for shore to learn more
from them, then ate while waiting further orders from a plane. The
Indians had seen the body on the beach. At 3 p.m. the helicopter
came over the first time, stopped, then went on to the beach and
came back to say that four other bodies had been sighted. We spent
that night with six guards on watch at all times.

The next morning, at 10:45 a.m. in our canoes, we rounded a
turn in the river and there on the right side of the beach was Nate
Saint's plane. I saw nothing that appeared to have resulted from a
struggle. Guards were posted and we went ashore after making
sure we would not disturb anything that might help in knowing
what had happened.

We were assigned different tasks. The plane had been stripped
and beaten down. There was a bullet hole in the windshield. Frank
Drown went into the treehouse and brought back the generator
for the radio transmitter, two candles, two large notebooks, a pair
of socks and a bottle of gasoline. Indians wading in the river lo-

cated first a camera, then a weighing scale, a smaller camera and two spears.

At about noon, Dr. Johnston and I left in two canoes to search for the bodies. With us went three soldiers and two Indians. The soldiers did not want to go, and only obeyed when the sergeant went himself.

We sighted the first body at the first bend, lodged against a large tree. A second was at the second bend, also lodged against a tree. Tension mounted with each turn of the river. The top sergeant sat in the forward part of the canoe and did not take his eyes from the thick jungle for a moment as the Thompson submachine gun lay cradled in his lap.

I frankly confess that I never felt so many shivers go up and down my back. Around another bend, we discovered a third body. Finally, we turned back as we could locate no more. Ahead of us lay the long and difficult trip upstream with the added weight of the bodies. I do not wish to go into any details about the bodies nor their recovery, except to say they were decomposed beyond recognition. Some still had spears in them. One spear had a page of a Spanish New Testament carefully tied around the handle.

A fourth body had been found in the river almost across from the plane. The fifth body, the one first sighted by John Keenan and the Quechuas, had disappeared and was never spotted again.

Thank God we know that when the trumpet shall sound they shall all stand there, whole, in glorified bodies, with a glory I'm afraid many of us will never know.

The trip took an hour and 20 minutes. We returned at 1:20 p.m. The bodies were laid out on the beach and identification made by Dr. Johnston solely through rings, wrist watches, belts and notebooks in the pockets.

While we had been gone, a common grave had been dug by the Indians under the treehouse. The bodies were then ready for their final rest, in accordance with the wishes of the wives that they be buried there.

It also started to rain — the fiercest storm I have ever been in. The rain came in torrents and it became as dark as the inside of a tunnel. The lightning and thunder literally shook the ground.

It seemed as though the devil was pouring out his last bit of hate. The Indians said that the Aucas were able to send rain through their witch doctors. Oh, how good to trust in God, the greatest power of all!

Internment was completed with a prayer of committal. Believe me, those were heart-wrenching moments as we laid to rest the bodies of these four saints of God. It was with heavy hearts and weary hands that the last shovels of dirt were thrown on the grave. There, far from those who loved them, far from their wives and children, we laid their bodies to rest. There were no gentle hands to lay flowers on their grave. Nothing but a cold, dreary rain and the noisy rushing river.

I have prayed and wept before the Lord many times since, that He would give me a love as these men had for the lost. They so willingly and courageously gave their lives, while many of us are afraid even to open our mouths to witness for Him where no danger at all confronts us.

Without a doubt, Jack's unforgettable experiences at Palm Beach challenged and sharpened his own ministry. In the years that followed the Auca episode, Jack became involved from time to time in Indian ministries himself, including Gospel campaigns among the Highland Quechuas. On one unforgettable occasion in the jungle near the border with Colombia, he baptized the first 13 of the Secoya tribe to put their faith in Jesus Christ.

Jack's description of the time he helped line up the human remains of the martyrs on the beach by the Curaray River was often in these words: *"As I looked on the bodies of those four saints of God, I felt as if I was looking at Calvary. They were men who had dedicated their lives to their Father in Heaven. They had gone forth to serve Him. They had obeyed His command. And now they are WITH Him, having fulfilled the Great Commission."*

Ruth's readiness to accept God's will for both Jack and herself as "a good soldier of Jesus Christ" continues to challenge us today! As a young, recently married woman with a toddler and another baby on the way, she had been prepared to accept His will, even if Jack were to be martyred also and she herself were to become a widow.

"The Lord gives, and the Lord takes away," says Job 1:21. Ruth, just like the widows of the martyrs, trusted God strongly enough to be able and prepared to echo the conclusion of that verse: come what may, *"Blessed be the name of the Lord!"*

Is *our* faith in God this strong?

CHAPTER 7

Mighty Shouts
1954 - 1980

From late 1954, Ruth and Jack's main ministry for more than 27 years was to be through the medium of radio to Russia — a type of ministry whose impact can scarcely be too highly rated.

By the mid-1950s, when they had taken up their new responsibilities at HCJB, missionary radio had already matured enough to have developed its own quite distinctive reputations in Christian circles — reputations which differed considerably from one Christian group to another.

To the *average church member* in the Western world, radio was — and perhaps still is — a powerful and somewhat mysterious medium lending an aura of prestige and even glamour to the radio missionaries. This was understandable, for still today regular broadcasters of any kind quickly become household names and enjoy some measure of celebrity status.

To *church leaders and mission boards* in the mid-1950s, radio was a wonderful, God-given medium whereby large numbers of believers could be strengthened and encouraged and unbelievers challenged — in a relatively cost-effective way. In the decades immediately after World War II, SGA recognized that this was the main — and in many cases the only — means through which the Christian message could be shared with Russians and most other Slavic-speaking peoples behind the Iron Curtain, that fortified frontier which communist countries had draped across Europe to defend and protect their personal, freedom-depriving ideology.

Last but not least, to the *radio missionaries themselves*, their chosen medium of ministry was a source of distinctly mixed emotions. Certainly it was *exciting*, because of its ever-present potential to help change the lives of many of its listeners. But in a way that laymen could never do, Ruth, Jack, and their other radio missionary colleagues also appreciated how very *exacting* it is to work in radio, with both program preparation and presentation calling for the highest professional standards. And soon after their arrival in Quito, Ruth and Jack had also come to realize how *testing* it can be for missionaries to be far away from the people they have been called to help, unable to interact with them face to face in time-honored ways. Indeed, for many years receiving feedback of any kind from listeners in the U.S.S.R. was to prove more difficult than from virtually any other major region of the world.

These particular problems arose because the 1950s, '60s and '70s were to be the most frigid years of the Cold War in international politics. Relations between the Soviet bloc on one hand and the Western bloc on the other truly fell into deep freeze. But how and why did this come about?

From the late 1940s, communism — principally promoted by the U.S.S.R. — was on the offensive everywhere. It quickly strengthened its newfound grip on the countries of Eastern and Central Europe, claiming country after country as its own. The whole world then tightened with tension as new nationalist liberation movements in Poland, Hungary and Czechoslovakia — all of which briefly promised their peoples greater freedom to think, act and worship as they wished — were brutally suppressed by communist-led forces. Further afield, Russian missiles were shipped to newly communist Cuba in the United States' very own back yard. This caused the tensest ever eyeball-to-eyeball confrontation between the United States and the U.S.S.R., when the entire world teetered on the brink of nuclear war. Soon afterward, one government after another in Asia, Africa and South America was overthrown by a People's Army or Patriotic Front, financed and armed by the Soviet communists and their new allies. Many armed conflicts flared up in which Western forces became involved, only to be defeated and even dangerously humiliated in the process. And as astonishing as this now seems, the ideology of communism — though so fundamentally flawed both in respect of its denial of God and its misplaced faith in human nature and our supposed potential for self-improvement — proved sufficiently magnetic to attract growing numbers of adherents, even in the longer-established democracies of the so-called Free World.

One consequence of all this was that life for Christian believers in Slavic countries became intensely difficult. Often it was even overtly dangerous. Although atheism was central to the creed of communism, the constitutions of many communist states spoke of religious beliefs being permitted or tolerated in their countries. However, the reality was very different. Great pressure was exerted on entire populations to renounce any faith in God, to give up church attendance, to cease religious education of the young, and to refrain from overt evangelism of any kind. The penalties for acting otherwise — in accordance with Christian conscience — were often physically and emotionally severe. In some cases, they were even fatal. Many children were removed from homes of Christian parents and placed in the "protection" of the state. Christian wives or husbands were fined or arrested, to be brainwashed or exiled to hard labor camps, never to see their families again. Church leaders were severely persecuted. Pastors were pressed to resign, or compromise their messages and betray their parishioners. Many were tortured for their unwavering faith in Jesus Christ and also became martyrs for Him.

It is not surprising, therefore, that traditional types of missionary work were impossible in most Slavic countries during this time, and certainly in Soviet Russia. Peter Deyneka Sr. had been free to travel and preach the Gospel there in the mid-1920s. There was to be no such freedom thereafter from the darkening days of the early 1930s until a new, more democratic dawn began to break in the late 1980s and very early 1990s. For more than half a century — as Ruth herself was to experience — visits to the U.S.S.R. by SGA missionaries could be no more than quite brief "tourist" trips, during which great personal restraint and extreme sensitivity to the difficulties under which local Christians worshiped, worked and witnessed were absolutely vital.

Throughout that long period, it was also intensely difficult to provide any practical support for Russian churches because of severe import restrictions. Making matters still worse, customs routines at the borders often exceeded even the strict letter of the law. In the case of the U.S.S.R., for example, possession of the Bible was not illegal, but copies of it were usually confiscated from Christian visitors by Russian customs officers. Two questions usually being asked of all airline passengers during those days were: "Have you any *pornography?* Have you any *BIBLES?*" In this way, the eternal Word of God was often equated with the most undesirable type of manmade material. Thus, the Bible became in practice — if not in principle across the Slavic world — a proscribed book. One result was that, as in the days of the Old Testament prophet Amos, there sprang up *"a famine through the land — not a famine of food, BUT A FAMINE OF HEARING THE WORDS OF THE LORD"* (Amos 8:11).

In view of this bleak situation, the rise of radio as a new ministry medium available to Christian missionary societies was truly a great and timely gift from God. As Peter Deyneka Sr. had realized during his very first visit to HCJB in 1941, radio enables the Gospel to be effectively communicated to listeners even in distant continents. And as Ruth, Peter Jr., Lydia and Vera Deyneka and others in Chicago had discovered by listening to Peter Sr.'s first Russian-language broadcast, Christians can be encouraged through radio and fed by others of God's family even though several thousand miles divide them.

It had been primarily to preach to Russians that Constantine Lewshenia had been sent by SGA to HCJB in 1942. And as the techniques and technologies of broadcasting improved and more young Russian-speaking missionaries completed their basic training in Toronto and elsewhere, it became possible to begin broadening the range of program types and formats. From the moment Ruth and Jack arrived in Quito on Christmas Eve 1954, they were well-equipped to take this process further and help develop broadcasts more fully suited to the needs of people across the entire Russian-speaking world.

On their arrival in Quito, Ruth and Jack had been greeted excitedly by Helen Zernov, a sister of Elizabeth Lewshenia. For with the arrival of the Shalankos, the local team of SGA radio missionaries nearly doubled — from three to five! And with Ruth and Jack's help, the number of Russian programs produced at HCJB rose. This growth was repeated as still more new SGA staff were sent to Quito through the 1960s and '70s.

Peter and Vera Deyneka (in front) with the SGA Russian radio team at HCJB in 1956: (left to right) Const and Elizabeth Lewshenia, Stella Jarema, Helen Zernov, and Ruth and Jack Shalanko.

By the time Ruth and Jack eventually relocated in 1980 to SGA's U.S. office in Wheaton, Illinois, SGA-sponsored radio program transmissions to Russia alone had topped 1,000 every month! The most from any station, about one-third that total, was from HCJB itself.

From the outset, Jack's principal programs were expository and evangelistic. A good Bible teacher, he had a special personal interest in prophecy and often preached about this when on the air. In response to requests from church leaders in the U.S.S.R., the Second Coming of Christ was a major doctrine he frequently addressed. Jack's eschatological themes were especially appreciated by hard-pressed Christians in the Soviet Union. Life here on Earth was so difficult for them, and seemingly held so little hope for the foreseeable future, that thoughts of Heaven were particularly welcome! This is how one Russian emigré wrote to SGA after a brief visit home to the U.S.S.R. in 1970:

> Late in the afternoon, the first day of my stay in my uncle's house in the U.S.S.R., I was rushed across the field to the home of a cousin. The entire group of people who had been there to greet me went too. Crossing the field to my cousin's home, I noticed a group of women pitching hay and obviously very tired from having worked in the hot field all day. On entering the home we went straight to the living room where, in a central position, was placed the radio. We all gathered round it and sat intently while the man of the house tuned the set. At last, the sound was clear and a voice filled the room.
>
> I wish you could have seen the looks on those dear people's faces! They were transformed — away from the pressures and cares of their meager lives, and into a blessed realization of what the love of Christ had secured for them now that they were *joint heirs with Him of all the glories of Heaven!*
>
> Midway through the program, the door creaked open and in walked another poor, tired woman, one of those who had been working in the field we had passed. She quietly took her place in an empty chair, and soon the tired lines were erased from her face. In their place came a radiance as she listened reverently to the message and the singing.
>
> That was a moment I will *never forget!* I realized then just how much the radio ministry meant to those poor people, so void of any other contact with the Word of God.

After the end of World War II, printed copies of the Word of God were in very short supply in the U.S.S.R. This dearth was nothing new. Even before the Bolshevik Revolution in October 1917, Russian-language Bibles had been extremely scarce. Under the Tsars, in most towns and villages it had been common for there to be just two copies of the Bible — one in the possession of the local Orthodox priest, the other chained to the pulpit in his church. Thus, there had been no reservoir of Bibles from which to draw when the communists ousted the Tsars and assumed power. After the Revolution, limited quantities of the Bible were printed in the U.S.S.R. with government permission, perhaps averaging a couple thousand annually. However, it has always been believed that many of these were exported, or merely displayed at international exhibitions, to fool the world into thinking there was religious liberty in the Soviet Union.

In response to the keen hunger for God's Word in the U.S.S.R., Western Christians began to take Bibles into the U.S.S.R. by one means or another — some overt, many covert. But the totals were very few in relation to the need. By the 1950s, after decades of anti-Christian teaching and propaganda, many Soviet believers had never even *seen* a copy of the Bible. Meanwhile, many unbelievers had become intensely curious about that book of which their government so strongly disapproved! Radio was to help satisfy the needs and wishes of both groups. Because the Soviet Union was so large, shortwave radio had been adopted as the main means of mass communistic propaganda within that country. Thus, most families came to have access to a shortwave radio receiver. SGA recognized that by this medium, the Gospel of Jesus Christ could be shared with unbelievers and God's Word could be shared with many of the "household of faith" who longed for it so much.

Thus, another regular type of production which the mission sponsored was the Bible-reading program. In each one, a short passage of the Word of God was read at dictation speed. We can picture young and old alike in the Soviet Union, grouped around their radio receivers with pencils and paper at the ready, eager to note down each precious word of Scripture as it was read aloud. Afterward, the newly recorded passages would be read and reread, memorized and absorbed by the recipients before the next program of that type was scheduled. Then listeners across the vast Soviet Union could echo the psalmist with extra understanding: "*I have hidden Your Word in my heart that I might not sin against You. Praise be to You, O Lord, TEACH ME Your decrees*" (Psalm 119:11-12). "*I rejoice in following Your statutes as one rejoices in great riches. I meditate on Your precepts and consider Your ways. I delight in Your decrees; I WILL NOT NEGLECT YOUR WORD!"* (Psalm 119:13-16).

Music has long been an integral part of the worship of God, already evident long ago in Old Testament times. The Bible also clearly shows that singing is part of the worship of God in Heaven. It is therefore worth practicing it on Earth! Ruth was very fond of music, and this was to become one of the most appreciated of Ruth's many contributions to the Russian-language broadcasts from HCJB. Previously, most of the musical elements in the Russian programs from Quito had been prerecorded somewhere else, but Ruth and Jack — joined a little later by Stella Jarema from Canada — began to record original items, often in response to requests from their listeners. At first, Ruth and Jack sang duets to the accompaniment of Ruth's piano accordion and Jack's guitar. When Stella arrived, she added solos in her beautiful soprano voice and often joined Ruth's alto in duets. Later still, Delores Baklenko, during her tour of duty at HCJB, helped enrich the Russian musical ministry still further through trios with Ruth and Stella.

Ruth with her HCJB singing partners Delores Baklenko and Stella Jarema.

Russian Christians have a special love of church music and are often moved by its beauty. For these and other reasons, Russian believers under persecution often wrote of the great encouragement they received through hearing triumphant songs of faith and hope in Christ broadcast by radio. Here are a few excerpts from such letters to HCJB:

Ours is a large family, and every day there are so many cares. When evening comes and we are all tired, we look forward to sitting down in front of the radio to hear your words of encouragement . . . and we are never disappointed! Your singing and your words of exhortation renew and inspire us.

Although we are separated from you by a great distance, we hear you in our homes and sing together with you.

We are learning many new songs which you sing on your programs, and then we sing them in our church.

And unbelievers also expressed their appreciation of such music. The following was penned by a Russian Orthodox priest . . .

Once I accidentally tuned into your evangelical broadcast and your message interested me so much that I continued to listen. I especially enjoyed your beautiful music.

This letter was from a professed atheist writing about himself . . .

There are many misgivings I have about your messages and I have many questions to ask about them, but your songs and hymns quiet my heart, and for this I must thank you.

And this came from a Christian writing about a non-Christian friend . . .

One of our lady neighbors came to visit one evening while your program happened to be on the radio. She was very impressed with everything. The singing especially touched her heart. She wants to start attending Gospel services!

Feedback via the mail was particularly valuable in those relatively early years of broadcasting to the U.S.S.R. Letters were both a vital source of information on the quality of reception and a great help to the radio staff in designing and developing their programs. In the days of militant communism, letters from listeners were unfortunately rare, for mail was almost always censored and much was never delivered. However, the ingenuity of many letterwriters ensured that some letters did reach their destination at HCJB and that what they wanted to say would be clear to a Christian reader. Some of the letters — particularly from the U.S.S.R. — were answered over the air in a program called *Mail Box*. The first names of the letterwriters would be given, and one or two sentences from their letters would be read. In this way, receipt of mail by HCJB could be confirmed. Points raised by the writers were then answered, and requests for particular Christian songs were met.

Russian letters received at HCJB were often mailed outside the U.S.S.R. by Russians visiting other countries. Others were mailed on behalf of those living in the Soviet Union, by other Eastern Europeans upon returning home. Because letters written and mailed within the U.S.S.R. had to be very circumspect, their writers often resorted to a kind of biblical code — quoting Scripture verses to make their meaning clear to other Christians, although not to the censors. Many letters made reference to the severe hardships Russian Christians were suffering. For example, one letter read:

> By the grace of God, we are alive and safe in His hands. The Lord is wonderfully blessing His true children, and He does not forsake them in trials. So says David in Psalm 23. We are now encountering everything in our lives — read 2 Corinthians 6:3-10. Praise the Lord also for this wonderful time when you, God's children, can still proclaim the truth.

The following letter likewise carried one message for God's enemies, and a totally different one for brothers and sisters in Christ:

> Praise be to our Father for His food, for the bread and the water, and His whole table prepared for us! Here we have complete freedom to pray, meet together, worship and praise God, just as in the time of Saul before he became Paul (Acts 8:3).

Ruth recalls one letter which read particularly strangely. The writer was seemingly complaining about his hearing, saying: "Oh, I just can't hear very well these days and I find this so hard. I am asking God to help me hear much better!" Suddenly the staff realized that the letter was trying to draw their attention to poor reception conditions, but without arousing the censor's suspicions. The problem was discussed with HCJB's engineers who immediately did what they could — by a slight frequency change — to improve transmissions to that region. Several months later, Ruth recognized the handwriting of the same person who wrote excitedly: "My hearing has now cleared up! I am rejoicing and thanking God that I can now hear very well again!"

Other letters cloaked their true meaning so carefully that the real message they were trying to communicate became clear to the missionaries only after much puzzlement. One of these was addressed to Jack. It said: "If I could meet you on the street, *I would really hit you in the face!*" The whole letter had a harsh tone and ended with this statement: "It is clear that no intelligent person can have an intelligent argument with another if he does not have access to the same material on which the other person is basing his argument." After much thought, Ruth and Jack concluded that the writer was *asking them for a Bible!* But they felt the need to reply in a similarly oblique way to avoid making problems for that fellow should a censor read their letter too.

Ruth still remembers the special thrill they felt that day in 1956, more than a year after their arrival in Quito, when they first received mail directly from the U.S.S.R. itself. This was a postcard from a medical student in Moscow. Although not a Christian, the writer had played the favorite Russian game of scanning the wave bands on his shortwave radio receiver to find something more interesting than communist propaganda. On hearing the Russian-language program from HCJB, he had written to describe the reception. Ruth says: "I cannot explain the *joy* we experienced that day! Although we had all been faithfully broadcasting to Russia and the other republics in the Soviet Union, here was the first direct evidence that we were being heard in Moscow. This spurred us on, and it was with greater joy and faith that we continued our programs. We could not see our audience — only the microphone — but now we were *sure* people could hear us, and were listening!"

Some of the most fruitful years of Ruth and Jack's ministry were to people they could never see.

As time went by, increasing numbers of letters were received by HCJB, confirming the cumulative effect which the radio broadcasts were having in the target areas in the U.S.S.R. Although expressions of gratitude from the listeners were great encouragements in themselves, little gifts began to come in too. These warmed and encouraged the radio missionaries all the more, confirming the love the listeners had for them. Almost anything which could fit into a modest-sized envelope arrived, including embroidered or crocheted doilies, scarves, and even little oil paintings.

But more than anything else, Ruth, Jack and their colleagues were thrilled as letters began to arrive telling how people had been born again as a result of the radio programs. This one was postmarked Khabarovsk:

> I am 18 years old and was brought up in a family of active atheists. Until recently, I was one, too . . . Someone suggested that I listen to your Christian radio programs. I laughed, but took their advice. At first, the programs seemed boring and dry. But as I continued listening, they became very interesting and real to me . . . Then, in a very wonderful moment it seemed as though something came upon me from above. This "something" or "someone" changed my outlook in that moment and gave me real purpose in life. I realized how great a sinner I was. I fell on my knees and asked Jesus Christ for forgiveness. I asked Him to teach me how to live. Even though my prayer was disjointed and I did not know anything about Christianity, my pleas came from my heart.
>
> My relatives and friends are amazed at the changes which have taken place in my life. Not only they, but I too am amazed! For instance, if someone goes too far in arguing with me, I no longer want to hit them in the mouth as I once would have done. Now if the other person is wrong, I try to explain this to them gently. If I am wrong, I prefer not to argue, whereas before I would have kept on arguing. I have also quit narcotics and alcohol and am trying to help my friends do the same.

Thus, the Russian-language programs prepared by Ruth, Jack and others at HCJB increasingly met a great need and yielded a growing spiritual harvest in the U.S.S.R. It was an added bonus that the same programs came to be a real blessing to Russian people elsewhere too. Many additional transmissions were directed toward North and South America, where they were appreciated by large Russian audiences. Listener response from them began to pour in. In contrast to letters from the Russian homeland, personal answers could be written in reply to those from North and South America and a correspondence built up with their writers. But whether replies were sent by mail or could only be given over the air, Ruth has affirmed that she and Jack came to have many friends among their audiences:

> Most missionaries go to a mission field and work day by day, and the people they have gone to help are all around them. They attend the same church as those people, visit their homes, and work in their hospitals. Our main ministry was different. Radio alone does not allow direct personal contact with the people being ministered to. But I must say that as the years went by, Jack and I increasingly felt that we *personally entered* the homes of our listeners. As they wrote to us, we would feel very close to them. Their handwriting became familiar. So, too, did their personal situations, their hopes, fears and needs. Some told us their life stories. Many pled for our prayers. Most of the time we never saw our radio audiences, but they became very personal friends. Many times Jack and I cried over their letters. At other times we had to laugh! And as our listeners reported answers to the prayers which we and the staff at HCJB had prayed on their behalf, we would *rejoice* — particularly with those who wrote to say they had come to trust Christ as their personal Savior and Friend!

Although Ruth and Jack's main ministry was in the Russian language, soon after joining HCJB they were asked by a fellow missionary, Ben Cummings, if they would join him to prepare a weekly 15-minute program for the English department. This they began to do under the title *Old Fashioned Melodies*. Judged by listener response, this was to be for many years one of the most popular English-language programs of its length.

The purpose of *Old Fashioned Melodies* was to encourage English-speaking Christians and challenge non-Christians through the singing of well-loved hymns. Listeners were encouraged to send in their requests, which Ruth and Jack honored whenever possible. Mail flooded in from the United States and Canada, the Caribbean and Central America, Australia and New Zealand, as well as the United Kingdom and even many countries on the continent of Europe. Consequently, from the early 1960s, HCJB sent Ruth and Jack to one of these regions after another to hold special Radio Rallies.

Back in Costa Rica for such meetings, Ruth remembers that because there was still only one railroad line in that country of Central America, they often had to travel for the meetings at night and get off the train very early in the morning. "But hundreds upon hundreds of Costa Ricans walked through the rain forest areas to our rallies in Costa Rica," recalls Ruth. "And we had a blessed ministry of testifying and singing, and Jack preaching the Word of God."

Of nearby Nicaragua and Honduras, Ruth says: "The most exciting thing was that many people actually found the Lord in those rallies! These people who had listened to our music in the *Old Fashioned Melodies* programs came to the churches we were visiting, and accepted the Lord as their Savior when they heard God's Word preached in more detail."

In Australia and New Zealand, there are large numbers of Russian and other Slavic immigrants. In the former, it has long been reckoned that there are more Slavic-speaking people than Australian aborigines! Ruth and Jack were glad of opportunities to minister in Russian-speaking churches. But they also met with many other people who regularly listened to their English-language programs. In 1976, on their way back to the Americas from Australia, Ruth and Jack's flight itinerary took them through South Korea and the Philippines, then to New Delhi, India, necessitating them spending one night in the Indian capital. While dressing the next morning, Jack turned on the little shortwave radio receiver they had taken with them to monitor HCJB reception in different parts of the world. Suddenly, at 10:30 a.m. he picked up the half-hour signal which HCJB transmits. It was followed by the Russian theme song from one of their own Russian-language programs! They were able to listen to one of Jack's recorded messages coming over loud and clear, along with Ruth's voice providing the program announcements. Ruth and Jack marveled at the quality of the reception. It confirmed that their broadcasts were reaching across that area toward the central Asiatic regions of the U.S.S.R. But they also questioned each other: "It's good we are being heard here, but are there any *Russians* in New Delhi?!"

Unexpectedly, at the end of their trip they received an answer. While they were visiting SGA headquarters and Ruth's parents, Vera Deyneka said to them: "I want to read you both a very interesting letter which arrived in Quito when you were traveling in Australia and New Zealand." It had been forwarded to Vera by Const and Elizabeth Lewshenia, who knew how interested Ruth's mother was in responses to the Russian broadcasts — she prayed for them often! The letter ran along these lines:

Dear friends, you will be surprised to hear from me. I live in New Delhi, India. I am stationed here to work in the Russian Embassy. Here, for the first time in my life, I have heard religious broadcasts in my own language telling me about God. Before, I never heard anything positive about God. I am very interested in all you say, and am deeply troubled in my soul. Please send me more information about this.

As Vera read aloud that letter, Ruth and Jack were astounded. Yes, even in India God was using their Russian ministry to point others to Himself! And this illustrates the *main miracle* of missionary radio: messages prepared in one place can be heard in so many more — prompting them to bear fruit even in regions and countries not directly figuring into our human plans, but *clearly prominent in the much greater plans of God.*

After each of their journeys to a transmission target area, Ruth and Jack returned to Quito much encouraged. Therefore as the years passed, their confidence grew more and more regarding the role of radio in relation to the needs of God's children everywhere. And although it would not be until after they had left Quito that Ruth would be able to pay her first visit to their prime target regions in the U.S.S.R., letters from their listeners continued to mount up, steadily deepening Ruth and Jack's understanding of the needs and aspirations, hopes and fears of their Russian audiences. More types of new programs were developed so that, if at all possible, no large group of people in the U.S.S.R. would feel neglected. Ruth participated in new programs designed for Russian women, and programs for children which featured the names of young listeners with birthdays as well as Bible stories which encouraged whole families to listen together.

As a teen-ager, Ruth had committed her life to Christ so that He might particularly use her to bless her own Russian people. In Quito, from her mid-20s until she was over 50 years of age, Ruth filled a very specialized Russian missionary niche. It became clear that through her obedience to the Lord every step of the way, she had grown up and been trained to fit that niche to perfection. Ruth loved the Russian people. She spoke their language and understood their customs. She had been trained in music, speech, education and drama. She had learned how to organize an office and make and keep files and records efficiently. She had become a clear and effective public speaker, but was also a good correspondent and knew how to counsel others one-to-one. Last but by no means least, she was a naturally supportive wife to her missionary husband, passionate to complement his skills and talents rather than promote her own. Likewise, she became a caring, sympathetic mother to John and Lydia, as glad to serve God whole-heartedly in the home as through her very public Christian ministries.

In Matthew's Gospel, Jesus explains in His commentary on the parable of the talents that God grants responsibility for major things to followers of His who have shown themselves faithful in respect of seemingly minor things. So it was with Ruth and Jack. Before moving to Quito, they had both proved their commitment to Christ through service in some of the most private, personal and unglamorous of all SGA missionary spheres — refugee camps for displaced persons in Western and Central Europe. Never had they thought that one day their names and voices might be destined to become known all around the world because of their role as Russian and English radio missionaries. And never did they think that their *faces* would also become well-known — not just because of their wide travels, but because of their own Spanish-language TV show!

Early in 1961, Gifford Hartwell, a TV engineer for a commercial company, had the foresight to buy up television equipment no longer needed by his company. He and his wife then donated this equipment to HCJB. Later, the couple raised support to move to Quito as missionaries of World Radio Missionary Fellowship to maintain and operate the TV system for Voice of the Andes. To accommodate it, Bob Clark, son-in-law of Clarence Jones, had supervised the building of TV studios. Thus in May 1961 under Bob Clark's directorship, Ecuador's first TV station — and the first missionary TV station in the world — went *Sound On, Vision On!* Soon after this, Ruth and Jack were asked if they would prepare and present a regular, Spanish-language TV show for local transmission. Although they had gone to Ecuador never expecting to work in television, their very varied Russian radio experience, plus their well-developed public speaking and singing skills, perfectly equipped them for this new medium.

After much thought and prayer, *Melodias del Rancho de Cowboy Jack* (Melodies from Cowboy Jack's Ranch) was conceived and born. As its title indicates, and like Jack's trade-fair pilot performances in 1959, the new show had a Western theme. Its scenes were either outdoors by a campfire or indoors in an early frontier-style log cabin. Transmitted live every Wednesday and lasting for a quarter of an hour, each program included hymns sung by Ruth and Jack to the accompaniment of their trusty accordion and guitar. Between the songs, there would be a conversation with a guest focusing on one aspect or another of the Christian life. Each guest was introduced as a visitor or friend from a neighboring ranch. Every edition had its own particular theme, normally with some activity to introduce and illustrate it. For example, one visitor stopped by as Ruth was making bread, with her hands in a bowl of dough. The conversation naturally turned to the need we all have for Jesus, the spiritual Bread of Life.

Ruth confirms that "this program series was very well received. It was an added blessing for us to have this Spanish-language ministry for several years on HCJB television. It was also a joyful experience to be able to be a member of HCJB's choir. On Sunday evenings this choir participated in a Spanish-language evangelistic program, *Platicas Dominicales*, for simultaneous transmission in Ecuador over both radio and TV."

One very visible outcome of the TV presentations of the Gospel was a new local church in Quito itself. At first, this was known as the "TV Church" because many people who had been born again through the Christian television program clamored for special Sunday afternoon meetings in which they could ask questions and learn more of their new faith in Jesus Christ. A thriving church began to blossom. Today, it is worshiping and going forward in its own building in that city.

Thus, although Ruth and Jack's foremost ministry for more than 25 years was by radio to Russia, additional rich opportunities opened up for them in English and Spanish, and via TV as well. Unquestionably, God greatly blessed their efforts across much of the world, from Ecuador to the Far East, and from Australia and Argentina to Canada and the United States — though nowhere more than in the U.S.S.R., as Ruth would later discover on extensive journeys to the Russian homeland.

CHAPTER 8

The Wheaton Years
1980 - 1987

Despite all the joys and blessings that had gone before, the next decade opened with what Ruth describes as "very dark, yet interesting days." At the end of April 1980, Ruth and Jack moved from Quito, Ecuador, to Wheaton, Illinois, an affluent western suburb of Chicago. Described by some as the "buckle on the American Bible belt," Wheaton had hosted the U.S. offices of SGA since their move from North Kedzie Boulevard on the north side of Chicago in 1975, and was to do so until 1993.

By 1980, the Western world as a whole had become thoroughly appraised of the horrific plight of the Slavic national churches under communism, and support from Christians in the West for the whole range of SGA ministries was strong. Leadership of the mission had passed from Ruth's father, Peter Deyneka Sr., to her younger brother, Peter Jr., in 1973.

The move of Ruth and Jack Shalanko from Quito to Wheaton corresponded with a new SGA policy of concentrating as many of its radio and related personnel as possible in one place. An even wider range of Russian-language programs than before was under development. Most conveniently, each individual program, including Jack's, could now be recorded on cassette in SGA's own radio department studios and mailed to the major Christian radio transmission stations all over the world. In this way, carefully prepared material could be broadcast to more areas and sections of society in the U.S.S.R. than had been possible before.

Ruth accepted the changes which affected her so directly, but certainly found their personal and practical consequences very difficult. For son

John and daughter Lydia, both already studying in the United States, the effects were happy: for the first time in several years the whole family was once more on the same continent! But Ruth and Jack, although they had been brought up in North America, had never lived there as adults. They had lived elsewhere so long that the United States was like another foreign country to them — very different from Ecuador, which they had grown to know and love. Ruth felt the United States was an entirely new place, a country she did not really understand or even know very much about. She recalls that after shopping for so long in open markets, even visiting an American grocery store was at first a strange and daunting experience.

Moving to Wheaton also meant that the Shalankos had to leave behind all their closest adult friends, plus the homes in which they had lived for over 27 years and where they had raised their family. To make matters worse, all their household items had to be left in Quito, along with the little jeep they had used for traveling to Gospel meetings.

A few days after arriving in Wheaton, it suddenly struck Ruth that most of the things she had counted dear had been left far away. In particular, she had come to think of their apartment in Quito as her "little nest." Undoubtedly, it contained much that had become precious to her. As odd as it might sound, this was more true of *one of the closet doors* than of anything else! Why? Because this was where Ruth had recorded the heights of their children as they had been growing up. Every six months she had measured John, then Lydia, and marked their upward progress with a pencil.

Ruth admits: "As I had been preparing to leave that apartment, I had thought to myself that *I would give anything in the world* to take that closet door with me, on which I had made all those little measurements across the years! Through this I had watched the children growing, maturing and going through all of their schooling. It was all very sentimental to me, very moving. But I had to leave it! As I walked the streets of Wheaton, I had no idea what lay before me. I suddenly realized how very heart-rending it had been to leave behind our home, life and ministries in Quito. This was one of the darkest experiences of my life.

"All of a sudden the verse '*Where your treasure is, there your heart is also*' came to me very strongly — and I remember weeping as I walked down the street toward the SGA offices. I was shocked by my own feelings. 'Lord,' I said, 'I did not realize that I counted all these things as treasures. I did not know that part of my heart and love have been in the wrong place!'

"It became very clear to me that I had been so wrapped up in the trees I had planted in the yard, the color schemes I had devised in the apartment, friends I had counted dear, and even a door to a closet, that I had been *loving all of that more than Christ!* As I began to consider this, I suddenly realized that God had had to tear me away from all those earthly treasures so that I could love Him all the more. But I also knew that He had taken all these things away from me *in love,* so that I would have more thought for things of eternal value — *and COMPLETE AFFECTION for God and His work."*

So Ruth, like many others before and since, came to see that she had become so preoccupied with everyday matters and relationships that her sight of the Lord and her love for Him had been dimmed. It is so easy for emotional commitments and the sheer busyness of life — even in the context of full-time Christian service — to impair a personal relationship with the Lord! As Ruth further agonized, she came to see that without due care even work for the Lord can lessen our love for Him.

But *recognizing* a problem is the first step to *solving* it. Thereafter, as she consciously sought to put Him first in everything once more, little by little He began to warm and encourage her in new and unexpected ways. Her quiet times became refreshing and joyful again, and the Scriptures sprang to life with extra, deeper meaning than for some time past. Ruth particularly remembers being helped and encouraged by Matthew 24:35 — *"Heaven and earth will pass away, but My words will never pass away"* — and other passages of similar meaning. Many of the psalms became like special friends through their words of comfort and assurance.

Meanwhile, the Lord began to strengthen her physically as well as spiritually. Ruth and Jack's top priority on moving to Wheaton had been finding a place to live. Finding somewhere suitable proved very difficult. Wheaton, an increasingly popular residential area for downtown Chicago commuters, had become an expensive city. It was not the most natural environment for a family seeking to subsist on a basic missionary salary — one which was somewhat short of expected support from prayer partners and home churches! However, the Lord guided them to a small, simple home which was affordable because it needed a lot of fixing up. It was about two miles from the SGA office buildings which were just the other side of the downtown area, a couple of blocks from Wheaton College.

Work-wise, the plan was that Jack would continue with his radio programming in the Russian language, preparing his messages for recording at scheduled times. Meanwhile, Ruth would be working normal office hours, assisting not only with the answering of letters from Russian radio listeners, but also with various projects in SGA's Russian literature department. Seeking as always to see new possibilities for God to bless, Ruth decided to walk to and from the office — whether it was spring, summer, fall or winter! Morning and evening, this was her opportunity for exercise. The daily walk to and from work soon became an enjoyable part of her daily routine, particularly invigorating at the end of a day anchored to a desk. So in all weathers, Ruth came to sample and appreciate the fresh air. Sometimes, especially in the frigid depths of winter, cars would draw up alongside her as she briskly strode to or from work. Feeling sorry for her, the drivers would ask if she wanted a ride. But she always declined, knowing that the walk benefited her health. She also knew that since the walks took almost 45 minutes in each direction, they would be good opportunities to meditate alone on the things of the Lord.

And the Lord began to reward Ruth's reinvigorated faith in all the other key areas of her life — family and friends, work and church.

All parents who love their children miss them when they move away — for higher education, work, or to get married. Ruth and Jack were no exceptions. Their apartment in Quito had felt strangely empty as first son John in 1973, and then daughter Lydia in 1974, had left to study at colleges in the United States. However, after Ruth and Jack moved to Wheaton, Lydia returned to live with her parents for a while after graduating from college. Ruth describes the time she had together with Lydia as an adult as wonderful! Even when Lydia left to complete a master's degree in sculpture at Northern Illinois University, mother and daughter were not very far apart. Then, when Lydia married Steve Heilmer, there was the excitement of the wedding from the Shalanko family home in Wheaton. Next, John, a middle school physical education teacher, returned to live with his parents after being appointed to a new teaching position in the nearby suburb of West Chicago. He later married Maria Erickson, and has continued to live in Wheaton longer than either Ruth or Jack themselves.

Ruth and Jack with (left to right) daughter-in-law Maria and son John, son-in-law Steve and daughter Lydia, and first granddaughter Gemma.

It was an added blessing to both Ruth and others that in Wheaton she was now so much nearer to her sister Lydia, brother Peter Jr., and most especially her parents.

Her sister Lydia, now Mrs. Tom Felter, was living in Arlington Heights, Illinois, not far from Wheaton. Ruth was glad of this proximity. As children, with six years difference in age between them, Ruth and Lydia had not really been on the same wavelength. While Ruth had matured and gone to college, Lydia had not yet become a high school student. After that, for three decades they had lived thousands of miles apart. So it was not until Ruth and Jack moved to Wheaton that Ruth and Lydia were able to begin a grown-up relationship as sisters, a friendship which deepened into a real love for one another and for which they now both thank the Lord.

She also appreciated being near her brother, Peter Jr. — and he was glad of this too. For over 30 years, Peter Jr. had been the one who had kept an eye on Rev. and Mrs. Deyneka Sr., helping them whenever they needed it. However, her brother was now more than fully occupied with the demands of his top executive position at SGA. The mission staff had grown to over 250 full-time workers. It had active fields in every continent except Africa and Antarctica. Working in the Wheaton office, Ruth could now see her brother more often — at least as frequently as most other people did! And she could also relieve him of some of the caring responsibilities for their aging parents, helping them in the twilight of their lives.

Ruth with her parents in 1984 at SGA's 50th anniversary celebration in Wheaton.

Her father, Peter Sr., was now in his eighties and declining in strength. Although he still visited the SGA office from time to time — especially to participate in the monthly Day of Prayer held by the staff — he could no longer speak in churches or personally encourage SGA supporters to pray for the work of the mission. Meanwhile, Ruth's mother Vera, now in her seventies, was in good health but finding it increasingly difficult to meet all the needs of husband and home as her strength also began to decline.

Last but not least in the area of personal relationships, Ruth came more and more to praise God for wonderful new friends. "I thought I'd never have close friends again after I left Quito," she tells us, "but God showed me that I was wrong, and He had *many pleasant surprises* in store for me! Many dear people crossed my path during the years I spent in Wheaton. Many of these were ladies working in the SGA office. In the case of Barbara Christensen and others, our friendships extend to the present day, with the closeness only God can bring as Christians work together and desire to glorify Him above everything else. And so, whereas I thought my friends were being taken away from me because of our move from Quito, God added to my life some very wonderful relationships which have continued even after we eventually left Wheaton. I was also glad to be able to renew fellowship with former HCJB missionary 'Aunt LaLa' — Alice Christopher — and her daughter Camille VanHoose. Their home in Fort Wayne, Indiana, is an oasis whenever my path leads to that area."

In her new work, there was also much for which Ruth came to thank the Lord. A first-time ministry for her was helping with the preparation of the Russian-language magazine *Evangelski Vestnik*, which SGA had been publishing for many years. The magazine was edited by Andrew Semenchuk and Platon Chartschlaa, assisted by Ruth's former teen-age friend Pauline Mazur — who had long since become Mrs. Andrew Semenchuk. Ruth was able to assist in a variety of different ways — from researching and selecting material for inclusion in the magazine, to helping lay it out and paste it up.

More familiar, and even more important to Ruth, was her ongoing work with all the mail being received from the Soviet Union. Most of the incoming letters at that time were responses to SGA radio transmissions, which were then at their most numerous. The range of program types was also at its broadest, including many especially designed for different groups of unbelievers, including women, children and the intelligentsia (particularly scientists and technologists).

As the long-icy relations between the world's superpowers began to thaw in the early 1980s, the trickle of letters from listeners in the U.S.S.R. turned into a rising stream. Ruth was increasingly involved in helping to monitor and classify their contents, mainly because mail from reception areas in the Soviet Union was being used more and more to shape the contents of the broadcasts themselves through the feedback it gave the scriptwriters. Because several of the scriptwriters did not speak the Russian language, key passages from letters were translated for their guidance, and Ruth helped with this too. Last but certainly not least, replies to many of the letters were prepared by Ruth and others, a ministry Ruth increasingly found joyful!

Then early in 1985, a long-desired opportunity came Ruth's way. Elizabeth Lewshenia and her husband Constantine, for so many years co-workers with Ruth and Jack in Quito, were now based in Wheaton too. One day, they told Ruth they were planning a group visit to the Soviet Union. The Lewshenias had been to the U.S.S.R. twice before in recent years, to encourage the churches and to guide Constantine as he prepared a book on Christian doctrine. This book was specifically intended to meet the needs of Russian pastors and church leaders who had not been able to receive formal Bible college training. Ruth, despite her Russian heritage and her many years of ministry to Russians, *had never been to Russia!* Elizabeth invited her to join their party for the new trip. The group would not be large, only about 10 people in all. One of them was Elizabeth's sister, Jenny, and a lady was needed to room with her.

Ruth was *ecstatic!* At last it might be God's will for her to meet face to face with some of their listeners and letterwriters in the Soviet Union! Discussion and prayer with Jack encouraged her to go.

The care and sensitivity required on such visits to the U.S.S.R. cannot be exaggerated. In 1969, Const and Elizabeth had driven into Lvov, Ukraine. Elizabeth had memorized the address of one lady in Lvov and had gone to her house. When the lady opened the door, she immediately recognized Elizabeth from the sound of her voice and from photographs received from HCJB. She then gave Elizabeth the address of a person in the next town, which Elizabeth again committed to memory. This pattern of memorization continued on to the last city on their itinerary.

Elizabeth Lewshenia recalls that on the new trip in 1985 they found few changes in the U.S.S.R. compared with their earlier trips: "The country was just as antagonistic to the Gospel, and life just as difficult for the churches," Elizabeth affirms. "It was difficult for us, too! We took Bibles and Christian books with us, but many were confiscated by customs, leaving only those for 'personal use.' We had to be very discreet when participating in church services. We could still not preach sermons, only 'bring greetings.' So Const would often take 10-15 minutes over his 'greetings,' and include many references to words from Brother Paul, or Brother Peter or Brother John!

"The only significant improvements we found in 1985 were that we were allowed to go to a few places by ourselves, and were overseen less closely by the government-run travel agency, Intourist."

The 1985 itinerary took the group to six cities. In each one, the group managed to attend Evangelical Baptist church meetings. Fearfully, the leaders of some of the churches refrained from naming the missionaries among the visitors to their services. But all at least announced that they included broadcasters from Voice of the Andes. Ruth recalls "the OOHS and AAHS from the audiences when they heard that! In most churches, we were invited to sit on the platform and bring brief greetings. This was a great delight for me, as I faced those people who had been listening to our programs. But I felt very much the tension of the communist government around us. We knew people were following us, looking to see what we were doing and whom we were visiting."

The missionary visitors spent the Easter weekend in the city of Kiev, capital of Ukraine. That Saturday evening, they decided to have an English Easter service of their own in Ruth and Jenny's hotel room. With two sitting on chairs and the rest on beds, they quietly sang Easter hymns, read the Scriptures recounting the crucifixion and resurrection of the Savior, and prayed around the circle. Some of the younger members of the group then whispered that they were going to slip out of the hotel to witness the midnight service in a local Orthodox cathedral. The older ones, including Ruth and Jenny, decided to go to bed.

At about 11:45 p.m. their telephone rang. A very gruff voice demanded: "*WHERE ARE THE OTHERS?*" Ruth was taken aback, but acted rather dumb. She said she and her lady companion had been asleep, and would he excuse them for they were trying to rest! But the voice persisted: "Where are the *younger* people? They were in your room before! *Where are they now?*" Ruth became sure the room had been bugged. So she replied that she had been asleep and wished to go back to bed again, then gently replaced the receiver. Ruth and Jenny were not troubled again that night, but the incident raised their guard. From then on they were all the more careful with what they did and what they said, even in their own rooms.

The next day, however, the Easter Sunday morning service at the Russian Evangelical Baptist Church in Kiev was a wonderful experience for them all. They arrived by taxi about 45 minutes early, thinking it would be interesting to watch people arriving for the service. But even by then, the church was already packed. Many people were to stand for the whole two hours of the service. The resurrection hymns sounded magnificent! Meanwhile, in contrast to the extreme hardship and persecution the whole church in the Soviet Union was suffering, the prayers and sermons were poignantly triumphant. But most memorable, spine-tingling and spiritually thrilling of all was the simple opening affirmation, repeated three times from the pulpit: *"CHRIST IS RISEN!"* . . . and the exuberant confirmation from the whole congregation, responding as with one mighty voice: *"HE IS RISEN INDEED!"*

Because of the strict laws in force during the communist era, Pastor Dukonchenko could not directly involve all the visitors in the morning worship service. The normal requirement was that every church should submit its proposed order of service to the police prior to each Sunday meeting. However, as Ruth reports, the pastor "took the risk of asking Constantine Lewshenia to bring greetings to the church." Const included Scripture plus encouragement from God's Word in his five-minute address. He also greeted the congregation in the name of Jack Shalanko "and his wife Ruth, who is here this morning, too."

After the service, Ruth was mobbed and kissed many times over by warm, sweet sisters in the Lord. She also received many firm, hearty handshakes from hard-working brethren: "Thank you, *thank you*," they repeated, "for EVERY radio program!"

In the U.S.S.R. in 1985, HCJB radio listeners greeted Ruth like a beloved friend.

Ruth edged out of the crowded church into the sun-drenched court-yard. A young couple approached her, their four-year-old son jumping up and down with excitement between them. Shyly, the young wife extended her hand and began to speak. Tears welled up in her eyes: "I just want to welcome you to our country of Ukraine, and *thank you* and your husband for your faithful radio broadcasts! I spent several years praying for the salvation of my husband. Your programs gave me courage and hope. For a long time they guided my broken heart."

At this, her husband lovingly put his arm around his wife and took up the story in a faltering voice:

"Yes, *Ruth Petrovna*, for years I resisted the voice of the Lord. But slowly, as I began listening to your radio programs, I began to understand the love of Christ. My wife's testimony and prayers, and your messages and explanations, brought me to Him. Today, we are a happy Christian family, bringing up our son in the things of the Bible, and we thank you for your faithful witness. I want to give you a remembrance!" With that, he took a bunch of keys out of his pocket, removed a small metal tag from the ring and handed it to Ruth. That ostensibly insignificant little scrap of metal is still one of her most treasured mementos today.

Another city they visited was Rostov-on-Don in southern Russia. Using a public phone booth, Const Lewshenia was able to establish contact with a local pastor. The pastor promised to come the next day and take them to his church for the Sunday morning service.

Early the next morning, about 3 a.m. Ruth's phone rang. She had been sleeping soundly and thought that perhaps others traveling with them needed help. "Hello," she said, as brightly as possible. A threatening male voice replied, "WHO ARE YOU? *What are you doing here?*"

She was startled, but simply told him she was a visitor to his lovely city. She also observed that, since she was a legitimate visitor, the hotel had her passport, then hung up.

She fell asleep, but was awakened again by the shrill tone of the telephone. Perhaps the young couple in their group had been frightened by the same man and needed reassurance.

"And as I was saying," repeated the same menacing male voice, "who *are* you? WHAT ARE YOU DOING HERE?" Ruth repeated that she was a tourist and that her passport details had been recorded. She excused herself and hung up once more.

Five minutes later, the phone rang again. This time Ruth ignored it. After several deafening rings, it stopped.

That experience was on her mind when two cars arrived later that morning to take them to the Baptist church. Ruth rode in the pastor's car. In the course of conversation, she recalled her nighttime escapade. The pastor slowly smiled. "Yes, *Ruth Petrovna*, I receive these kinds of nighttime visits myself, almost every other night! These people feel they can intimidate and scare us. They want you to know they are aware of you. But it would be better not to relate this to anybody else, because you have no idea who it is you may be meeting and who is listening to your conversations. It is for this reason we have come for you ourselves today, to be able to talk to you in private in our cars."

Driving along the streets of that major Russian city, watching the emotionless faces of the crowds outside, Ruth stole a glance at the profile of the pastor — a middle-age man who, despite every problem, was full of God's love and praise. His congregation had just finished building a big new church building. It had taken many, many years!

The pastor shared something of God's miracles in that regard with his passengers. For five long years, his church board had submitted petitions to the city, begging for a piece of land on which to build. For five years, their requests had been denied. One day, a legal letter arrived to tell them that the only plot they could have was near the outskirts of the city. He and the elders and deacons eagerly went to investigate the site. They found it was a rubbish dump! The men were discouraged, but the pastor encouraged them to take heart. They had prayed and God had answered — this was the area on which they should build their new church. Later investigation revealed that it had excellent train, bus and trolley-car connections with all parts of the city. So together they prayed again, thanking God for it, and asking Him to bless their new undertaking.

The first task on that forbidding building site was to fill and level the dump in preparation for foundations of the church. The pastor described how many members of the congregation, both male and female, had come from work every evening to assist in the work. They had erected floodlights so construction could continue into the night. On Saturdays, even the children and young people had come to carry bricks, buckets of water, boards and nails; to push wheelbarrows; and to pour cement and saw timber. The ladies of the church had brought vegetables from their gardens and cooked large pots of borscht which they served to the workers with sour black bread and large glasses of hot tea. Young people of the church had been sent to evening classes to learn how to plaster, lay parquet floors, and even how to make huge chandeliers to be hung in the sanctuary. Older members of the congregation had fasted in order to increase their meager donations toward the purchase of building materials.

Now, several years later, Ruth and her party were being taken to that new church. Ruth confesses she was quite unprepared for the lovely three-story, white-painted church peeping through the trees as they drove down the side road to it. Many people were milling about — older ladies with brightly flowered scarves covering their heads . . . younger women wearing chiffon-like head scarves folded into bands (a slightly more modern form of head covering) . . . teen-age girls wearing their hair long and simple, pinned back into fashionable buns, or decorated with big bows . . . men wearing their dark Sunday suits.

At exactly 10 a.m., the pastor, deacons and elders strode into the sanctuary. The entire congregation stood to their feet as the pastor opened the service with prayer.

"Thank you, Heavenly Father, for allowing us to enter this House of Prayer of ours today, to worship your Holy name," he prayed. The congregation quietly, but audibly said their *Amens* in agreement as he prayed.

Ruth found that tears were flowing down her cheeks as the poignancy of that plain prayer hit home. She was so conscious of the presence of the Lord and the joy of those people in that place — a do-it-yourself church on a former dumping ground! Did *she* thank God every Sunday for the privilege of entering her church building? Why, she *usually took such things for granted!*

During the two-hour service, she carefully watched the behavior of the congregation. Although the building was large, every seat was taken. Late-comers had to stand in the aisles. From time to time, though, some who were seated would offer to exchange places with others standing nearby. Despite such movements, there was dignity and reverence throughout.

The choir sang several lovely hymns. If a song was a prayer to the Lord, the entire congregation would respectfully stand as it was rendered, for during any type of prayer in any Russian home or church, people either stand or kneel to pray — even at the meal table before and after eating.

There were three sermons during that memorable service at Rostov-on-Don Baptist Church, as well as special music, and a designated time of prayer when members of the congregation could publicly participate. Many prayers were offered tearfully as, one after another, people opened their hearts to the Lord.

At one point, Ruth noticed a slight distraction on the platform as a man passed the pastor a note. As the choir sang, he slipped out, returning shortly afterward. Later he explained to Ruth that the KGB had called him out of the service to ask who the 10 Western visitors were. The presence of Ruth and her compatriots in the service had been reported. In those days, the KGB continually posted informers in most of the churches. The pastor had cautiously replied that they were Christian believers from North America who follow the custom of attending religious services on Sunday mornings and were just doing what they would do at home. He told the officers the name of the hotel where they were staying and that their passports were being held there.

When the service was over, Ruth and the other visitors were invited to the lower floor. There, on large planks, ladies of the church — so eager to show their own love for their special guests — had laid out a generous lunch for them: huge bowls of soup and fried eggs, accompanied by black bread and tea. Once again, speeches were made at the table, especially thanking the visitors for the Russian radio programs.

As Ruth left that church and others on her first journey across the U.S.S.R., her feeling was not just a parting from friends, but from her own family — fellow members of the family of God. To her, the people of the U.S.S.R. would never again be the unseen masses "over there." They would be much easier for her to visualize. They would be much more *real*. For she had now met some of the people who had listened to the radio broadcasts . . . she had shaken their hands . . . she had felt their embraces . . . she had been warmed by their smiles and touched by their tears . . . she had been thrilled by their kindness and deeply touched by their spiritual longing and desire.

Ruth's first trip to Russia affirmed her resolve in this: she would try *all the more* to reach the Russian people for the kingdom of Heaven — in any way she could!

Not long afterward, under the leadership of President Mikhail Gorbachev, the attitude of the Soviet government to many aspects of Soviet life — both external and internal — at last showed signs of significant change. Internationally, friendlier overtures were made to the Western great powers than for several decades past. In the late 1980s, warmth between the major power blocs of East and West was increasing fast. With astonishing speed, the Cold War was melting away into history. Meanwhile within the Soviet Union itself, Gorbachev's policies of *glasnost* (openness) and *pere-*

stroika (rebuilding) were beginning to bring real relief to believers in Jesus Christ.

Some of the earliest and most obvious effects of these changes, as witnessed by the Wheaton office of SGA, involved Russian mail. For several decades, censorship of mail from the U.S.S.R. had been strict. This was strongly witnessed in the letter from one radio listener who said, "I have written to you *40 times without reply!*" Fortunately, censorship had not been uniformly that effective! But in the second half of the 1980s, the stream of letters received by SGA from Russian radio listeners grew to a veritable torrent. As before, many of the correspondents were pleading for Christian literature. The two excerpts below are contrasting, but both typical examples of their kinds. The first is from Galina, a young woman in Novosibirsk, and the second from Dina, a girl from the city of Leningrad (now St. Petersburg):

Ruth at her desk in Wheaton, Illinois, answering mail from radio listeners.

Just recently I have become very interested in learning about the beginning of life on Earth. Until now I have been brought up as an atheist, but I have been trying to find books about God. In our country we have very few writers who can write about God, and it is difficult to get books about God or religion. I was told you would not turn down my request: please send me a Bible in the Russian language. I think I will find answers to my questions in this book. I ask you to forgive my boldness in this important matter to me: *you are my only hope!*

I live in the U.S.S.R., but the love of the Lord has united us with you. I have asked the Lord to save me. I want to know everything I can about God, but here in the Soviet Union it is difficult to find Christian literature. Please send me a Bible in the Russian language. Also, I have a younger brother who as yet has not accepted the Lord. He would really like to have the children's illustrated New Testament which I know has been printed in Russian. Please send one of these if it is possible. I have many friends who now believe in the Lord and wish they could have Bibles too, but are too scared to write.

And the following letter, a special encouragement to Ruth and Jack, was written by Vasili from Krivoi Rog in Ukraine:

We are grateful . . . most of all for your radio programs! I shall never forget my first encounter with them when I heard the voice of Brother Jack Shalanko. I cried uncontrollably. I fell on my knees by the radio receiver and prayed with tears. Then I heard the Shalankos singing their song *When His Glory Paints the Sky* and it, too, tore at my heart. I cannot write all that is laid upon me, but that first broadcast *changed my entire life* and I shall never forget it! We pray for you and wish you God's blessings. We are in great need of Christian literature. Please send us whatever you can.

Benefiting still further from Gorbachev's policy of openness, Ruth's team in the SGA office began to find that they could now mail not only letters, but also small packages in reply to such requests — and be reasonably confident they would be delivered. As more and more listeners' letters arrived in Wheaton, Ruth found herself working harder and harder, even with the help of others, to keep up with the demand for Bibles, New Testaments and other Christian books. For children, copies of David C. Cook's lovely illustrated New Testament — of which SGA had prepared special Polish and Russian editions — were often requested by name.

As general director of SGA, Ruth's brother, Peter Deyneka Jr., kept abreast of these encouraging developments and the new challenges they presented. He himself had served for a year at HCJB. Recalling that many listeners' letters received from the U.S.S.R. even in those days had requested literature, but that most of the books SGA had sent in response had not been delivered, Peter was given a new vision: as many as possible of the letterwriters — *especially the earlier ones* — should be sent Russian-language Bibles and other Christian books. HCJB was contacted for the addresses of all those who had requested Russian-language literature over the years. Many friends and churches were donating money for the printing of Russian-language Bibles, and SGA therefore had stock in hand. Ruth realized, though, that there was one snag: the cost of postage would be very high!

She then had a bright idea. Whenever she and Jack were invited to speak at a meeting, they would take prepared Russian literature packets with them. They would then invite individuals or churches to take a number of the packets — whether one, several, or maybe many — and mail them out from their local post offices to the U.S.S.R. This was a simple, yet appealing way in which American Christians could help meet the needs of those so hungry for the Word of God. The idea spread. Soon, Sunday schools of all ages were mailing out these packets in large numbers. Hundreds upon hundreds of Bibles, New Testaments and other books were being posted every week.

Grateful recipients began to write back, full of thanks for the books they had received, sometimes after waits of several years. Many letters came from people who had long been Christians, but who had never before owned any part of the Word of God. Peter Jr., Ruth and all those involved in this expanding ministry were encouraged and gratified. And they particularly praised God for all the new letters from the U.S.S.R. which explained how the newly delivered books helped people get to know Him or to know Him better.

One such letter came from a man who had been brought up by devoted Christian parents. Despite their love and witness, he and his brother and sisters had rejected the faith of their parents and strayed — and then stayed — far from Christ. After explaining all this, the letter continued:

> Can you imagine my surprise one day, not long ago, when we received a parcel in our mail box addressed to my mother. She had already died and gone to be with the Lord she loved. As we opened the package to see what someone had sent her, we found it was a Bible. It was as if a ton of bricks had hit me! I had not listened to my mother's teaching. Since she had died, I no longer heard her prayers each day nor saw her living testimony in front of me. So I was running further and further away from God.
>
> As I opened that package and saw God's Word, it brought back to me images of my mother on her knees praying for us children. I took that Bible in my hands, fell down on my knees, and cried out "Lord, the God of my mother and father who are with You today, *I don't want to run away from You any longer!*"

Continuing, he went on to relate how receiving that unexpected Bible, truly a message from Heaven, had caused him to confess his sins to the Lord and accept Jesus Christ as his Savior. He concluded emotionally:

> I want to *thank you* for the Bible you sent my mother. She does not need it because she is with the Lord. But *I* need it and will read it, and *with all my heart and strength I will TRY TO LIVE FOR HIM MYSELF!*

For a while, this ministry of mailing literature into the Soviet Union continued to expand. As people began receiving packages, many of their relatives, neighbors and friends clamored for the SGA office address so they could write for some themselves. Thus, the torrent of letters from that great nation which had been so deprived of God's Word for nearly three-quarters of a century rose to become a flood.

As the chains of communism began to fall away from the minds as well as the everyday lives of the people, their hunger for spiritual food became ever more overt. Fifty years earlier, Peter Deyneka Sr. had been implored by Russian Christians to send them more *Hleb zhizhni*, the Bread of Life! Now not only Christians, but non-Christians too, were pleading for this. Decades of atheistic teaching had failed to convince the Russian people that God did not exist. A Moscow taxi-driver had once expostulated to Nick Leonovich: "If there is no God, why does our government spend *so much time and money* telling us not to believe in Him?!"

In *Scientists Who Find God*, a recently published collection of testimonies excerpted from SGA's evangelistic *Radio Academy of Science* (RADAS) programs, Alex Yusov, a one-time Red Army lecturer in atheism, tells his own conversion story. While searching for suitable material to support his atheistic dogma, he chanced across a copy of the New Testament. The more he read it, the more deeply he began to question his once firmly held antireligious beliefs . . . and the more he began to wonder if the Bible might be true. Not long afterward he became sure it was true, and acted on its instructions to repent and trust in God.

Therefore, there were many reasons why, through the late 1980s and early 1990s, SGA placed as much emphasis as possible on the printing and distribution of Russian-language Bibles and New Testaments. Translating and publishing a wide range of books to explain the messages of the Word of God and how these could be applied to the lives of individuals was also accorded high priority. Ruth was excited by the part she was able to play in helping to get those precious books to people who had yearned for them so much. Yes, much of her work was now relatively simple and straightforward, even sometimes mundane. But it was vital nonetheless, calling for both care and commitment to each task in hand.

At the same time, however, one other part she played was much more public, drawing not only on her deep concern for the Russian people but also on her considerable gifts of description and persuasion. By now the chief market economies of the world were beginning to move into recession, as eagerly awaited "peace dividends" from the end of the Cold War seemed to give way so quickly to some "peace penalties." Even in the prosperous United States, many families began to feel the pinch. Almost everywhere, donations to churches and missions began to decline. Consequently, it became more and more important for Ruth and her colleagues to visit churches to present the challenge of the opening up of the Russian empire to the Gospel of Jesus Christ. Without increased help from donors, many of the new opportunities to spread His Word would have been lost during that exciting period.

But far more radical changes were about to burst onto almost the entire Soviet scene, and far beyond . . .

In Wheaton, the Lord came to bless and encourage Ruth in her new life, not only in respect of home, family and friends, but also in her ongoing work for Him with SGA. He came to use and bless Ruth and Jack in their new church life too — most unexpectedly.

On their arrival in Wheaton in 1980, they had decided that although for many years they had attended Spanish-speaking churches in Quito, they would now worship in an English-speaking church. They had learned to love the Ecuadorian people and to worship with them happily, but the time seemed right for a total change. So they began a search for a church where they would feel at home and make new friends. Soon they settled at one of the smaller fellowships in the Wheaton area, Pleasant Hill Community Church. Here they enjoyed and appreciated the preaching of God's Word for almost two whole years.

Quite suddenly, though, they nostalgically remembered Ecuador and felt an urge to visit a Spanish-speaking congregation at West Chicago Bible Church. Ruth speaks smilingly of the moment they walked into that church, for they instantly realized how much they still loved Spanish-speaking people after all their years in South America! Ruth and Jack were welcomed warmly by the minister, Pastor Roberto Vergara and his wife Cornelia, and by many of the congregation. They just had to go back, again and again! Very quickly, Ruth and Jack began to be involved in the life of this Hispanic church — assisting with the music, Ruth helping in the monthly meetings for women, and Jack often taking the pastoral prayer in the Sunday morning services. For over six years, Ruth affirms: "We enjoyed a wonderful work with the Spanish-speaking people in the West Chicago Bible Church." To this day, the church considers Ruth one of their own missionaries.

Thus, in many ways the longer Ruth lived in Wheaton, the more content she became and the happier with her ministries both inside and outside SGA. But she did not forget those very difficult days she had known immediately after arriving back in the United States. This was fortunate — for *lessons she had learned from them were soon to be tested to the very hilt.*

Just before that, though, the Lord who alone *"knows the end from the beginning"* (Isaiah 46:10), prompted her to seek a new practical qualification — her very first driving license! Those changes in her life which lay just around the corner would soon make this so vital.

Before moving to Wheaton, Ruth had neither the necessity nor the occasion to learn how to drive a car. It had been early on in Quito that she and Jack had purchased a 1957 jeep. She recalls that there was only one problem with it at the time: it was not in working order when they bought it! So it had been towed to the HCJB mechanics shop where Jack and Andy Newman, a missionary colleague, had taken the engine out. Every Saturday they had worked on it, repairing and rebuilding, until it ran again. Jack was very practically minded. He had not only been a motorcycle fan in his late teens, but also something of a private boat-builder in his 20s. Bringing that jeep back to life had been something Jack had greatly enjoyed, another truly therapeutic activity after the time-watching, tongue-controlling intensity of the radio recording studio. Afterward, Ruth and Jack had used the jeep for many years, mainly to take them to the various Spanish churches where Jack was to preach and where they were to sing together. Because they had almost always traveled together to those meetings, Ruth had never felt the need nor the desire to learn to drive.

Now, some 30 years later, and for no reason apparent to her at the time, Ruth informed Jack she wished to learn to drive a car! Aware that older people do not learn as quickly or as easily as youngsters, her "fingers did the walking" through their Yellow Pages directory and she selected a driving instructor whose advertisement was somewhat reassuring. It read: *"Specializes in teaching senior citizens!"* At 57 years of age, she had not really joined that rank yet and was a naturally calm, poised person — but the whole idea had begun to make her very nervous. She was sure she needed a teacher with more than average patience!

It was in the summer of 1985 when Ruth first took to the driver's seat and began to edge her way ever so tentatively around some of the quieter streets in the sedate city of Wheaton. She recalls that by the end of each hour's lesson, the back of her dress would be drenched with perspiration. But little by little, she made progress, and one day her instructor said, "Well, Mrs. Shalanko, I guess you are ready for the driving test."

Ruth's response must have come as a considerable surprise — a unique proposition the instructor had probably never heard before from any of his pupils: No, *SHE would tell HIM* when she was ready to take the test! For at that precise moment, she did not feel confident enough for it. First, she wished to have some lessons on the multilane roads in the region. And driving in downtown Chicago was another type of daunting challenge she wished to confront while still benefiting from the tutelage of the teacher by her side.

However, the agreed day of her driving test finally dawned. Encouraged by the prayers of her friends at the SGA office, she passed the first time, praising God for what she considered to be a "tremendous accomplishment at the age of 57!"

Ruth did not know how very soon her new skill was to become a real tool of ministry in helping others, as well as a means of helping herself when some near and dear to her could no longer help her in any way . . . or even help themselves.

CHAPTER 9

Homes in Heaven
1987 - 1993

As the 1980s advanced, effects of old age and failing health had more and more begun to take their toll on Ruth's parents. At first, Ruth had joined Peter Jr. in keeping watchful eyes on Peter Sr. and Vera, and helping in whatever way they needed. Soon it became her practice to visit her parents' apartment every day. Being able to drive a car was then such a blessing when there were trips which had to be made for her parents to shop or to visit the doctor. However, Ruth's pleasure in sharing with them news of SGA, and reading the Bible and praying with them in the Russian language, were the things they appreciated most.

Ruth was sad to see her father, who had been so vigorous and active in the Lord's work, growing weaker and no longer able to respond to calls for help from the mission field. One day while Ruth was visiting her parents' humble two-room apartment, such a request arrived from the Australian and New Zealand offices of SGA in relation to a particular project. This need was mentioned to Peter Sr. as an item for special prayer. "Oh, if I were only 10 years younger," he sighed, "I would go there immediately, right now, and give whatever help I could! But now I am like a prisoner in my own body. My *heart* wants to go, but my *body* will not let me!"

However, like many of an older generation, Peter Sr. could still exercise the vital ministry of prayer, and do so effectively. All his life, he had preached its purpose and its *POWER*. Ever since he had transferred the leadership of SGA to his son, Peter Jr., his mind had remained clear, enabling him to go on ministering in the most important sphere of intercession. Time and again, Peter Sr. called on the Lord concerning the needs of the mission all around the world. He repeatedly cried from his heart that Russian and other Slavic peoples would hear the Gospel and repent.

As time went by, though, two things became ever more obvious to Ruth, Peter Jr. and Lydia: not only was their father growing weaker, but their mother could not care for him much longer. Vera had always been a tiny lady. Now 80 years old herself, she found her enfeebled husband's needs an increasing strain. She told her children she could no longer tend to him properly. However, Lydia was working, and Peter Jr. and his wife, Anita, were often traveling for SGA. Also, Ruth was growing ever more conscious that her own husband Jack, although only in his 50s, was — for unclear reasons — physically slowing down. Thus, there was no way in which any of the three Deyneka children, with their many ministry and family responsibilities, could care for their parents in their own homes.

So Ruth began the search for a nursing home in Wheaton where Peter Sr. could be better looked after, yet could still be visited every day. In August 1985, a suitable place was found only a mile or so away. However, Ruth confesses that as she took her Papa there from the environment he knew and loved, "THAT WAS THE HARDEST DAY OF MY LIFE. It was *so difficult* for me to take him from the little home he had shared with Mama to live among people he did not know. It was *so difficult* for me to see him unable to do much for himself, let alone for others."

True to her own personal resolve, Ruth went to visit him every single day, often both morning and evening — a pure expression of daughterly devotion. And even there in the nursing home she found opportunities for witness and testimony. Every evening after work, Ruth would spend an hour with her father until dinnertime at 6 p.m. She would sit with him, take him to his table, and say a word of prayer with him before he began his meal. Other residents in that secular home took note and came to insist "say the prayer, Ruth, say the prayer!" before they would eat too. So she would lead them all in thanksgiving for the daily providence of God.

One special friendship she built up in the nursing home was with a lady whose name was also Ruth. Ruth Shalanko told her that their name was found in the Bible in honor of a special woman, and many times she told her that God loved her too. She encouraged her with Scripture verses and told her she would pray for her.

One evening, as they awaited the dinner bell, Ruth-the-patient motioned Ruth-the-visitor to come closer. The television was blaring and there was noise all around. Ruth Shalanko went across to speak to the old lady who had a distraught look on her face. Bending down, she asked: "Hello Ruth, how are you tonight?"

"Not too good — I think I'm going to die soon and I'm scared," was the reply. Ruth Shalanko immediately knelt down beside her and began to explain that if she was ready to meet God she did not have to fear death. To get right with Him all she had to do was invite the Lord into her heart, asking Him to forgive her sins and accept her as His child. Ruth offered to pray with her friend, but first of all asked if she wanted the Lord to enter her life. "Oh, yes!" was the reply. Ruth spoke with her a bit longer . . . and the old lady opened her heart to Christ. Leaning over, closer to her ear, Ruth prayed for her. When she had finished praying, she asked her friend if she wanted to pray too. She did, finishing with the Lord's Prayer. The two hugged and kissed each other joyfully! Then the dinner bell rang and the residents went off to the dining room.

Visiting her father the next day, Ruth looked in vain for her friend. When a nurse passed by, she asked where the other Ruth was. "Oh, she died last night," said the nurse as she continued down the hall. Ruth was startled! But she silently thanked the Lord for the time of prayer she had shared with the old lady the evening before, and that she had not died in her sin.

Ruth confesses that "after that occasion I tried to speak with more of the residents, realizing this was now another ministry God was giving me, even while I was visiting my father."

One Thursday in July 1987, Ruth and Jack left for Canada to visit with some of his relatives. Over the previous month, Peter Sr. had become increasingly frail following a series of slight strokes. Ruth's cousin, Nick Leonovich, by then director of SGA's Russian radio department, was also now living in Wheaton with his wife Roz (Frozina Kucher, Ruth's first missionary colleague in Europe). That Sunday, Nick went to visit Mr. Deyneka. Immediately afterward, he phoned Peter Jr. to say that the grand old warrior was failing rapidly. Peter Jr. hurried to be with his father, and read God's Word aloud and prayed with him. Peter Sr. could no longer speak, but responded by squeezing his son's hand from time to time. Just before midnight, the Lord took His servant home to his reward in Heaven. *"Precious in the sight of the Lord is the death of His saints"* (Psalm 116:15).

Ruth's first thought the instant she heard the news from Peter by telephone the next morning was about Heaven: "Papa is *with the Lord!*" With thanksgiving, she recalls today: "This wonderful man, whose prayer life, whose dedication to Christ, and whose desire to serve Him were the greatest object lessons I could have ever seen with my own eyes. More than anything else it was his prayers, his example, his encouragement, that made me fear God and do what was right in my life for Christ. Through the grief and loss I experienced when he died, I was encouraged by the realization that right then he would be meeting not only with the Lord, but also with brothers and sisters in Christ whom he loved so much — his fellow saints and fellow workers, people for whom and with whom he had prayed much and had striven hard for the kingdom of God."

As Ruth and Jack traveled back to Wheaton, many thoughts and pictures sprang to their minds. In particular, Ruth tried to envision her Papa meeting his own mother in Heaven. Because she had not wanted to know Christ at the time, there had been difficulties between them on his first trip home to White Russia from the United States in 1926 . . . but later, she did come to know the Lord. And Peter Sr. would be meeting Ivan Prokhanov again, who had so encouraged him to minister more widely to the Russian people. Ruth imagined her father being reunited with Clarence Jones, Reuben Larson and Lance Latham, those men with whom he had worked and who had challenged and helped him so much . . . and she could picture all of them walking over to Dr. Paul Rader — the one who had not only led her Papa to the Lord, but the one who had also inspired that whole group of young men to become missionaries for Him. Ruth imagined her Papa with Oswald J. Smith, with whom he had shared many a missionary conference at The People's Church in Toronto, and with whose help the Toronto Russian Bible Institute had been established . . . as well as with Paul Rood who had been the first chairman of SGA.

There were many others Ruth thought of at that time too, with whom Peter Sr. had fellowshipped and prayed. Last but by no means least, there were the thousands upon thousands of Russian-speaking people who had found the Lord as a result of her father's vision and faithfulness in taking or sending them the Word of God, through personal evangelism and Gospel preaching or by literature and radio.

So at the age of 89, Rev. Peter Deyneka Sr. — a missionary pioneering giant even among a generation of such giants — had gone to claim his everlasting inheritance in Heaven, as a *"co-heir with Christ"* of all its treasures, just as Paul affirms in Romans 14:17.

Merely two months previously, on the very day he and Vera had celebrated their 61st wedding anniversary, Peter Sr. had attended an SGA staff

Day of Prayer for the last time. He had joined with his fellow-laborers in prayer until the very end. In a special letter to her own prayer partners, Ruth wrote as follows in September 1987:

> When I think of my father, I think of commitment; I think of sacrifice; I think of PRAYER.
>
> As Jack and I stood at the casket of my dear father, we renewed our covenant before the Lord to continue the work of taking the Gospel to our Russian people — to carry on his vision of reaching men and women with the message of salvation.
>
> With the psalmist I can truly say: "*The lines have fallen unto me in pleasant places; yea, I HAVE A GOODLY HERITAGE*" (KJV).

After the earthly remains of Peter Sr. had been laid to rest in Wheaton Cemetery, Ruth and Jack, together with Nick Leonovich's son, Jim, joined in singing that song which Jack had written about the resurrection of believers in the Lord, that song which Ruth and Jack had sung so often over the radio from HCJB — the same song which that radio listener's letter confirmed had helped make many a sinner conscious of their need of a Savior:

Ruth and Jack with Jim Leonovich, singing at Peter Sr.'s internment in July 1987.

> *I could see him through the twilight,*
> *At the closing of Earth's day.*
> *I could almost hear him whisper,*
> *As to Him I knelt to pray:*
> *"Only wait a little longer,*
> *Falter not in faith, nor sigh,*
> *I will meet you in the morning —*
> *When HIS GLORY PAINTS THE SKY!"*

Vera Deyneka was able to continue living in her own apartment for another 18 months or so after the passing of her husband, but age was increasingly taking its toll of her too. Her mind remained very clear, but as time passed she could no longer live by herself. Ruth faithfully and cheerfully visited her daily, and monitored very closely the progress of her mother.

One Monday evening at the end of her visit with Vera, Mr. Murdoch, the manager of the apartment complex, invited Ruth to his office. "Ruth," he began, "I don't know if you are aware of this, but we are anticipating selling these premises. We will be redecorating them first. To do this, we need to vacate some of the apartments — including the one your mother is in." He then made some suggestions concerning Mrs. Deyneka's future accommodation, but thoughtful and caring as they were, Ruth knew that none would be suitable.

She returned home to Jack deeply concerned by one question: "*What are we going to do with Mama?*" Now 84, Vera could still walk and talk, dress and feed herself. But she needed care in other ways. Above all else, she deserved peace and quiet in the twilight of her life.

Sadly, this was not the only serious family health concern Ruth had at the time. Earlier that year, it had been discovered that Jack needed surgery. This had been performed at the end of February 1988, but there had been post-operative complications. Doctors then advised that he should be protected from stressful situations. Having worked very hard on his radio recording schedule in the Wheaton studios, he had already prepared enough new recordings for two and a half more years of programs. Therefore, he had been temporarily assigned less intensive jobs at the SGA office buildings and their grounds. But Ruth recognized that even these tasks were stressing him.

The night after Mr. Murdoch's revelation, Ruth awoke several times with that same question running around in her mind: "*What shall we do with Mama?*" Each time, she committed the problem to the Lord. Then all of a sudden, in the morning when she was dressed and ready to leave for the SGA office, she says it was as if the Lord Himself prompted a new thought in her mind. In Ashford, Connecticut, there is a home for the aged called Gilead Home, run by the Russian-Ukrainian Evangelical Baptist Union (RUEBU). This would suit her mother very well. Ruth knew it was run by loving people, and everyone there spoke the Russian language. Her mother would really appreciate that!

There was just one small problem: Ashford was in the northeast corner of the United States, more than 1,000 miles from Wheaton. In a flash, Ruth knew that she could not just *send* her mother there, she would have to *take* her — meaning Ruth and Jack would have to move too!

Unlike the move from Quito to Wheaton, this time the thought of moving away and leaving their family, friends and church behind did not disturb Ruth. She had learned much from that earlier experience, and how kind and gracious the Lord is to His children when they obey Him. As she set off on her usual walk to work that morning, it occurred to her that a move to Ashford could bring at least one other major benefit: along with being best for Vera, Jack could retire and enjoy the peace and relaxation which his state of health increasingly required.

Later that morning, Peter Jr. looked into Ruth's office. "How are things?" he asked. "Please come in and shut the door," Ruth replied, "I have something to tell you." Peter's eyes widened at Ruth's serious manner. "Something wrong with Jack?" he inquired anxiously. Ruth put his mind at rest on that — there was nothing more to report other than what Peter already knew. Then, as she summarized her conversation with Mr. Murdoch, Peter quickly echoed Ruth's own original concern: "*Whatever shall we do with Mama?*" This was Ruth's cue to share the outline of the thoughts she had had that morning. Her brother suggested they pray about it during the day, then meet again at 5 p.m.

As the day progressed, Ruth became increasingly joyful in anticipation of such a suitable new place for both Jack and Vera. Her mind began to race and her heart beat more quickly as she suddenly realized that, because the home in Ashford was Russian, it was also likely to open up new Russian ministries for her. Amazingly, even before the end of work that day, Ruth found herself clearing out her desk and putting many things in order — just as if it were to be her last day in the Wheaton office!

At 5 p.m. her brother returned. They prayed and began to talk. "You know, Ruth," Peter began in his soft voice, but also with his usual decisiveness, "as much as I would hate to see you leave the Wheaton area, I think you have been given a really great idea!"

Ruth was quick to reply. "Peter," she continued eagerly, "my heart is *really peaceful* with the anticipation of this wonderful place, where Mama will be surrounded by her own people and where they have daily prayer meetings. For, oh, she has always *so loved* to pray! I know she will participate and enjoy it all so much!"

So the decision was made, and sealed again with prayer. Ruth says there was one other reason to remember that day — it was the hottest day of the summer in Wheaton, with a high temperature of $104°$ F, $40°$ C. Ashford, meanwhile, was in a cooler corner of the country! After a further chat with Jack, she phoned the home in Ashford. Yes, there was a room available for Vera. Every sign was positive. Once again, God was guiding — quickly, clearly and decisively.

Of course, humans often move more slowly. Many things had to be arranged before the move could take place, including a long weekend trip to Connecticut to see Gilead Home and meet the staff and residents. Also, proper arrangements had to be made for Ruth's responsibilities at the SGA office to be passed on to others. At last, several months later in May 1989, Ruth, her sister Lydia, and Jack drove with many of their possessions to Ashford, while Peter flew there with Vera.

Vera became extremely happy in her new environment. For the first time in many years, she was living with a whole community of Russian people. Because they were Christians too, she considered her new home to be truly next door to Heaven! She loved her fellow residents and was lovingly cared for by Ruth and the entire staff.

The last picture of Vera Deyneka, taken just a few days before her passing in February 1993, with Ruth and Alex Leonovich.

It was not until nearly four years later that the Lord called Vera home, on February 15, 1993. She had recently celebrated her 88th birthday.

The previous day — a Sunday — Ruth had spent as usual, caring for her mother and the other Gilead Home residents. As evening approached, she had seen that Vera was too weak to go to church. Instead, Ruth had walked her to her room and helped her into bed. As Vera was being moved, she had bowed her head and kissed Ruth's hands. A few hours later, the night nurse called Ruth to say that her Mama had just died, peacefully, in her sleep.

Three days after, a memorial service was held for Vera in Wheaton, attended by about 80 relatives and friends. Ruth deeply grieved the loss of her mother, but chose the encouraging words "MOTHER IS IN HEAVEN" for the front cover of a special commemorative prayer letter. In it, she noted that the memorial service had been "a very uplifting and joyous evening of prayer, Scripture and testimonies."

At the funeral the following day, over 100 people gathered for what became a triumphant time. Dr. Torrey Johnson, who had been chairman of the SGA board for many years and a close Deyneka family friend, warmly praised the way that quiet little lady had served her Lord so completely and had supported her husband so unswervingly and unselfishly. Pastor Larry Powell of Midwest Bible Church in Chicago, where Mrs. Deyneka had been a member after Crystal Street had closed, remembered Vera's membership application many years before. In answer to one of the questions concerning possible areas of Christian service, she had replied with the simplest understatement imaginable: "*I would be glad to help in the kitchen.*" Although usually in the background, Vera, throughout her long life, had always been ready to serve the Lord simply and unobtrusively — yet wholeheartedly and therefore effectively — anywhere she could.

Such humble service seems all too rare in the church today. Yet among the spiritual gifts which the Apostle Paul names in his letter to the Romans, one is *serving*. Indeed, this is every bit as vital as others which may seem much more glamorous.

As Ruth thought of all the wonderful times she had enjoyed with her mother, another spiritual gift of Vera's came to her mind. Paul called it *encouraging*. Ruth's mind crossed the decades to her college days, and one evening in particular when the Bob Jones campus was very quiet. The night watchman was on his rounds, checking the doors and windows of the dormitories where most of the girls were already sleeping. He was quietly whistling the old hymn which goes: "*His eye is on the sparrow, and I know He watches me.*" Because Vera had often sung that hymn to her children, Ruth remembered thinking of her mother then and how she had believed those words with all her being. Vera had often warmed her children's hearts with the conviction that if God cared even for little sparrows, then He cared for them too.

As Ruth continued to think of both her Mama and Papa, she praised God that she had been blessed with not one, but *two* wonderful parents. In a special prayer letter, she wrote this on behalf of all the Deyneka children: "They taught us to LOVE GOD. They taught us to have a BURDEN for people without Christ. And they showed us we needed to be CONCERNED for the Slavic people." Indeed, Ruth, Peter Jr., and Lydia had been strongly encouraged by both their parents to *"seek first the kingdom of God and His righteousness"* (Matthew 6:33), and then to go, as He directed, *"into all the world and preach the good news to all creation"* (Mark 16:15).

Ruth stood by her mother's coffin and wondered what the coming days held. But these words from Jeremiah 29:11 uplifted her spirit: *"For I know the plans I have for you, declares the Lord, plans to prosper you and not to harm you, plans to give you HOPE and a future."*

As Ruth began to adapt to an additional area of emptiness in her life, she had one particular date in her diary to help her through the next few weeks. On May 28, 1993, she was due to leave for her second visit to Eastern Europe on a CIS ministry tour organized by Alex and Babs Leonovich.

All the Slavic countries had undergone huge political, economic and social changes since Ruth's previous trip eight years before. The closing years of the 1980s had witnessed the opening of a whole new era in the U.S.S.R. As the 1990s dawned, God began to breathtakingly answer decades of prayer for a softening of official attitudes toward Christianity across most of the great communist empire of Eurasia. By 1993, the former Soviet Union had broken up, and many communist governments had fallen! Several of the former Soviet republics had already declared — and mostly won — their independence from Moscow, including the Slavic nations of Belarus, Moldova and Ukraine. Many regions of the old U.S.S.R. had mutually agreed with Moscow to be partners of Russia, but only in a looser association than before, as the Commonwealth of Independent States (CIS).

Meanwhile, all the former Soviet satellite states in Central Europe — Albania, Bulgaria, Czechoslovakia, East Germany, Hungary, Poland, Romania and Yugoslavia — found themselves quite cursorily abandoned by the Kremlin, cut loose both economically and militarily. New governments of much more democratic ilk had quickly arisen in almost all of them. Across vast territories, hosts of Christians began to find themselves unexpectedly liberated to build new churches, openly serve their local communities in the name of Jesus Christ, and evangelize as freely as their brethren in the West! Whole populations were no longer being taught that there is no God. At long last, they were free to believe whatever they chose. Millions upon millions were eagerly seeking spiritual truth.

So SGA and other missionary personnel began to rejoice in the fact that travel to the former Soviet Union was now much easier than before, freed from many of the worries which had surrounded their previous visits. However, in the same prayer letter in which Ruth announced the home-going of her mother, she felt led to request special prayer for her second journey to Europe — due to begin so shortly — for she was now deeply concerned about Jack's health. His condition still baffled his doctors. Although it had been diagnosed and treated as Alzheimer's disease, it presented symptoms which were far from classic. Ruth had been very loathe to place Jack in the hands of others, and had continued to care for him in their apartment in Ashford. He was able to stay at home alone while Ruth worked at Gilead Home. She would run in and check on him about every two hours, and this had seemed to work out well.

However, as the time came closer for the newly scheduled trip to Europe, she came to realize that Jack would have to be placed in a nursing home during her absence. On May 12, just two weeks before her departure date, she entrusted him to the competent care of medical staff in a nearby town, intending to bring him home again upon her return to Ashford in June.

Ruth left New York for Moscow on May 28, 1993, with the Slavic Missionary Service tour group as planned. For two wonderful weeks, along with her brother Peter and other missionaries, she visited and testified in several churches — in central Moscow and Khimki (a Moscow suburb); in Kiev, Ukraine; and in Minsk and Kobryn in Belarus. As on her previous trip, every church was packed to capacity with people standing throughout the aisles. But she and others were thrilled by a completely new experience: they were now able to preach freely in the services! There was freedom and openness everywhere, and Ruth found new joy in being able to meet Christian families right in their own homes, sharing with them about the Lord without fearing negative consequences, either for her hosts or for herself.

Ruth with Dr. Alex Leonovich at the Evangelical Baptist Church in Minsk, Belarus, June 1993.

After each meeting, people crowded around Ruth and said how much they had been blessed and helped by the Christian radio broadcasts from

Voice of the Andes. Older people could not talk to her about this without tears. Younger people said they had grown up under the sound of Jack's messages and Ruth and Jack's music. People old and young alike said they had accepted the Lord as Savior as a result of their radio ministries, and thanked and hugged her warmly.

The group visited the site of a new church and Sunday school buildings under construction on the outskirts of Minsk, the Belarussian capital. One of its young pastors shook Ruth's hand and said: "Sister *Ruth Petrovna*, please tell your husband how grateful I am for all his Bible teachings on the radio as I was grow-

ing up. My school friends often ridiculed my faith and tried to persuade me into joining the Young Pioneers communist youth club. I got to the point where I was almost ready to give in! But that same morning, your husband's voice came so strongly over the radio say-

New ministry facilities in Minsk, Belarus, under construction in June 1993.

ing: 'Young man, what do you plan to do today? Is it something that would please God, or dishonor Him? Stay true to Jesus! He will strengthen you. *Be faithful to Him.* Remember, He died on the cross for you!'"

Tears came to the pastor's eyes. He explained how he had felt that Jack, though so far away, had been speaking directly to him! He gripped Ruth's hand as he continued: "Sister Ruth, please tell your husband how *grateful* I am for his faithfulness in preaching God's Word, for it helped me stay true to the Lord. This is why I am one of the pastors of this church today!"

The ultimate destination of that missionary tour group was the city of Kobryn, Belarus. After many years of consistent, laborious efforts, the Evangelical Baptist Church in Kobryn was planning the dedication of its new church building on June 6, 1993. Ruth's brother, Peter, traveled from Moscow by train to join Ruth and her colleagues for this joyous occasion. Their Mama had lived close by, and had often spoken of the ministry of an earlier pastor of that church when she was young.

Over 3,000 people attended the day-long event. It was an emotional experience for everyone.

The next day, Ruth and Peter left the tour group to begin their own search for the villages where their parents had been born, as described in Chapter 1. "WE FOUND THEM!" Ruth wrote to her friends afterward. *"WHAT an experience!"*

Following those memorable visits to Chomsk and Staramlynia, Peter and Ruth made the long, 14-hour journey back to Moscow. That very same evening, a phone call came from the United States: Jack had taken a turn for the worse. He had stopped eating and drinking. From the spiritual mountain tops of previous days, Ruth found herself cast down into a deep, dark valley. The day after, the news was even worse. Rev. Andrew Semenchuk, Pauline's husband, phoned with a report from Jack's doctor.

Jack was dying.

The next morning, June 11, 1993, Peter took Ruth to Moscow's international airport. Bidding her goodbye, he handed her two Russian-language books and said, "These might come in handy." She was placed on standby with the Russian airline, Aeroflot.

Ruth realized they would soon be closing the flight and very nervously addressed the ticket agent: *"Pazhalusta . . . please,* I really need to get on this flight! My husband is dying and I need to be with him." With that plea, she placed the two Christian books in front of the ticket agent, putting the one by Billy Graham on top, facing the young lady. As soon as the girl noticed Billy Graham's name, she spoke positively to Ruth for the first time: "Why don't you go speak to my supervisor!" Shortly afterward, Ruth's seat on that flight was confirmed. Late that same night, she was back with Jack in Connecticut.

As soon as possible, she spoke to Jack's doctor on the phone. "I do not understand what is happening to Jack," she said. "From the books I have read, Alzheimer patients die from other related conditions."

"Well, Mrs. Shalanko, Jack *does not have* Alzheimer's," were his surprising words. "But we are not sure what he has." Later, an autopsy was to prove he had had arteriosclerosis, which causes restriction of proper blood flow to the brain. Jack had suffered for over seven years from this.

For two days before he died, Ruth sat by his side, holding his hand, recounting all that had happened on her journey. She enthused him with the news that on May 30, 1993, he had become a grandfather again with the birth of Gracia Faith, their daughter Lydia's second little girl, joining Gemma who was then nearly four. Jack tried to smile at that information and squeezed her hand to show he understood.

On Sunday morning, June 13, Ruth phoned two pastors, Rev. Larry Powell of Midwest Bible Church in Chicago and Rev. Philip Somers of New Castle Bible Church in Mackinaw Creek, Illinois, and asked them to pray for Jack. Phil Somers knew Jack had read the Bible from cover to cover many, many times during his life. He made this suggestion: "Ruth, take your Bible and read it to Jack. You will see an amazing sight, I am sure." Ruth did that. Slowly, she began to read Psalm 23. With the very first verse, Jack's eyes flew open and he struggled to lift his head. He became extremely excited, and showed much emotion. When she paused to comment on the verses, he quieted down and lay back very still. As she resumed reading, he became very excited again. This continued during the entire psalm. Ruth's immediate reaction was, "I could see the POWER of the reading of the Word of God!"

Next, she related the thank-you message from Pastor Pavel in Minsk, Belarus — the one who had decided not to join the Young Pioneers communist youth organization after hearing Jack's radio messages. With tears streaming down her cheeks, Ruth shared with Jack how so many in the former Soviet Union had testified to the blessing they had received because of radio and how they wanted her to thank Jack for his long, faithful radio ministry to *his own Russian people*. His grip on her hand tightened; she knew he had understood. Then a few minutes later, she realized he had lost consciousness. Several hours later, he died peacefully in his sleep.

Jack's funeral was held in Ashford at the Evangelical Baptist Center on June 18, 1993. About 80 of his relatives, friends and colleagues attended his memorial service. This was led by Dr. Alex Leonovich, Ruth's loving relative. His wife Babs played the piano. John and Lydia gave beautiful testimonies about their dad. A tribute to Jack was written and read by his brother, Leonard Shalanko.

Leonard told of the way in which Jack had been trained as a mason and bricklayer and had quickly become a church-builder, helping with the construction of Redeemer Bible Church in Niagara Falls, Ontario. Jack later became the first overseas missionary of that church, which went on to support him throughout his entire missionary career. After his passing, the church continued their support for Ruth, and does so to this day.

Jack had loved the open air and had an ardent interest in a wide range of outdoor pursuits. One summer as a young man, he motorcycled across Canada, from Niagara Falls to British Columbia. There, while hunting, he slipped and fell into a crevice in the rock. Miraculously, he escaped injury. That night, sitting by a camp, he realized that God had preserved him from possible death. He also knew he had not been living as he should for Him. There on that mountainside, he committed himself completely to the Lord and promised to serve Him among his Russian people.

The very next day Jack had set off for home, and was soon training for the Christian ministry at SGA's Russian Bible Institute in Toronto. After graduation, he had traveled to Trieste to work as a missionary among displaced persons. Above all, Jack became a beloved Russian radio missionary, appreciated most for his Bible teaching programs and his musical presentations with Ruth.

However, as Leonard Shalanko went on to stress in his tribute, Jack had also been an effective personal worker, especially concerned for the spiritual welfare of his own close relatives. "Jack was a brother to me, not only in the flesh, but also in the Spirit," he explained. "The Lord used Jack's ministry to lead my wife and me to know Him as Lord and Savior in 1960. He was my big brother, but greatest of all, a true and dedicated servant of our Lord Jesus Christ. His experience now is indeed: '*For me to live is Christ, and to die is gain*'" (Philippians 1:21).

Though Jack was rejoicing in his new situation, Ruth, John and Lydia were mourning their new loss. Ruth, for the second time in just four months and the third time in six years, was bereft of the love and companionship of someone very near and dear. Although in each case she knew that a weak body had been supplanted by a glorious new one, each passing of a close relative had been a shock to her — particularly since she had cared so fully and self-givingly for her Papa, her Mama, and beloved husband.

But the loss of Jack was the hardest blow of all. "*I miss him!*" she wrote plaintively to her prayer partners. "This November would have been our 40th wedding anniversary and of serving the Lord together, but the Lord chose to take him HOME!"

Three blows . . . two blows . . . or even *one* such blow can be enough to depress and defeat people who have no knowledge of the love of God and no assurance of new life with Him in Heaven. Such blows may also affect Christians, for they are human and suffer much from the loss of those they love. But God's chosen people are promised an eternity in the presence of their Lord, the "*blessed hope*" Paul mentions in Titus 2:13. How good it is for every believer to know that all their family members and friends who have left this life knowing and loving God are already enjoying their new, much better life with Him!

When her father died, Ruth had fortified herself with Psalm 116:15 — "*Precious in the sight of the Lord is the death of His saints.*" This had been the verse chosen for the memorial cards sent out to their friends. After her mother had been called home, Ruth's certainty that "MOTHER IS IN HEAVEN" had been printed in capitals on the special prayer folder prepared for that occasion. After Jack had gone to Glory, Ruth opened her newsletter in this way:

> In Ecclesiastes 7:1 we read, *"And the day of one's death is better than the day of one's birth."* On June 13, 1993, Jack had THE VERY BEST DAY OF HIS LIFE. That was the day the Lord called him to HEAVEN.

The Lord loves all His children. He *"binds up the broken-hearted . . . and comforts them that mourn"* (Isaiah 61:12). He *"knows all our needs, and that we are as frail as dust"* (Psalm 103:14). We may grieve for ourselves when those dear to us are called home; but we should not grieve for them, for they are in a place which is *"better by far"* (Philippians 1:23). And we certainly must not cease serving the Lord. As Ruth was about to see again, the end of one chapter of life can be the opening of another, previously unimagined.

The moment the nurse had telephoned Ruth to say that Jack had died, her first thoughts had been: "Jack is WHOLE. He is HEALTHY now!" Just as suddenly, though, she had realized: "But Lord, the life I knew for 40 years has just ended too! I am a *widow!*" Falling down on her knees, Ruth prayed again: "Lord, what do You have for me NOW?"

His answer, although she did not know it at the time, was to involve new and very special ministries, both in the United States and abroad — ministries which she had become uniquely equipped to exercise and for which she was now free.

Then in the Lord's good time, there was also to be a whole new sphere of family togetherness, to supplement the old.

CHAPTER 10

Camps, Curtains and Conferences

1989 - 1994

Because of the needs of her mother and husband, Ashford, Connecticut, had become Ruth's new home and sphere of Christian service in May 1989. For five and a half years, this was also to be the primary place in which Ruth was to continue serving the Lord among the Russian people. Then, quite unexpectedly, it was also to become the springboard from which her most unique ministry was to be launched — a ministry which was to become possible because of the vast changes which were synchronizing in both international politics and her own personal circumstances.

While Ruth was in Ashford, the political revolutions which had begun to affect the communist world before she had left Wheaton accelerated rapidly. The earliest consequence for Ruth was a continuing need for her to help translate and answer radio listeners' letters from Russia, for these were flooding into SGA more and more. Although this work became increasingly demanding, she was happy to continue with it for a while. However, even wider-reaching consequences of the disintegration of the former Soviet Union were beginning to ensue. For the first time in generations, many of its regions were opening up to traditional missionary work of almost every conceivable kind. By the time Ruth found herself a widow in June 1993, the Russian-speaking world had become more open to the Gospel than had ever been the case before. Thus, Ruth would soon be called to minister in the former Soviet Union in a very special way.

Upon Ruth's arrival in Ashford, she immediately began to find new Russian ministry opportunities in the local area. The Russian-Ukrainian

Evangelical Baptist Union (RUEBU) organizes many Christian activities in Ashford, home of its Evangelical Baptist Center where it owns 140 acres of land. In addition to Gilead Home — RUEBU's home for the aged — its Slavic publications offices are there, plus a campground and a conference center where retreats and other special events for church groups or young people's organizations take place.

From her very first summer in Ashford, Ruth was invited to help in the children's camps. Many of the youngsters attending them were new immigrants, recently arrived from eastern Europe. Because Russian was the native language spoken by most of the children, Ruth was asked to teach the camp Bible lessons in the Russian language.

She captured some of the atmosphere of those cheerful days in a prayer letter to friends dated December 1990:

> The window was open. Soft summer winds were sweeping in. The stillness of the morning lent clarity to young, happy voices: "Ludmila, Elena, Luda . . . time to get up . . . *hurry!*" Beautiful Russian names, and the Russian language being used. Was I in some village in Russia? No, I was sitting in Ashford, Connecticut, in our apartment.
>
> It was CAMP TIME. Here at the Evangelical Baptist Center this last summer, we averaged 90 children a week for six weeks. The majority were recent immigrants from the former U.S.S.R. They preferred playing, conversing and memorizing their Bible verses in Russian. The last morning of camp, I saw teen-ager Peninnah sitting alone on some steps. Her Jewish family moved from Russia to Israel some years ago, but now lives in New York. I asked her if she had learned anything that summer. "Oh, *yes*, Aunt Ruth," she replied. "Pray that I will remember it all and live for God!" After words of encouragement and prayer, she hugged me and we said goodbye.
>
> I thank the Lord for the privilege of being involved in the camp program. Rejoice with us in the salvation of many children and the spiritual commitment of others. Quite a few are from non-Christian homes and particularly need our prayers.

Some of the children from non-Christian backgrounds who went to camp at Ashford were special vacation visitors from southern Belarus, close to Chernobyl in northern Ukraine. This city had been the scene of the world's worst nuclear accident on April 26, 1986, when one of the four reactors of an aging Soviet nuclear power station had blown up, dusting radioactive material over wide tracts of Europe. Even hurriedly evacuating an area of 1,000 square kilometers around the station, involving over 135,000 people, proved to be too little and was carried out too late. Indeed, more than a decade later, effects of the radioactive fallout are still being felt as far away as Italy, Norway and the British Isles. But not surprisingly, the most deadly consequences were, and still are, concentrated close to Chernobyl itself. An epidemic of cancer soon broke out in this region. Some cases were relatively slight, but many were severe and quickly terminal. Since travel restrictions into former Soviet bloc countries were at long last easing in the late 1980s, SGA and other missionary and aid organizations were able to send help to the local medical services and many individual sufferers.

RUEBU, spurred on by its roots in the U.S.S.R., plus family ties which linked many of its members in North America with people in eastern Europe, also helped in every way it could. One of its most imaginative acts was to fly traumatized children from the worst affected regions to Ashford, Connecticut, for a vacation on the RUEBU campground. Children likely to benefit most from its fresh air, relaxed atmosphere, and lovely surroundings were handpicked for this trip. In another prayer letter dated July 1991, Ruth wrote about the Chernobyl children and how they and the camp staff responded to each other:

Children affected by the Chernobyl fallout visit with Ruth in Ashford, Connecticut.

It is impossible to describe how BLANK the minds of these children were to the things of the Lord.

"What is sin?"

"What is he doing?" (as the teacher was praying with head bowed at the end of his class).

These are just a couple of the questions the children asked. When they first arrived, we felt it best to begin by telling them about creation. The next day, one boy was overheard saying to another: "They told us GOD created the world. Imagine *that!*"

But we should realize THEY HAD NEVER HEARD ANYTHING POSITIVE ABOUT THE LORD BEFORE! They had never seen a Bible or New Testament!

So, we have to start from the beginning. It is all new to these eight- to 15-year-old children. One 15-year-old girl is having the hardest time of all. After our Sunday morning Russian service, she left the church in tears. When a counselor spoke with her she said, "This is too much for me. I have been told all my life there is no God. This is all so confusing. Now I don't know what to think!"

Yesterday I drove them in the camp van to the Salvation Army store to pick out some used clothing from a stock given by the Willamantic Chapter of the Salvation Army for the Chernobyl children. When I opened the door and said "Go on in," the first girl drew her breath, stopped and exclaimed, "Oh! Look at ALL those things!" Her reaction brought tears to my eyes.

Yes, they have material needs and SPIRITUAL needs. Please pray! Such a wonderful opportunity, but such darkness. What a joy to tell them about the Lord, but what a RESPONSIBILITY! We are counting on your prayers.

Meanwhile, there were many more opportunities for Ruth to help members of the small Russian-speaking community permanently residing in Ashford. Many of the older ladies were particularly grateful for Ruth's readiness to take them to the doctor and to interpret for them on those often anxious and sometimes worrying occasions. Residents of Gilead Home, where her mother lived, also appreciated her piano playing in chapel on Thursdays and Sundays. She played not only in the services themselves, but also quietly before them as the little congregation began to assemble. She encouraged the residents to request their favorite hymns and they enjoyed her renderings of them as they sang along.

Then at the end of 1991, the management position of the home fell vacant. Ruth was invited by the RUEBU executive committee to become the home's new director effective January 1992. After much thought and prayer, Ruth accepted the offer, although only on a temporary basis. For one thing, it was during this time that Jack was growing progressively weaker and his future needs were very uncertain.

Ruth did not find her new job easy. "Day by day I had to learn things I had never known before," she affirms pensively. "Neither 27 years in radio nor 11 years clerical work in Russian had prepared me for them. I cannot over-emphasize how often I prayed and pleaded for wisdom from the Lord! Every morning as I awakened to face a new day, I knew there would be situations arising that I had never encountered before. But I was very aware that if that was what the Lord wanted me to do, He would help me. So I leaned on Him, and tried."

Simultaneously, of course, all the residents of Gilead Home leaned on Ruth. "It seemed as if I became their mother and they became my children," she has said. Ruth's basic approach to her new role was to act

Ruth stands with Mary Selody (seated), the founder of Gilead Home, and her assistant Lydia Sheyda.

as if every one of the residents was a guest in her own home, even part of her own family just like her mother, Vera. Ruth viewed it her responsibility not just to provide as much care for everyone as she could, but also to love each one as an individual. In return, the residents loved her and deeply appreciated the attention she paid to all their needs.

Ruth was very thankful for "the wonderful staff we were able to gather around us. The majority of them were new Russian immigrants, recently arrived from the former Soviet Union. One, Marina, was a good cook. We had a wonderful couple, Vera and Vladimir, who helped both in taking care of the residents and with the maintenance. Galina from Kirghizstan joined us as a trained attendant, using her skills for the practical, physical care of the elderly. She had the heart of a missionary and accepted her new role in Ashford as her first missionary assignment. Paula Darras became my right hand, serving as afternoon attendant and taking over both the financial management aspects of the institution and the ordering of food and medicines. I was so glad for all their help, and that of others, too. We all worked together well as a team — mainly because we regularly met for times of prayer to commit ourselves, our ministry, and our elderly residents to the Lord."

In many areas, Ruth positively took the lead. When Ruth and Jack first arrived in Ashford and saw the many needs, she had been happy to join in with others on the maintenance side, such as helping paint, scrub and clean the dormitories for the boys and girls before the camping season began. In one year alone, Ruth sewed 26 pairs of curtains for one building and enough for 40 windows in another! So when appointed manager of Gilead Home, she began a particularly energetic yet also enjoyable period renovating it. This was made possible by a memorial gift in honor of Ann, a former resident who had gone to be with the Lord. Some of the happiness and satisfaction Ruth rightly felt at that job well done shines through her personal recollections: "We painted the hallways, some of the bedrooms, and the kitchen. My love for sewing was transferred into making new valances and small curtains. I loved getting new tablecloths with matching flowers, anything which would brighten up the home. We bought a fish tank and some goldfish, and introduced two birds to our little menagerie. I often smiled as I passed through the sitting room and saw Adele and Christina, two of our dear ladies, tapping on the fish tank. As the fish came to them, they would greet them and talk to them so sweetly. During special holidays, we dressed the rooms up in different ways and brought in several small things to make life for everyone a little more interesting."

Ruth's staff during her tenure as manager of Gilead Home (left to right): Galina, Nadia, Zoia, Marina, Paula, Willey, Bea, Vladimir, Joe, Sally, Vera and Jo.

When the chaplain could not be present for church services at Gilead Home, Ruth frequently led the entire services herself. Outside chapel, her loving counsel and encouragement were often appreciated too — for example, by the lady in her mid-80s who had cancer but no living relatives to comfort her. Ruth encouraged her with reminders that she would not die alone; her whole Ashford family would be by her side. Every such conversation ended with a hug and kiss of assurance.

All this time Ruth was also responsible for making key decisions concerning the health treatment the residents required, at whatever time of day or night an emergency arose. If someone became ill or fell down, could they be treated in the home or not? Every evening, Ruth went to bed both mentally and practically prepared to get up in the night if necessary, even to take someone to the hospital. She became good friends with the staff of the local volunteer ambulance service, the doctors, the dentists, the pharmacists . . . and the funeral director.

Being able to serve God in Ashford in such varied ways was also a real blessing for Ruth herself. One day, sitting at the chapel piano, a warming thought came to her mind: "From Quito, Jack and I had a ministry to maybe millions of people, and truly God used us there. But here in Ashford, I know this ministry to a few people is just as important in His sight. Even playing these hymns is meaningful to these dear people."

Ruth was glad, too, that she could serve her own loved ones every day. Concerned as she had been over the health of both her aging mother and ailing husband, she was now able to care for them both, yet not having undue time to fret about them.

"Most of the residents had favorite chairs in the lobby of the home," Ruth smiles. "My mother chose one nearest the hallway leading to her room. Every morning as I came into the home, my eyes searched quickly to see if Mama was sitting in her chair, which she usually was. She would be so happy to see me and I to see her. As I greeted her with a morning kiss, she always asked me, 'How is Jack today?' If he was not too well that particular day, I would say, 'Not too good, Mama,' and she would beam and say, 'It's all right. *I am praying for you!*' I would take this phrase with me all day as I went about my work. So it was that God arranged for me to be the one to be with our mother, to help her in the last years of her life, the one to see her smile and hear her prayers for others — most especially for her own family."

Then on February 15, 1993, one year after Ruth had become manager of the home, Vera went to be with the Lord. Jack followed four months later, on June 13. Ruth suddenly found herself relatively alone, freed from two of her greatest responsibilities of recent years.

What had the Lord in store for her next?

Naturally, a time of sorrow and grieving followed. Through this, Ruth began to learn new lessons not previously possible. A year later, in July 1994, she wrote this to her prayer partners:

"The Lord raises up those who are bowed down . . . He supports the fatherless and the widow!" (Psalm 146,:8-9). I am *amazed* how often WIDOWS are mentioned in the Bible. I hardly noticed this before. There have been lonely times, but I can testify to the Lord's nearness and care during this past year of becoming accustomed to widowhood.

I want to especially THANK each individual and each church who has stood by me with their prayers and financial giving through this period. You have all encouraged me so much.

Like many a person after losing their spouse, Ruth rightly considered that her life might be at a new crossroads. Throughout most of the previous 40 years, her work for the Lord had been closely tied to that of her husband. Since Jack had been forced to retire four years previously, managing Gilead Home had been something of a departure from that pattern. Though her work there had developed with his needs and those of her mother firmly in mind, Ruth had known Ashford to be the Lord's place for her at that time. Now Jack and her parents needed her no longer, her personal situation had radically changed once more.

In the meantime, of course, the political situation in the Russian homeland had also changed radically and remarkably.

From the early decades of this century, the Russian world had been dominated by a family of atheistic and materialistic creeds, collectively dubbed communism. As the European continent struggled to rebuild after World War I, this basically social and economic system had begun to extend revolutionary tentacles across Central and Eastern Europe, then far beyond. Led by Vladimir Lenin, communists in Russia established their international headquarters in Moscow. This city soon became the capital of that new super state, the U.S.S.R., which stretched across the whole breadth of the Eurasian land mass from the Baltic Sea in the west to the Pacific Ocean in the east.

At first, communism proclaimed praiseworthy principles: fairness and equality for all. It had even sought early support from some Christian churches. However, it quickly evolved into a one-party political system which took offense at the slightest whiff of opposition. In turn, this system was furthered by fear, and fostered for the chosen few — the card-carrying Communist Party members and their friends. Some of the severest religious persecution in the whole history of the world was to follow from the early 1930s, initiating a veritable new dark age more than half a century long. By the early 1990s, militant atheism had deeply influenced all of Ruth's previous four decades as a missionary with SGA.

Today, it is widely recognized that as long as politicians or political systems continue to deliver improvements in living standards, the common people can be quite tolerant of associated limitations on their personal liberties — including the freedoms of speech, religion, and meeting together when and where they choose. For a while, this kind of tolerance had been seen even in the communist world. However, as the second half of the 20th century unfolded, the inefficiencies of centralized economic planning had become more and more burdensome to the peoples of the U.S.S.R., as well as many of its satellite states. Living standards in these countries actually began to fall, not only compared with those in more market-oriented countries, but even with their own recent internal levels. Predictably, pressure for change began to rise.

By the end of the 1980s, national lids had begun to blow. One by one, the communist governments of Central and Eastern Europe were overthrown. In some cases, as in Hungary, Poland and the former Czechoslovakia, there were virtually bloodless, post-communist revolutions. Elsewhere, as in Romania, Bulgaria, and the U.S.S.R. itself, fierce though mostly brief civil wars were fought, with considerable loss of life before calm was restored under new and radically different leaderships.

In most former communist countries, it became clear that it would take many years to rebuild national economies. But much more happily, whole populations were once more able to believe and say what they wished without fearing for their liberty, or even their lives. Prisoners of conscience were released, and almost overnight, Christians who had been heavily persecuted were able to worship, witness and work for the Lord with almost total freedom. Countries long closed to traditional types of missionary work opened up to the Gospel and related help from outside.

After democracy became infectious in Eastern and Central Europe in the early 1990s, changes affecting church life were ones for which many believers both within and outside those countries had long prayed. Yet few, if any of us, who had so prayed for Christians persecuted by communism ever dreamed that these prayers would be *so suddenly and dramatically answered!* In fact, only recently has the true scale of this miracle been fully recognized within the perspective of the whole history of the human race. With the wisdom of hindsight, we can now see that it ranks alongside major miracles of both the Old and New Testaments — including the safe return of the Israelites from captivity in Egypt, and the rapid growth of the early church despite the severest treatment the Roman Empire could mete out.

What encouragement this should be to any who beg the Lord to intervene in any situation, from the individual to the international! And what a thrill it was for Ruth and many others to *finally* be able to visit and freely minister in lands which had been so hostile to the Christian church and missionary work!

In the light of all the changes in her own life that occurred at the same time as those in the Russian world, it is not surprising that Ruth began to wonder before the Lord if some new ministry opportunity might possibly open up for her, perhaps even in the CIS? SGA had become able to base workers within the former Soviet Union. The mission had even established an office in Moscow itself — something unheard of throughout the previous 60 years of SGA's existence.

Because the Lord knows so well the needs and abilities of His children, it is not surprising that a new and very special invitation came to Ruth from Eastern Europe for the autumn of 1993 — at the precise time she most needed some personal encouragement. Neither is it surprising that it came from an earlier visitor to the home for the aged, for all who visited Gilead Home were deeply impressed by its manager's care for all her "children."

In 1992, Rev. Grigori Komendant, president of the Union of Evangelical Christians-Baptists in newly independent Ukraine, along with his wife Nadia, visited Ashford to speak at the annual conference of RUEBU. Ruth had shown Nadia around Gilead Home, and discussed with her all the other ministries in Ashford in which she had been involved. An instant friendship sprang up between the two. One year later, when Nadia heard of Jack's death, she sent a message to Ruth asking

Rev. Grigori and Nadia Komendant.

her if she could come to Kiev, Ukraine, for their Autumn Conference for Women. Nadia thought this would not only be a great blessing to many in her country, but would also help Ruth through her time of grieving.

Ruth was glad for the invitation . . . and dismayed when just four hours before her scheduled departure from New York to Moscow on October 4, 1993, the flight was canceled. The White House, home of the Russian parliament in Moscow, was in flames! A determined attempt to wrest power from reforming president Boris Yeltsin was being repelled by tank corps loyal to the president. Quickly, members of parliament were arrested and Yeltsin's power was enhanced. Fortunately, that crisis was short-lived. Few people were as brave as Ruth, though — she flew to Moscow as soon as permitted, merely two days later!

In Kiev, the Ukrainian capital, Nadia Komendant took Ruth to many meetings. One was a conference for pastors. This was presided over by Brother Dukonchenko, a previous, much-respected leader of the Ukrainian Baptists. He invited Ruth to share in one of the sessions. Ruth was deeply moved as she scanned the sea of over 200 faces, knowing that during the communist era many of those men had suffered much for their faithfulness to the call of Jesus Christ.

Recalling the dark decades of the 1950s, 1960s and 1970s, Ruth told her audience that every time the radio staff at Quito had come to the microphone they had prayed that God would bless His Word as it was broadcast to the U.S.S.R., and that many would hear it and be helped by it. She confirmed that, particularly in the earlier years, it had been a real act of faith to broadcast at all, not knowing if anyone was listening. Ruth, Jack and their colleagues had simply prayed before each radio program that someone would find it a real blessing.

When the conference session ended, Ruth was almost mobbed by the ministers! They eagerly clustered around, anxious to confirm what a *tremendous* blessing the broadcasts had been. Many of the pastors were from small towns or villages, or even far out in the countryside. They recounted, one after another, how they would awaken early to catch the morning programs from Voice of the Andes. Many of the younger men exclaimed how they had accepted the Lord as children while listening.

Ruth rejoiced! "It was a *very moving experience* for me, so soon after Jack's promotion to Glory, to be among those soldiers of Christ and to hear their testimonies of the value that all our years of broadcasting had been to these wonderful people!"

During her visit to Ukraine, several day-long women's conferences were held. One of the most memorable was at Alexandria, an overnight train journey from Kiev. Ruth and Nadia were met at the local railroad station at 6:30 a.m. After a 20-minute walk, followed by a van ride from the pastor's house, they arrived at the church compound. Like many in that region, the church stood in a yard surrounded by a high wooden fence. As the gate opened, they found many ladies of all ages already inside, awaiting their arrival.

The early breakfast was a highlight of the conference in Alexandria, Ukraine.

First, there was breakfast, laid out on simple tables of wooden planks. As was the Russian custom, prayers of thanksgiving were offered with everybody standing up. Glasses of hot tea were then passed around, followed by thick slices of dark bread and a homemade butter of lard and garlic. After once more standing to pray when the meal was finished, the meetings began in the church.

Women had gathered from eight different communities. Sisters from each one contributed to the program — telling their testimonies, reciting Christian poems, singing or praying. Nadia Komendant, her mother and Ruth all gave messages. The morning session, which began at 10 a.m., had been due to end by 1 p.m. for lunch, but the ladies said, "Let's not stop!" because the presence of the Lord was so prevalent.

It was 2:45 p.m. before some of the women said, "Nadia, we MUST stop now for lunch. The borscht is boiling over and over! We need to eat it!" The benches were taken to the side room once more, where the plank tables had been set up. These were now laid with a simple, traditional meal: steaming bowls of that deep red vegetable soup, ample boiled potatoes, more of the dark bread, and glasses of tea. Apples were the dessert.

The second session lasted from about 4 p.m. until 7:30 in the evening. It only finished then because of train departure times for ladies from some of the more distant villages.

Ruth and Nadia's train was not due to leave until 2 a.m. the next morning. After informal fellowship at the pastor's house, their group, including others from the conference with later trains to catch, walked the remaining distance to the station, arriving there sometime after midnight. The two dozen or so Christian women gathered in the waiting room and began softly singing hymns. Some of the songs were new to Ruth, but she joined in when she could. Other passengers in the waiting room listened. Then a stranger approached the informal choir.

"You're Christians, aren't you?" she said. "I would like you to pray for me because I'm sick. I know that when *you* pray, something happens!"

The ladies gathered around her in a circle and said they would pray. But there was something much more important than the healing of the body. Did the woman know that God sent His Son Jesus to die on the cross for the spiritual ills of mankind, and yes, for her too? They clearly explained to her how she could be spiritually healed and begin a personal relationship with the Lord. The woman had many questions and was deeply touched. There, at that train station about 1 a.m., the ladies prayed for her and encouraged her to accept Christ. There was joy on her face as she thanked them and kissed them and assured them she would seek the Lord.

Ruth remembers: "Soon afterward, our train was announced and there were quick hugs, kisses and goodbyes before Nadia and I ran off to find it. It took so long to find the right numbered car that we barely tumbled in before it began to move! We just collapsed with laughter! It had been such an exciting and blessed day that even with many hours to spare after the conference had ended, we nearly missed our train! We made ourselves cups of tea from the samovar in the corridor, and there, between 2 and 3 o'clock in the morning, shared the wonderment of joy in serving the Lord."

Flying back to North America, Ruth had more time to marvel at the previous two weeks. This is what she wrote in her diary that day on the plane, October 17, 1993:

> During the past two weeks, every lady I met in those services had heard the names Deyneka and Shalanko! I did not meet one who did not know my Papa's name.
>
> As I sat drinking tea in the home of Pastor Nikolai Kidovich in one of the little towns, he stood behind me and patted my head softly. I felt that was like a benediction from the Lord.
>
> No, I cannot forget my dedication to Russian ministries. This is my life's calling. I must consider these last two weeks as my rededication to Russian missionary work, even in the future. Whatever I do, *it must be for the benefit of furthering the Gospel to my Russian people.* My heart cries out for them!

Romans 14:12 tells us that: *"Each of us will give an account of himself to God."* We have to answer, I am accountable to the Lord. I am thankful for this past invitation to Ukraine, and for the opening of the window of ministry that I feel God will give me in the future days.

In the meantime, of course, Ruth had passed her 65th birthday. In the United States, this is a common retirement age for people not already retired. Though suffering from a significant breathing problem, Ruth concluded that: "Somehow I still had reasonable health and strength. I also had a *great desire* to keep serving the Lord among my people. So I continued to pray about this, thinking and wondering what new kind of work the Lord might open up for me."

Her brother Peter, with his wife Anita, had recently rented an apartment in Moscow and had been spending increasingly long periods of time there with his newly formed organization, Peter Deyneka Russian Ministries. From early childhood, Ruth and Peter have had a very close relationship. The fact that both had come to dedicate their lives to serve the Lord among their own peoples had further strengthened their kindred spirit. Ruth has often turned to Peter for advice. So it was natural that after her visit to Ukraine, and now that Jack was gone, she should again turn to Peter for suggestions concerning the possible future ministries she might exercise in the newly formed Commonwealth of Independent States.

Since the downfall of the old communist government, the need for professional Russian people in the former Soviet Union to be able to communicate more easily with the English-speaking world had become ever more widely recognized. Thus, one suggestion Peter offered involved the possibility of Ruth teaching English in Russian schools in the new CIS. There was a growing demand for it. The education authorities were now even willing for the Bible and other Christian books to be used as English textbooks! Peter's idea appealed to Ruth. However, not being a teacher, Ruth would first need some training and certification.

Accordingly, she began to telephone colleges and universities in the Ashford region — seven in all — asking if they had evening classes on the teaching of English as a second language which she might attend that summer after her day's work at Gilead Home was done. One after another, the answers came back, no, *no*, NO! Every time, this was the answer. Ruth recalls replacing the telephone onto its cradle for the final time and exclaiming out loud: "Well, Lord, I've tried to do this my way. Now I will leave it in Your hands, so You can do it YOUR way!" From that moment on, she stopped trying to think about or work out herself how she might enter Russia for further ministry. She just kept on *praying* . . .

Several months passed.

Then one evening, on returning to her quiet little apartment in Ashford, she found the red message light on her telephone answering machine was blinking. Idly pressing the recall button before beginning some chores, this message jolted her to attention:

"Hi, Ruth! My name is Micki. I am calling you from Moscow. I am on the committee of PROJECT 250. We are involved with special church-planting seminars for pastors and Christian workers, which your brother Peter is organizing. We are planning a seminar in Ukraine, and this one is different because the men are bringing their wives and several women engaged in missionary work are coming too. We feel we need some sessions on subjects of particular value to the women. Your brother suggested we ask if you could come and be the women's speaker. *Please call me back!*"

Almost in disbelief, Ruth rewound the tape and played it through once more. Then she dropped to her knees, bowed her head, and whispered: "Lord, THIS is Your way!"

But what could she share in those seminars? She had never had that kind of public ministry before. In Europe many years earlier, she had often spoken in services, but biblical exposition had not been her responsibility. After their marriage, Jack had been the leader, the preacher, the Bible teacher, and the evangelist. She had been primarily his helpmate. Until asked to manage Gilead Home in Ashford, she had considered that her varied roles and functions had all been supporting others. She had done many things in her life . . . but had never exercised a teaching ministry of her own to adults in the Russian language. Even if she were capable of this, what messages would be most helpful for those Russian ladies? Calling Micki back, she agreed to go, but asked for suggestions concerning the topics she should address. Ruth and Micki agreed they would both pray for the answer, and set a time to talk again.

Ruth recalls what happened next.

"As soon as we finished that phone call, I took my Bible in my hand. Leafing through it, I saw the books of Ruth and Esther. Then I noticed the names of Mary the mother of Jesus, Lois, Anna and other women in the

Bible. Wasn't there *great potential* to encourage women in Russia through the experiences of those women who had served God in so many different ways? Even women who had met Jesus and whose lives had been changed through knowing and serving Him? A great desire came over me to study the lives of these and other women in the Scriptures. After a few days, and much more thought and prayer, I called Micki in Moscow again and shared these thoughts.

"Her response was immediate: 'Why, Ruth, our committee has met and prayed and has come to the *same suggestion!* We have concluded that the ladies need to be taught things from the Bible that they would probably not hear from the pulpit in church services. Studying women in the Bible will be so good for them!'"

Thus, the Lord's leading was crystal clear — at least for the next step along Ruth's way. "A new and unexpected phase of my ministry was beginning. God was leading me further along this pathway called life." The seminars were scheduled for August 1994. Ruth was very conscious that she should not contemplate that new venture without the Lord's help and guidance. She also knew she could not give other women anything she had not first acquired herself. So began another chapter of learning in Ruth's own life. Her anticipation and excitement grew as she studied, one after another, the lives of many of the women in the Bible and meditated on the messages they might hold for Russian women in the modern world.

As expected, about 60 women attended the eight-day series of seminars in Rovno, about 200 miles west of Kiev. Organized by Light of the Gospel, the oldest national mission in Ukraine, the course was attended both by pastors' wives and single Christian lady workers. Ruth soon discovered that, although mostly quite young, many of them had been regular radio listeners. Thus she found her audience particularly eager and attentive. Her carefully prepared messages, developed lovingly and appropriately for those types of ladies, were a great success. But Ruth was overwhelmed by the response. In a prayer letter that fall, she remarked that it was impossible to describe her feelings as she saw the tears of the women and heard their prayers of response to her ministry.

She received several invitations to speak in churches in the region around Rovno during the week which was to follow the end of the seminars. When accepting, she specifically requested that the extra meetings be for women only. She was so new to this type of public ministry, and still felt unsure of herself as she stood before each congregation! In Ecuador, her speaking had been into a studio microphone. Now there were faces before her — faces of people with varied, individual needs. She felt even more challenged and moved for her Russian audiences than ever before. As it happened, though, during that second week her audiences were often mixed. She appealed about this to the pastors, saying that her heart's messages were for the women of their churches. But they would smile and say, "You go ahead and talk to the women. We men will just observe in the background. You see, we also heard your radio broadcasts in years past and want to be part of these meetings too!"

The day before her scheduled return to the United States, Ruth stayed with her dear friends, Grigori and Nadia Komendant. That evening they chatted about the new opportunities which were opening up so thick and fast for Christian service in the CIS, and how God was drawing many people in those countries to Himself. All of a sudden, the president of the Ukrainian Baptist Union looked across his kitchen table and said, "Sister *Ruth Petrovna*, FREE YOURSELF from your ministry in Ashford, and come to the CIS — especially to Russia, Belarus, Ukraine and Moldova — and MINISTER TO OUR WOMEN HERE! They NEED you! Come this winter, as soon as possible, for it may soon be too late!"

He paused for Ruth to think, then continued.

"Yes, we only invite you in the winter, because during spring and summer our women need to work in their gardens, planting potatoes and other vegetables so their families may have food on their tables the rest of the year. We only hold special services in the winter. Come after Christmas, and stay until Easter!"

His wife Nadia took up the theme. "Yes, come for our ladies conferences in March. Encourage our ladies on how we should live as Christian women in this new era, where there are so many new opportunities to witness for the Lord which we never had before!"

Ruth's heart stood still.

What an invitation! *What a challenge!*

Much of the night and the next day on her long flight home were spent in thought and prayer. Could this be the open door for which she had prayed ever since Jack had gone to be with the Lord?

She could not escape from Nadia Komendant's final words of farewell, called out to her at the airport in Kiev: "Remember, Sister Ruth . . . *come back*, COME BACK!" That night, by the time she had reached her apartment in Ashford, she knew God was giving her the desire of her heart . . . to go back to the CIS, to the land of her parents, to her Russian people, to serve Him among them.

Taking up this new challenge meant ending the responsibility of her present position. She called her special relative, Dr. Alex Leonovich, president of RUEBU, to submit her resignation as manager of Gilead Home. When she told him her decision, he expressed his deep dismay — then quickly added: "But who am *I* to say I'm *sorry* when I myself know the overwhelming needs of the CIS and have given my own life to minister to our people there?!"

Already at that time, in September 1994, Ruth was planning another visit to Belarus so she could attend the dedication of a new Sunday school building in Minsk, the capital of Belarus. This facility was desperately needed because of the recent rapid growth in the numbers of children wishing to attend Sunday school. Under the long decades of communism, Sunday schools had been illegal across the entire U.S.S.R., as well as church attendance for anyone under 18 years of age. Now these restrictions had been swept away, and large new facilities were needed since the fastest-growing Christian work in many places was among young people.

And Ruth had a special reason of her own for wishing to attend this dedication service — this was the building Ruth had seen under construction in Minsk the year before. It had been there that Pastor Pavel had given Ruth his message of gratitude for Jack's ministry, with which she had been able to encourage Jack during his final hours in this world.

So on Friday, September 9, 1994, Ruth flew Air Austria from New York to Vienna, then on to Minsk. Friends were gathered at the airport to warmly greet her, filling her arms with a beautiful bouquet of gladioli. Her heartbeat quickened: once more she was in the land of her roots!

The next day she was taken to the dedication service of SGA's new Regional Ministry Center in Belarus. Dr. Bob Provost, who had become president of SGA in the United States one week earlier, was also present. Meeting for the first time, Bob and Ruth quickly found warm fellowship in the Lord and oneness of heart, mind and spirit in Him. Dr. Provost readily agreed that Ruth's recent call to ministry to women in the former Soviet Union had truly been from God. Encouraged by this, Ruth knew she could set out on her new missionary assignment to the CIS in January 1995, just as the Komendants had originally proposed. Yes, *she would soon be going back again!*

That evening, Ruth attended the regular Saturday night service at Minsk Baptist Church. Just before the closing prayer, her presence in the balcony was announced to the congregation and she was welcomed by the pastor. As soon as the closing prayer ended, she felt a tap on her shoulder. Turning around, she found herself looking into the sweet face of an older lady in the row behind. "Are you REALLY *Ruth Petrovna Shalanko?*" she inquired wonderingly. Ruth nodded. Without ceremony, the lady leaned forward and put her arms around Ruth, cradling her head and rocking her gently to and fro. "Oh sister, *Sister Ruth Petrovna*, if ONLY I COULD TELL YOU what the radio broadcasts meant to us in our village!"

Ruth felt the crown of her head being moistened by the lady's tears as she continued: "The persecution of believers in our village was so great we never dared to take our children to church. But every morning, we awakened them early to listen to your programs from the Voice of the Andes. That was their church!"

The lady's voice broke: "And do you know, dear Sister Ruth, because of your broadcasts, because of the faithful preaching of your husband Jack, one of my children who sat by the radio each morning has been helping with the construction of the new Sunday school building. *For my son is one of the PASTORS of this church!*"

All at once, Ruth realized that this must be the mother of Pastor Pavel, the young man who himself, on that very site 16 months before, had thanked Ruth so effusively for the radio broadcasts . . . that young man whose thanks she had been able to share with Jack just before he had lost human consciousness and slipped away to Heaven!

The following day, nearly 400 people jammed into the church's new educational facility for its dedication ceremony. This lasted several hours. The local press and TV crew were in attendance. Ruth was asked to bring a greeting. She spoke of her joy in being in the land of her parents once more, affirming that the new building was yet another answer to her father's prayers — that the Gospel would go forward in his homeland and that many in Belarus would find the Lord, just as he himself had done.

The new facility in Minsk, Belarus, shown under construction in Chapter 9.

After the ceremony, guests were invited to a simple meal. There, two professional women — administrators of a local hospital — approached Ruth. Though not believers themselves, they had been given Bibles and had been invited to the dedication service. They had been deeply moved by it all. But what had interested them most was that a lady from America spoke so lovingly of Belarus and so positively of God! They confessed a strong desire to find Him for themselves, and listened intently as Ruth told them her testimony.

Still later, after the evening service in the central church, Ruth was asked to address the regular youth meeting, for which about 50 had gathered in the choir loft. Ruth was excited to hear them planning outreach activities among university students. Describing the lives of several foreign missionaries in Ecuador, she stressed the time and effort they had to expend just to learn the languages and customs of the Indians and to translate the Scriptures. She challenged those young Russians to firmly grasp their new opportunities to be missionaries to their own people in their own country. They *could do so at once*, with no need to spend long periods preparing for it!

At the end of the meeting, several of the young people prayed with emotion — dedicating their lives to the Lord, to serve Him in their own country and to spread His Word, as their pastors and others were already doing so effectively.

Ruth found that throughout Belarus there was much evidence that God was blessing His people as they became more bold in their witness and evangelism. In Rahachov, a small community over 120 miles from Minsk, a church fellowship had long met in a house because the communist authorities had not permitted a church to be built in that district. Now things were different. A plot of land had been acquired for their first church building. Not being a very large plot, it was clear to Ruth that the members were imaginatively doing their utmost to use the land as fully as possible. Two three-story towers were already going up, one at each end of the plot. She learned that these towers were for the Sunday school. But Ruth wondered aloud if there were really that many children in this thinly populated area who would or could attend?

"Well," said her hosts, "we have about 300 children coming on Saturdays at present! Even the new rooms will not be big enough for them all, so half will come on Saturdays and half on Sundays. Most of them are children of unbelieving parents, who are nevertheless sending them, thrilled that their children can now study God's Word!"

Back in the capital itself, Ruth learned more about the Minsk Sunday school whose new premises had been dedicated just a short while before. "We already have a membership of 600 children," she was told by the superintendent. "Before the new building was opened, we had to hold classes from 8 a.m. to 7 p.m. every Sunday to accommodate so many children in four small rooms. In fact, we will still have to stagger classes in our new building. You remember the TV crew that was present at the dedication service? Well, the local TV station did a short spot on us in their news program. They also gave a phone number for viewers to call if they were interested in their children joining our Sunday school. The name of the church and our phone number were given just one time. Now, only three days later, we have already received over 500 calls from parents saying: 'We want to register *our* children in your Sunday school!'"

It thrilled Ruth to think that she would soon be able to play a fresh part in the life and growth of the churches in Belarus, Russia, Ukraine and other republics of the new CIS. It was clear that in many areas the Church of Jesus Christ — long bound by political chains, gagged by media restrictions, and punished by persistent persecution — was now quickly growing and being greatly blessed by God.

From Minsk, Ruth was then able to retrace parts of the journey she had made with her brother Peter — that summer of 1993 when they had searched for their roots — and was able to revisit the birthplace village of her father. In Staramlynia that chilly September day, cousin Anastacia was found in the fields with her husband, Peter. They were digging up potatoes. Because of her blindness, Anastacia had not seen Ruth coming, so Ruth knelt down to hug and greet her. Ruth knew that — but for the purposes of God — she might easily have spent much of her own life alongside Anastacia, working in the fields. She therefore prayed all the more that God would continue to bless her new ministry as she sought to plant and nurture God's Word in Russian-speaking lands and to harvest more souls for Him there.

Ruth finds cousin Anastacia harvesting potatoes in Staramlynia, September 1995.

They could not talk very long that day, for Anastacia was conscious that colder weather was approaching. The frost would damage the potatoes if they were not harvested quickly! So there in the potato field, Ruth once again told her cousin that God loved her. Sadly, Anastacia insisted her life was too sinful for God to forgive her. Ruth was disappointed, but promised to return the following March. With much reluctance, they parted.

Fortunately the neighbor, Vera, who had taken Ruth to the potato field, was also able to take her to the nearby cemetery where her paternal grandmother had been buried. On the tombstone of her *babushka's* grave, Ruth found this inscription:

DEYNEKA
ANASTACIA L.
BORN 1860, DIED 1960
"Blessed are the dead
who die in the Lord."
(Revelation 14:13)

Ruth drew yet more strength and encouragement from that headstone, for she had already come to know the story to which it alluded.

Ruth's father had returned to Staramlynia in 1925 for his first visit home since leaving for the United States 12 years before. Peter Sr.'s mother had responded very negatively to his newfound faith. She had even pressed him for money so that the village could celebrate his homecoming with vodka. In reply, he told her of the Bibles he had brought as gifts, and then proceeded to hold Gospel meetings in the Deyneka house where many people were saved!

Peter Sr.'s mother had been angry and embarrassed. Her son had been working in America — he must be RICH! Why would he not give her money so they could celebrate in the traditional Russian way? She had severely scolded Peter and mocked his newfound faith. She even threatened to throttle him with a chain while he was sleeping! Thus, Peter actually came to fear for his life while sleeping in his mother's hut. This continued until he married Vera and returned to the United States.

Later — *much* later — during Peter Sr.'s second return to his homeland, Grandmother Anastacia Deyneka had finally come to know God through faith in Jesus Christ. And in a memorable way she had been able to testify to this just before leaving this life to meet her Savior. Until 95 years of age, she had been very active but by then had lost her eyesight.

After this, she gradually found it more and more difficult to do things for herself. About five months before her death, she had gone to bed and had not been able to get up again. "She's losing her mind, too," people said, as they helped her as much as possible in her 100th year. Several times they had thought aloud about calling the Russian Orthodox priest to pray over her and "grant her absolution" before she died. One day, as they talked about this once more by her bedside, Grandmother Anastacia suddenly sat up in bed and announced in a clear voice: "Don't get the priest for me! I don't need him! I know Jesus as my personal Savior! When I die, *I am going to be with Him!*"

With that, she sank back onto her pillows.

"*Babushka*, grandmother," they fretted, for they had not understood the situation at all, "We don't know where we can get a Baptist pastor for you!"

But at least Grandmother Anastacia understood the Gospel. "I don't need a Baptist pastor either," she insisted. "*I KNOW I'M GOING HOME TO SEE JESUS!*"

Recalling all this, Ruth smiled as she stood before her grandmother's grave. She had never met her grandmother on Earth, but knew she was rejoicing in Heaven in the presence of the Lord along with Ruth's own dear Papa, Mama and Jack. Peter Sr.'s witness to his mother had eventually borne fruit! This was a timely reminder to Ruth that as a worker in God's harvest field, she might sow, or plant or water . . . but it would be God Himself — alone — who could bless her work and grant the increase. Sooner or later God would ensure a harvest, of that Ruth was sure, though much of this might not be until after she herself had gone to Heaven.

Driving back along the dry and dusty lanes of western Belarus, Ruth pondered again on the totally unexpected way in which God had chosen a teen-age lad from that remote region, had taken him to a new land to hear of Christ, and had then used him to spread the Gospel in his own native Russian language all around the world. Tears flowed freely down her cheeks as they left Chomsk and headed back toward Kobryn. She looked at her companion and said: "Why am I crying? I guess it is because I feel SO PRIVILEGED to be serving the Lord in this land of my forefathers!"

Once relieved of her caregiver responsibilities for her mother and husband, Ruth had prayed in Ashford that the Lord would show her what to do next. As so often happens, He had been doing so — just one step at a time. But now the next step was to be a GIANT step for Ruth. No longer would she be serving God as a helpmate for her husband or as a member — or even a leader — of a team. For a time at least, God was now clearly calling her more as an *individual* — one especially gifted, chosen and prepared by Him over many years for a particular, very specialized and distinctive ministry. All her former experiences had been part of her training for it. Echoing the words of Mordecai in Esther 4:14, they had been to prepare her *"for such a time as this."*

Thus, Ruth was able to conclude her Christmas 1994 prayer letter to family, friends and prayer partners as follows:

> WEEPING in 1993 . . . as I said farewell to my mother and dearest husband. *"Weeping may endure for a night,"* but JOY in 1994 as ministry in the CIS brought me extreme happiness. Indeed, *"joy comes in the morning"* (Psalm 30:5). The times in Ukraine and Belarus were the most blessed I have ever experienced in all my 44 years of missionary work!
>
> The Lord willing, I leave O'Hare Airport on January 5, 1995, for the CIS for my new ministry to the women. My *needs?* Most of all I need *lots of prayer*. I also need HIS blessing and help! It sure will be COLD. I need His protection.
>
> Please continue to share in my ministry as I go to the CIS! Thank you for your support. May you have a very blessed Christmas.
>
> Joyfully in HIM,
>
> *Ruth*

CHAPTER 11

How Should We Russian Christian Women Live?

1995 - 1996

Ruth arrived in Moscow on January 5, 1995 — two days before the traditional Russian Christmas Day. She was amazed to see the large banner in the GUM shopping mall near the Kremlin which greeted all: *"WITH THE BIRTH OF CHRIST."* Only a few short years before, its Soviet banners had still been proclaiming the old communist dogma, *"There is no God!"* What a change!

The senior pastor of Moscow Central Baptist Church knew Ruth would be attending the 9 a.m. service that Christmas morning. He invited her to sit with the leaders on the platform and to bring greetings to the congregation. Every single seat in the church was taken. People were standing at the back of the church, as well as three orderly lines down the aisles. Scanning the crowd of well over 1,000 people, Ruth was struck by how happy they were as they sang the beautiful Christmas hymns! For so many years, they had gathered for worship in fear. At long last they were able to assemble and praise God in freedom. Conscious that her father had spoken from that same pulpit, Ruth spoke of her long Christian heritage and her joy at being able to return to Russia to witness for the Lord.

Recalling that occasion, Ruth says: "Let me try to find words to describe my feelings: CONTENTMENT, as we sang the Russian Christmas hymns of my childhood . . . JOY, as the choir rendered favorite carol selections I used to sing in our Russian choir in Chicago . . . PEACE, as I watched the people enter the church for the service and saw their worshipful faces. Every chair in the church was filled. The love of the people was over-

whelming. How I thanked God for allowing me to be in the land of my parents, and for the opportunities He was giving me to speak in the churches.
"Being able to participate in that service was *the best Christmas present I could possibly have had!* I had no idea where the Lord was going to lead me in the next three months, but I knew He had taken me there. From the outset I gave myself completely to Him, to use as and where He would. That Christmas morning service was to be the beginning of a beautiful venture with Christ. From then until my return to the United States on April 4, 1995, I was to experience blessings, situations, miracles and answers to prayer that I had never known in my life before."

Certainly she could not have undertaken such a venture without help from on high. In the remainder of January she spoke at 22 meetings, 27 in February, 38 in March, and two in the first three days of April! Scattered across large areas of three countries — Russia, Ukraine and Belarus — Ruth's tally of 89 public speaking engagements in 87 days would have taxed even the fittest person. That an unwell lady in her 67th year could have completed such an undertaking, in the depths of an Eastern European winter and traveling long distances over land almost entirely by public transportation, is quite astonishing.

The venues for her meetings ranged from great cities including Moscow, Kiev and Minsk, through smaller cities and towns, down to the villages and even tiny hamlets which she preferred. The meetings themselves were also of many different kinds. Most, of course, were solely with women

Ladies eagerly gathered to hear Ruth in the town of Rahachov, Belarus.

— sometimes with older women, sometimes younger women, sometimes single women of any age, and sometimes all kinds of women at once. But she also spoke in a number of general church services and other meetings when men and children were also present. In the Crimean city of Donetsk, she had the opportunity to speak for an hour to the entire work force of a factory which produced stage clothing and theatrical costumes. In the city of Vinnytsya in Ukraine, she was invited to speak in a public school to a class of 10-year-old children learning the English language.

While in the Vinnytsya area she stayed with Valya, a newly converted young woman, and her son Igor. Valya had been witnessing to her mother who lives in a village about an hour's journey away. Her mother had been reading the Bible, but was only just coming to appreciate how much God loved her. She was not yet sure about committing her own life to Him. Valya pressed Ruth to visit her mother, and a Gospel service was arranged in her small house — the first Gospel meeting in the history of the village. That very day Valya's mother was born again, and others were touched by Ruth's ministry. Since then, regular services have been held in that settlement.

On another particularly memorable occasion, Ruth spoke at a military Palace of Veterans where, over tea, she was able to share the Gospel with a former general in the Red Army. At least as memorable, though for entirely different reasons, was her visit to the Bible institute in Samara, a major city on the banks of the wide Volga River, 500 miles southeast of Moscow.

One meeting in the Ukrainian Black Sea resort of Odessa was held in a tent because the group of believers in that suburb had only just begun to construct a building in which to hold their services. Tent meetings have been quite common in the 20th-century history of the worldwide church. However, as Ruth remarks, it is hard to even IMAGINE a service in a tent *in the depths of an Eastern European winter!* Amazingly, nearly 150 ladies attended that meeting in Odessa despite the severe cold weather. Not until the end was tea served, which warmed Ruth a little as she mingled and chatted with many of the ladies.

It had been early in Ruth's itinerary, at the close of another great women's convention in Kiev chaired by Nadia Komendant, that this announcement had been made: *"Sister Ruth has a few weeks to spend in Ukraine. If you would like to invite her to speak in your district, tell us afterward."* It was because of this that Ruth's Ukrainian schedule quickly filled to the brim. She was unconcerned by the sizes of the audiences she might have, for her greatest desire was to be an encourager of forgotten ones, whose greatest source of happiness was their faith in God. This was why she felt led to mostly visit the smaller towns and villages, especially places where visiting speakers from other countries rarely went.

Although the biggest of her congregations on that itinerary was well over 1,000 strong, many numbered under 100 and occasionally as few as 10. Everywhere she met people who had regularly listened to Christian radio. Many recalled having heard Ruth and Jack broadcast in earlier years from HCJB. Many were still regularly listening to the Christian programs, whether from abroad or — as had become possible in a limited way since the fall of communism — from mediumwave transmitters within the countries of the CIS itself. She found that for multitudes of people, especially the elderly and sick, and mothers with young children, radio programs are still their church services. The same is true for many hamlets and entire villages far from the nearest open church.

In sharp contrast to her meetings in the rural areas, one group of speaking engagements had been organized for Ruth in southeast Ukraine among a center of heavy industry on and around the Donetsk Basin coalfield. There, Ruth spoke in the city of Dnipropetrovsk as well as smaller mining towns including Nikopol and Dniprodzerzhynsk. On Tuesday morning, the pastor said they would be driving to Marganets for a 10 a.m. meeting. Surprised by the time, Ruth asked if this was common for such a service.

"Oh, no!" came the reply. "This is a special meeting because you are here and the church is so eager to meet you! We couldn't arrange an evening meeting because your schedule was full."

Quietly, Ruth wondered who would be able to attend a meeting in the middle of the morning in an industrial city in the depths of winter?

As they neared the church building, she saw warmly clad men and women tramping down the snowy streets wearing fur hats and head scarves and carrying little bags. Ruth sensed that the bags contained Bibles and that these people were heading for the service. Sure enough, at the church the people were streaming in! Inside, it was already virtually full. There was even a choir of young people. Ruth later asked Pastor Vasily how they could be there on a school day. He smiled and said they, too, wanted to be part of such a memorable service and had skipped classes.

With the congregation standing, the pastor opened in prayer. He recalled that their church in Marganets had been closed by the communists and many of the members thrown into prison for their faithfulness to Jesus Christ. Through all those terrible experiences, they had been encouraged and sustained by Christian broadcasts. He then introduced Ruth, remembering how she had been part of the SGA team at Voice of the Andes, and welcomed her as a very special guest. But Ruth was not only one of the radio team that had been such a blessing and encouragement to the believers in that region — she was also the first foreign visitor they had ever had in the history of their church!

This was the cue for one of the younger ladies to step forward with a bouquet of flowers, which she presented to Ruth as the young people's choir began to sing. At last the pastor turned to Ruth: "And now, Sister *Ruth Petrovna*, it's *your* turn!"

Ruth scanned the congregation. Many were still wrapped in coats and scarves. Some were smiling, some crying, as they riveted their eyes on the tall, gray-haired, American-Russian lady standing before them. In that moment, Ruth could see so much warmth in that sea of hardworking, careworn faces that she was in tears too — quite overwhelmed. As she struggled to find her voice, she found herself thinking particularly of the poor among her audience, who clearly found it a struggle to maintain a decent standard of life for their families, and of those who had been imprisoned for their faith in Jesus Christ.

At first in a whisper, she said, "I do not have words to tell you how I feel! My heart is so full! But *thank you so much* for all your love!" Then in the power of the Holy Spirit, she grew stronger and began to develop a lesson based on Abigail, one of the women in the Old Testament . . . for Ruth had become all the more certain that the lives of many women in the Bible have much to say to women in the CIS even to the present day.

Another of her subjects in such meetings was Miriam, called by God to serve His people in a leadership role — and who did so well for a while. But as Exodus 15 describes, she then began to think too highly of herself, even to the point of believing she knew as much as her brother Moses, the supreme leader of their people. Ruth pointed out that a lack of proper humility is still a danger for any Christian in a position of authority today.

Then there were Hannah and Peninnah, the two wives of Elkanah. Between them they cared for a godly man, and both went to the temple with him. Yet God had chosen to bless only Peninnah with children, and she in turn chose to ridicule Hannah in her childlessness and gossip against her. With her sharp tongue, Peninnah even reduced Hannah to tears in the temple! Describing these events from 1 Samuel 2, Ruth would then ask: "Might there be any women like Peninnah in our churches today?"

And from John 11 and 12 in the New Testament, Ruth sometimes spoke of Mary and Martha, those sisters who both enjoyed the company of Jesus, particularly pointing out how Martha, hard at work preparing a big meal in the kitchen, had too little time to listen to His teaching.

Ruth's talks were Bible-based, and chosen to be as pertinent as possible to each audience she found — timeless messages, as helpful for women in Eastern Europe as they have been elsewhere down through the centuries. Their success was evident from the reactions they invoked. Women of all ages peppered her with questions! Later, many responded audibly in prayer or visibly with tears. Ruth was an open channel for blessing from the Lord because her personal love and concern for others was obvious to all and her great patience evident for everyone to see.

The questions she was asked were many and varied. Often they sprang from difficult personal problems and deep spiritual needs. They included queries from wives and mothers, especially on how to live with an unsaved husband or how to bring up children in a society which — with little warning and absolutely no preparation — has become exposed to all the worst of Western influences. There were questions from single girls, particularly on how to manage in regions of high unemployment and few career prospects, and how to relate to others if they remained single.

Whole nations springing from the former Soviet Union are in a more rapid rate of flux than at almost any previous period in history. Entire societies and ways of life are under enormous stress. Even the churches themselves are being challenged in unexpected ways, for as Ruth discovered, more than half their congregations are new believers, still learning the very basics of their newfound faith. A high proportion of the new converts she met were from the professional classes, providing fresh opportunities for local fellowships, but also presenting new challenges especially to the longer-established, more traditionally minded congregations.

Ruth was deeply conscious of the tremendous challenge provided by each new meeting and every question asked. It was often hard for her to counsel simultaneously in both a frank and sensitive way. For example, younger girls often wanted to hear about people of their own ages in the West — their job opportunities, clothes, pastimes and general lifestyles. But how could teen-agers in small rural communities in eastern Europe even begin to appreciate the comforts and conveniences, the problems and the temptations, of affluent urban populations in the West?

Ruth was encouraged, though, by the realization that CIS Christian women of all ages generally had closer personal relationships with the Lord than their counterparts in the more prosperous countries of the world. Furthermore, they were also more eager and willing to go into even deeper relationships with Him. Meanwhile, the sadness and depression of those in the CIS who did not know the Lord always prompted her to treat even seemingly frivolous questions seriously. She always emphasized that getting right with God was of far greater and more enduring value and significance than money, status or material possessions.

Nor were men too shy to quiz their foreign lady guest! Both publicly and privately, many sought her advice. Writing to prayer partners on February 2, 1995, concerning that visit to the Bible institute in the Russian city of Samara, Ruth reported this:

> My first assignment was one I had never had before . . . to lecture to the students on what kind of husbands they should be! I

had just two hours to prepare. At first I was scared, but with the help of the Lord, we dived right in with Bible in hand. My lecture lasted one-and-a-half hours, with many questions following. In my weakness I realized that nearly 40 years of marriage to Jack was good material. Actually, we had a GREAT time as the men opened up their hearts. It was fun, it was surprising, and it was *blessed!*

On another occasion nearer Moscow, Ruth visited a family for lunch, and the conversation turned to the acute problems it was experiencing — the family was truly falling apart! Later that afternoon, she led a discussion with ladies from a church in the Khimki suburb on husband/wife relationships. This meeting was followed by a long prayer session and many petitions to the Lord for better family living. Afterward, it took Ruth another hour on the Moscow Metro before she arrived back at the apartment where she was staying — weary, and wondering whether any good would come of that difficult day's work for the Lord. As Ruth and her hostess, Svetlana Chartschlaa, were drinking tea and beginning to relax after such a long and taxing time, the telephone rang.

"Sister *Ruth Petrovna*," quavered the voice of the man whose home she had visited for lunch: "*Our family is restored, and WE THANK YOU!*" He explained how difficult life with his wife had been in recent years, but continued to tell how she had returned home from the meeting in Khimki a changed person. His wife had confessed that her attitude to him had been all wrong and pled for his forgiveness. His married life with his wife had been reborn in Christ, and they were now happy together in the Lord!

Little wonder Ruth concluded a prayer letter by marveling: "I am OVERWHELMED with the way God is blessing. I know I am in the right place, and that the Lord is with me! How I rejoice in all of this!"

And there were even opportunities for Ruth to witness while traveling, too. Contemplating a 14-hour train ride between Belarus and Ukraine, she prayed that God would give her a female fellow passenger in her train compartment. Her prayer was answered in the form of Valya, a woman of about 40 years of age who instantly recognized that Ruth was from another country. Valya wondered aloud, what was an American lady of retirement age doing traveling alone in that part of the world?

Ruth explained that her family roots were in Belarus, and she had come to share God's love with Russian-speaking people. Valya responded with the news that although she had been brought up as an atheist, she was now very interested in religion and in all Ruth had to say about God.

Being an atheist, Valya's father had not allowed her to have anything to do with religion when she was young. Her husband had been baptized as a baby in the Orthodox Church, but had had no active faith himself. After the fall of communism, as people began to talk much more freely about religion, Valya realized that something was lacking in her life. Although their own son was 10 years old, she and her husband had decided that he, too, should undergo Orthodox baptism, usually a rite applied to babies.

"For a while," Valya continued, "I felt I had really taken the step of religion. But my life still feels empty and I still do not know God in a personal way. I have managed to borrow a New Testament, but to this day I don't really understand it. Often I put it down, frustrated!"

Ruth and Valya talked for hours, until 2 a.m. At that point Ruth felt it vital to get some sleep, for she was speaking at a women's conference later that morning. So she encouraged Valya to focus on those Scripture passages which she could understand, and always to pray to God for wisdom to understand His Word more. When Ruth finally prepared to leave the train, Valya hugged and kissed her, and thanked her profusely for the helpful time they had had together. The Lord had blessed Ruth with a lady traveling companion . . . and that lady had been blessed, too!

In Belarus, Ruth felt drawn to return again to her father's village, Staramlynia. There she was able to spend two more hours with Cousin Anastacia and her husband Peter in their home. She had some little gifts to give to Anastacia, who, in return, reached under the bed. Despite her blindness, she quickly located some pumpkin seeds. These she gave to Ruth, along with eggs newly laid by the chickens (which came and went in and out of the little wooden home, just as they pleased).

Also revisiting her relatives the Leonovichs in Kobryn, Ruth asked Vanya Leonovich if he could take her to one of the villages where her father had preached some 70 years before. Although the building used for the services was locked, it was possible to peep in through the window. Inside, there was a small table set with a white cloth and a glass containing dried flowers. There were rows of simple blue-painted benches and other seats lining the walls. The wallpaper was peeling, the walls were

The small village church where Ruth's dad had preached in 1925.

cracking, and a hole had developed in the roof. Dust, leaves and twigs had blown in from outside. As Ruth stood there peering in, she thought, "If only the walls could speak, I could hear my father preaching . . . calling men and women to follow Christ. Where are these people now? Are they with the Lord?"

Suddenly, Matthew 24:35 sprang into her mind: *"Heaven and earth shall pass away, but MY WORD shall last forever!"* Her father, mother and husband had already passed away, but they had all witnessed faithfully for the Lord. Not only were they rejoicing in His presence, but many more were rejoicing with them too — souls saved and preserved because Peter, Vera and Jack had delighted to share the Word of God and His love with others.

As her itinerary progressed, Ruth came to thank the Lord increasingly for so many new opportunities to share that same Word herself with relatives, friends, acquaintances, and even complete strangers in that land. The treasures of His Word are lasting and precious — *yet available to all*, and *FREE!* It was with great reluctance that after three intense months, she returned to the United States as planned.

As eager as Ruth was to get back to her apartment in Ashford for a rest, she felt she should first report on her CIS experiences to some of the churches which have long and faithfully supported her as a missionary of SGA. These include Wichita Bible Church in Wichita, Kansas, and First Baptist Church of Freeport, Illinois. Both these churches had originally pledged their support to Ruth in 1950, when she first made her way to Europe, and have continued to support her ever since. Such faithful investments for nearly 50 years have been richly repaid.

Finally, Ashford beckoned in April 1995, and Ruth could write once more to all who had supported her mission to the CIS. She noted:

> I had not been in my own apartment for six months. It was good to get home and sleep in my own bed again, even though the hospitality in the CIS had been wonderful! I had stayed in the homes of the women who had invited me to their churches. They served me the best they could, and almost always gave me the best bed or sofa in the house. The linen sheets were always crisp, covered with homemade feather quilts. I was shown much Christian love, and I was grateful. At home in Ashford, it seemed strange to be surrounded by familiar things and to sleep in one bed for a while. Sometimes I wondered if my memories were just a dream. But

God had granted me such an experience that I could NEVER HAVE
DREAMED IT POSSIBLE!

And she was encouraged by the knowledge that she would be going
back to eastern Europe just five months later — leaders of the Ukrainian
Baptist Union had invited her to return in the fall. Ruth had been delighted
to accept, and was already looking forward to her return.

Although her speaking tour planned for the fall of 1995 would be for
two months instead of three, it would cover more ground, taking her to
Asian as well as European Russia, and to Moldova and Ukraine. And although it would be generally less of a venture into the unknown, as she
made her plans Ruth was more conscious than before of the great responsibility which rested on her in such a public ministry. Therefore, as
she began to prepare her messages, she felt a growing trepidation about the
task that lay ahead. This seemed so daunting that she continually prayed for
strength and wisdom. She sometimes even wondered if should she really
go back!

One day as she was reading in the book of Joshua, its very first verses
spoke to her in a clear, fresh way: *"Now it came about after the death
of Moses that the Lord spoke to Joshua, saying, 'My servant is dead. Now
arise, you and all your people. Go to the land that I am giving you . . .
every place on which the sole of your foot treads, I have given it to
you.'"* Suddenly Ruth felt the burden of responsibility lifting from her
shoulders and her trepidation falling away. The words on the page seemed
to change until they read: *"It has come about after the death of your
parents, and after the death of your husband, that I am telling YOU to
arise and go to the lands of your Russian people. Every place where
you go, I will give it to you."* Reading further, her eyes fell on Joshua 1:7,
"Only be strong and courageous," and on verse 8, *"You must meditate
on My Word night and day. The law of the Lord must not depart from
your mouth,"* and on verse 9, *"Do not tremble or be dismayed, for THE
LORD YOUR GOD IS WITH YOU, WHEREVER YOU GO!"*

As she finished reading those verses, she took them as God's purposes
and promises for her personally. It was the Lord who had previously opened
the door for her into the CIS. Now He was opening it again! She must therefore go, in His strength and His alone. She remembered how much her

father had prayed that the Russian homelands would open to the Gospel. How he would have loved to have gone back there, to freely minister in the churches as she could do now! His faithful prayers for greater Christian freedom, and those of so many others too, had been so amazingly answered. But it had fallen to his son Peter Jr., and then to his daughter Ruth, to take up the challenge, the responsibility, and the privilege of encouraging thousands of Russian-speaking brothers and sisters in Christ to grow in the Lord, and to witness to many who still did not know Him.

On September 26 , 1995, as she boarded the plane at Chicago's O'Hare Airport headed for Odessa, Ukraine, she prayed: "Thank you, Lord, for bidding me to be strong and courageous. Please help me to remember to do everything in Your name, not in mine, and that I must meditate constantly on Your Word."

She had no time for rest after her flight. Although she had traveled more than one-third of the way round the world, crossing eight times zones, her first meeting was 10 a.m. the morning after her arrival in the bustling Black Sea port of Odessa. This was followed by lunch at the same church, then by an evening meeting for women, held in a local school. The pattern and the pace were familiar. They were just like the trip before!

Even as she entered the building for the first meeting in Odessa, she was still not completely sure what kind it would be. In a large hall, she found the pastors, elders and deacons of the church, plus all their wives, sitting around in a big semicircle. They said they wished to begin by sharing with her — a representative of the entire Russian radio missionary team — their thanks for all the Russian-language Christian broadcasts. Many would give personal testimonies of how the Lord had saved and preserved them through the long era of communist persecution. After that, they would be anxious to hear a message from the Lord through Ruth!

As one after another got up to speak, it seemed as if at least half of them had served time in prison because of their faith and witness for the Lord. Finally the senior pastor rose to his feet.

"I was an 18-year-old young man when I was arrested and sentenced to 10 years imprisonment," he began. "My crime was professing faith in Jesus Christ and telling someone else about it. During the first five years, I spent time in four different jails. The authorities moved me often so that I would not get too comfortable in any one area. This was common practice. Because Christian prisoners were so well behaved, the guards often took pity on them. They treated them more leniently and were generally more friendly to them than to the average convicts! But the senior prison staff would see this happening and either move the Christians or move the friendly guards. Also, the Christians were usually sent farther from home than the others, to prevent their families from providing them with extra food and warm clothing — neither of which were adequate in prison.

"For the second five years of my sentence, I was sent to Siberia. Out there, some things were more lenient. We were put to work in the community, felling trees, building roads and office blocks, and so on. And we were allowed to find our own living accommodation, reporting once each week to the prison office in town. As I was walking down the street after my arrival, not knowing where to look for a room, I stopped to ask an elderly woman: 'Are there any Baptists here?' She was very scared at that, so I quickly added, 'I am a believer and I need help! I just thought they might help me.'

"When the woman saw I was sincere, she told me of another elderly lady who lived at the other end of the village. I went to see her the next morning. Looking over her shoulder through the doorway of her house, I saw a big Bible open on the table and was reassured. This lady invited me to live in her home. Often her unsaved sons would visit. I wanted to witness to them and teach them God's Word, but did not know how. Furthermore, I was fearful. For all I knew, they might have been KGB informants!

"Then I remembered the radio programs I had heard from Ecuador before being sent to prison. I saved up the little money I was paid and bought a shortwave radio. When her sons came to visit, at first I would turn the volume up for the singing and down for the prayers. Soon the men asked what times those programs were on and came to visit during them. This increased my courage! I began to copy down phrases and thoughts from the broadcasts and quoted them as I began to witness, slowly at first, to the unsaved friends and children who came to visit this *babushka*.

"Soon we began a home group church in that old lady's house in the depths of Siberia. The lives of many of the villagers began to be organized around the radio transmissions! Even milking times were changed, and the times children got up in the mornings.

"It was through listening to the radio messages that I was inspired to preach. When my prison sentence had been served out, five years after arriving in Siberia, I returned home and began preaching the Word of God there too."

By the time it was Ruth's turn to speak, all she wanted to say was "AMEN!" and go home! It had been so moving to hear how those dedicated servants of God had suffered for their faith. Whatever could she share with them? She realized, though, that these men and women were eager to serve Christ and share this Gospel with other people. But they needed advice and encouragement on how they might do so best, especially with all their new freedoms to live openly for Christ and share the Gospel with others. These dear people had learned many things from listening to the radio. Could they not learn still more from being able to question a speaker and discuss matters specifically concerning themselves?

Thus, Ruth became even more firmly convinced that she was in Eastern Europe once again by the will of God. "With much exuberance," she affirms, "I continued my schedule of special meetings! Often I was the only speaker, whereas in the usual services there would be two or three sermons. This meant I was often expected to speak for an hour, an hour and a half, or even longer. I just had to call on the Lord to help me. I was frequently amazed at the thoughts and words that were coming to me, knowing they were only from Him. Often I glanced at my watch and was astonished to find that an hour or more had already passed since we had begun to open His Word. We had question times at the close of the meetings. Many other questions were brought to me privately, being more personal in nature. Many of the ladies were so burdened for their children or unsaved husbands. How could they influence them for the Lord? Others were burdened for themselves, that they might grow more spiritually. My heart went out to them all."

Ruth sharing the Gospel during tea with a group of unchurched women in Lvov.

Ruth's itinerary continued on to the historic city of Lvov in western Ukraine for several women's meetings, then across the border into the new republic of Moldova. Previously the Soviet state of Moldavia, this little country of some five million inhabitants is sandwiched between Romania to the west and Ukraine to the east. It became independent in 1991. Since then, churches in Moldova have been growing fast, helped particularly by field workers of the British office of SGA through church-planting and leadership-training seminars. Ruth was one of the speakers at the large annual Baptist women's convention held in the Moldovan capital, Chisinau, and attended by some 350 ladies. What interested Ruth about this particular event was the large number of young women — besides the middle-aged and older ladies — who had gathered for it from many outlying towns and communities.

Reflecting the linguistic mix in Moldova, the conference was held in both the Russian and Romanian languages. As Ruth prayed about which women in the Bible she should portray, she felt led to speak once more about the New Testament sisters, Mary and Martha. Eastern European people are naturally very hospitable and Slavic ladies are also good cooks, very innovative in their recipes when there is little variety of food available. Thus it seemed appropriate for Ruth to describe the kindness and hospitality these two sisters showed Jesus, and debate the relative merits of the different ways they sought to serve Him. Ruth remarked on the eagerness of Martha to prepare an elaborate meal for the Lord — but also on how she spent all her time in the kitchen, fretting about her household duties. Martha was so concerned about the physical needs of her guest that she was unable to gain from Jesus spiritually, as her sister Mary did! Many of the Moldovan ladies took this message to heart, resulting in a lively prayer session as the meeting ended.

The convention organizer then expressed her wish for Ruth to speak next on the theme of relationships within the family, especially between wives and husbands. Ruth knew many of the young women present were recent converts, whose husbands were still without the Lord. In her next message Ruth chose to speak from the passage in Proverbs 31:10-31, and emphasized these Scriptural specifications of a *good wife*:

- Verse 11 teaches that because she can be trusted, her husband will give her his heart.
- Verse 12 insists she will do only good things for him all his life and never evil.
- Verse 13 says she is not lazy and works to make the house nice.
- Verse 14 shows she wishes to please her whole family and will search widely if necessary for special or tasty food.
- Verse 15 tells of her early rising, and kindness not only for her own family but also for those who in some way were serving her.

Later verses tell of her work in the garden as well as the home, and of her work for the poor and needy as well as for her husband and family.

A good wife is a happy, joyful person, wise and kind to all. No wonder, Ruth pointed out, that verse 28 asserts that the children of such a woman call her blessed, and verses 28-29 affirm that her husband highly praises her: *"Many women do noble things, but YOU SURPASS THEM ALL!"*

Ruth asked her audience in Chisinau how any woman could accomplish all of this — then pointed to verse 30, which gives the resounding answer: "*A WOMAN WHO FEARS THE LORD is to be praised!*"

For good measure, Ruth then asked her congregation to turn to one last verse, Romans 16:16. As they found it, a murmur ran around the building and there were some smiles. "Come, ladies," Ruth said, "let's read this verse aloud, in unison."

Almost inaudibly they whispered, "*Greet one another with a holy kiss.*"

Ruth smiled and said, "No, let's read it again, louder and clearer!" This time they responded well. The third time, they were resounding! Ruth emphasized how Paul had taught members of the early churches to greet each other with love and warmth, even with the sign of a sanctified kiss. Not waiting for an answer before she sat down, she finally asked the wives if they had kissed their husbands farewell as they had left their homes for the conference that morning. It was clear from their reactions that most had not.

So Ruth set out the necessity for Christian wives and mothers to express their love for their husbands and children in both very practical and overt ways — adding that by so doing, they were also teaching their children the right way to live. At the end of the session, there were many intense prayers of response.

Afterward, Ruth was flocked by scores of young women. "Sister Ruth, what should *WE* do? We are new believers. We love the Lord. We want to live for Him, but it is so hard with our husbands because *they don't understand!* Are you telling us that we should love them even if they won't trust Jesus Christ — even if they make things difficult for us?" Ruth affirmed the teaching of the Word of God: Christian wives should love and honor their husbands, even if the husband shuns the Lord and casts scorn on faith in Him.

Ruth found those sessions unforgettable, for so many of the new young Christian wives professed themselves encouraged to return home and live for Christ, come what may. Nor will she forget the manner in which one of the young ladies confided in her at lunch on the last day of the women's convention in Chisinau: "Sister *Ruth Petrovna*," she said, "I need to tell you that when I went home to my husband yesterday, I tried to show him by my smile and kind words that I love him. I must admit that I had grown tired of his criticism of me as a Christian and his frequent fault-finding, though I realized this came from his frustration that I knew Christ and he did not. Last night I told my husband I love him and I love the Lord. I told him that because I want to follow the Scriptures, I plan to be the *best wife* to him that I can be. My husband was so shaken by this that he embraced me, and we cried and cried."

With tears in her eyes, the girl continued: "I am encouraged to keep praying that he will be saved. I will try to do all that those verses in Proverbs 31 teach. I will keep reading them, to remind me to be kind, to be loving, and to be faithful to him. I am going to *trust the Lord for the salvation of my husband!*"

And there were many memorable occasions when young men, too, responded to the messages Ruth brought from the Lord. One such occasion was the very next day, at Grace Bible College in Chisinau, where Ruth addressed the student body of about 125 on the topic of personal commitment to God. As she was speaking, she became aware of one young man who was listening particularly intently. As the meeting ended, he lowered his head and silently cried. Afterward, Ruth tried to shake hands with as many of the students as possible, including that young fellow. But as he was thanking her for her visit, he suddenly burst into tears again, excused himself, and rushed from the room. That evening she found he and others had been invited for further fellowship in the home where she was staying. By then, he was more composed. He apologized for having been so emotional and abrupt that afternoon.

"You see, Sister Ruth," he explained, "I have had a problem in my life. I had committed it to God and had been fasting about it for two days, praying He would show me how to deal with it. During your message this morning, I realized that God was showing me what I should do. I couldn't talk with you after the service because I was so overcome with that answer from the Lord!"

There were some times on her travels when Ruth herself needed help and reassurance from the Lord that He was with her. Such occasions were most frequent when she had to travel alone. Rev. Platon Chartschlaa, with whom Ruth had worked in SGA's literature department in Wheaton, has served God for many years as a missionary supported by SGA and RUEBU. Platon has often witnessed to relatives of his in the small Black Sea republic of Abkhazia near Georgia, where he was born. Through his witness, the Lord has drawn one of his nieces, Svetlana, to know God for herself. A brilliant, well-educated woman with many qualifications, she was already living in Moscow by the time Ruth had begun her itinerant speaking ministries in the CIS. As soon as Ruth had arrived in Moscow, Svetlana had given her hospitality in the one-room apartment where she was living. Svetlana subsequently helped arrange many of Ruth's journeys within Russia, purchasing tickets, contacting the pastors, and organizing many of the accommodations needed in other cities, towns and villages. Svetlana therefore came to be Ruth's constant traveling companion and guide on the many buses, metros and trains she used in that country. Ruth's praise of her is heartfelt: "Svetlana really took care of me. Also, she and I had wonderful fellowship together. We always prayed before and after a meeting. She was a great help and blessing, and became a true sister in the Lord. How I have come to thank God for Svetlana Chartschlaa!"

There were, however, many times elsewhere in the CIS when neither Svetlana nor any other Christian friend could travel with Ruth. Some of these occasions provided opportunities to counsel others, as on that overnight train journey between Kobryn, Belarus, and Kiev, Ukraine, early in 1995. However, there were also times while traveling alone when Ruth was really scared!

One night she had to travel alone by train from Kiev to Khmelnytskyy in western Ukraine. At first she was the only passenger in her sleeping compartment, but knew there would eventually be three strangers sharing it. To her dismay, one after another they turned out to be men! Ruth was understandably nervous and dismayed. She asked an attendant if she could move into some other compartment where there was at least one other lady. No, came the reply, every one was full.

"So that was it," Ruth says. "I went back and sat down. I recalled again those words of the Lord which He had given me in Ashford when I had been preparing for that whole trip: '*I will be with you, I will not fail you, or forsake you. Be strong and courageous, and do not tremble or be dismayed, for the Lord your God is with you.*' And I added, '*EVEN ON THIS CLIPPERTY-CLOP TRAIN IN UKRAINE!*'

"I bowed my head, closed my eyes, and prayed: 'Lord, I didn't really ask to come on this trip! I'm here because I know You are leading me. I wouldn't have chosen three men as fellow passengers, but I boarded this train with a prayer for the right compartment, and this is the one I've been given. Please protect me, and help me have a calm and restful sleep tonight because I have a service to speak at tomorrow!'

"Soon afterward, the men went out into the corridor. I knew this was a sign of respect for me, so I could prepare for the night. I spread one sheet on the mattress, placed my small bag under my head to use as a sort of pillow, lay down, pulled the other sheet up over my head, and said, 'Lord, I place myself completely in your care.' And He sent me *such sweet peace*

I fell asleep immediately . . . and woke in the morning after the *BEST REST I EVER HAD* on a train during all my travels in the CIS!"

That afternoon she was taken to Zachintzi, a village an hour's drive out into the countryside. To reach the meeting place entailed a further walk of over half a mile along a muddy track. The lovely little chapel had been built by villagers themselves, mostly women. It stood atop a low hill, like a lighthouse for the region around — small and simple, but clean and freshly painted, a gleaming glimpse of God's purity and love in a wayward world. Ruth learned how each summer many children came from nearby cities to spend the school holidays with their grandparents in the village to enjoy the fresh air and fresh food. Daily Bible studies and classes are organized for these children by the pastor and his wife. Through them, many young people have already come to know the Lord. Ruth was particularly burdened for the local grandmothers who had not yet committed their own hearts to Christ. She encouraged the Christian women in the church to be faithful witnesses in deed and word to all their neighbors.

On Sunday, Ruth was invited to participate in a typical Ukrainian Christian wedding not far away in the village of Velikiy Chernyochi. Everyone in the vicinity had been invited, and about 250 actually attended! It was a great opportunity for witness and evangelism. Everyone knew the bride and groom were Christians. Both gave their testimonies, and the bride's father (the pastor) preached a long sermon. Other ministers also spoke, plus Ruth, who was asked to do so twice during the festivities. The choir sang several hymns and the Gospel was clearly proclaimed. The joyous event ended with a big meal featuring lots of dark bread, potatoes prepared with garlic and onions, cabbage rolls, tomatoes and cucumbers, and tea and small cakes — contributed by virtually the whole village.

Two local customs were also observed. In one, a bridesmaid handed the groom a head scarf which he then tied around the head of his bride. From that moment on, whenever she went to church she would be expected to wear such a scarf as a sign that she was a married woman. In the other, a large wooden bucket was passed around to collect gifts of money to help the newly married couple set up their new home together. The entire day clearly demonstrated that the Christian faith can bring real peace and joy not only into the lives of individuals, but also into marriages and homes, and through these into whole communities.

Despite occasional exceptions, Ruth was usually able to relax and enjoy the company and kindness of others she met on her travels. This was true in every home in which she stayed, for although conditions were often simple and facilities inconvenient — even sometimes rudimentary in the extreme — fellowshipping with dear saints of God was warm and precious.

On one occasion, after their journey had led northeastward deep into Russia, Svetlana asked their new host if he had a telephone in his little wooden house. He looked at her with a smile and a twinkle in his eye. "Well, dear sister," he replied, "except for two pigs, one goat and my house, I have nothing else!" Then looking around his family, he added: "Oh, yes, and I have a wonderful wife and eight daughters!"

Everybody laughed, but Ruth was touched yet again by the willingness of such dear Christians to share the very little they had with their guests. Like Peter in Acts 3, they certainly had no silver or gold to give away — but what they had, they were glad to give.

Ruth was also impressed time after time by the enthusiasm of the believers, especially in the country areas of the CIS — to attend church come what may, and really focus their minds and souls on spiritual things. Many members of those congregations have to walk to worship. Journeys on foot of half an hour, an hour, or even up to two hours in each direction are quite commonplace. Ruth also found that many of the churches filled long before the services were due to begin. But there was no idle chatter or time-wasting. Deacons read aloud to "redeem the time" — articles from Christian magazines, works by well-known authors such as Billy Graham, or passages of the Bible.

She also found that, as in the days of communism, hymnbooks are still generally in very short supply. However, a few members of some congregations had their own personal copies, and sometimes Ruth was lent one of them. She was intrigued to recognize hymns which had been introduced through broadcasts from Quito — hymns she knew had been written first in Spanish, then translated into the Russian language by Helen Zernov, former SGA missionary colleague at HCJB!

Perhaps it was in Siberia that Ruth grew most encouraged as she discovered still more of the parts which radio had played in the lives of individuals, families, and the growth of the Russian church. One pastor told Ruth how he had never had the opportunity to attend Bible school because under communism in the U.S.S.R. there had been none. But he had loved God's Word and his local church had wanted him to preach. Then the thought had suddenly occurred to him that he could make notes from the radio sermons and preach them himself. Many times people thanked him for doing so, saying: "We enjoyed that message so much when we heard it on the radio this week, and it was a real blessing when you retold it today!"

In another town, the father of Ruth's host came to meet her in the home where she was staying. Grasping her hands, he asked: "Are you REALLY Jack Shalanko's wife? I knew him, he was my *friend!*" He repeated the same question and statement several times that evening. It was left to others to explain the old man's excitement and wonderment. He had been one of the elders of the local church. When difficult questions or problems of faith, doctrine or practice had arisen over which the leaders could not agree, they had said, "All right! Let's send this question to Jack Shalanko in Quito. Whatever he answers, we'll accept!" So they had come to rely on God-ordained "Solomon" Shalanko on the other side of the world to resolve their disputes. No wonder they had considered him a friend!

Under communism, the Soviet state made sustained efforts to limit the influence and effects of Christian radio on the population. Radios were often confiscated to prevent people from listening to the Gospel, but some people were very brave in their defense of that privilege. One family told Ruth how the radio they had purchased for their elderly parents to listen to the Christian broadcasts had been taken away by the KGB. The entire family — adults and children — gathered round the local KGB offices in a brave demonstration of their deep dissatisfaction at being treated thus. They protested peacefully, but very loudly: "What is wrong with you? *What kind of land is this?* You say you want to help the people: WHY CAN'T WE OWN A RADIO?" Shaken by such a rare display of public disapproval of their dubious strong-arm methods, the KGB relented! The radio was returned, and tuned in once more to the Christian programs.

Other radio listeners were less fortunate. One was a man who told Ruth that his house had been invaded by the KGB. "Who are you listening to?" they demanded. "Jack Shalanko," he replied. They sent the man to prison for 10 years.

Across the whole former Soviet Union there had been a system of radio transmitters controlled by local government, to which community-owned receivers and loudspeaker systems had been pre-tuned — an efficient means of mass thought-control. But Ruth learned of one village in which, time and time again, the local loudspeaker system would suddenly begin broadcasting Christian programs from HCJB — somehow the dial in the local radio station was being reset to signals not from Moscow, but distant Quito! So everyone in earshot would hear hymns, prayers and Bible messages instead of communist and atheist propaganda. Recalling those amazing times, Ruth's friends smiled and said, "You know, they *never found* the person responsible for that!"

Yet even unbelievers could generally tell when the Christian programs were on because they would see the believers leaving their tasks of planting vegetables, pulling weeds, plowing or whatever. "It must be nearly time for the religious radio," they would remark to one another, "*the Christians are going home!*" In this way, many non-Christians had learned when to listen to their shortwave radio sets at home, too.

During her travels in Siberia, east of the Ural Mountains separating Europe from Asia, Ruth found that Omsk and other cities in western Siberia were planned and laid out better than many of their counterparts in European Russia. This was because of the cheap labor which had been available from prisoners, beginning with the millions who had been exiled to Siberia by Josef Stalin during his reign of terror in the 1930s. Many Siberian cities have wide streets, fine public buildings and even some impressive factories — among the better legacies of those terrible times when there had been such pernicious persecution of the Christian church.

But today in Siberia, there are far superior legacies of those times in the lives of men, women, families and churches, for many have benefited from the forced influxes of Christians from elsewhere in the old Soviet Union. After believers were exiled to Siberia for their faith in God, they lived out their Christian faith among the local people. The Christians were particularly good workers. Their colleagues and bosses observed this and asked questions about relationships with God. When their years of exile finally ended, many believers married and stayed on in Siberia, encouraging others to trust in Christ.

Meanwhile, Red Army officers who had access to shortwave radios on their bases often used them to listen to programs from the West. Wearing earphones, these tough, unchurched, ungodly men had been able to tune in, safely and securely, to Gospel broadcasts. Many had been born again as they listened, and then quietly began to seek out other believers and local fellowships to join.

Yet life for Christians under communism in Siberia had usually been very difficult indeed. Ruth was told a little of the history of the large church where she spoke in downtown Omsk. While the persecution of Christians had been gathering pace, this church had been requisitioned for use as a courthouse and jail. Conveniently for these purposes, it was next door to the police station. Women in Ruth's meetings recalled how many of the church men — their brothers, husbands, fathers, sons and uncles — had been arrested simply because they wished to worship God. Insult had then been added to injury as the men were tried and sentenced in their own church building. Humiliated and hurt, they had then been imprisoned in the very place in which they had sought to worship and honor the Lord.

The Baptist church in Omsk, now restored for worship after being used as a courthouse and jail during the communist era.

Then in the late 1980s, as Soviet politics began to soften, members of that former church in Omsk had requested that the jail be returned to them and restored to its former use. As in many other places across the former Soviet Union, that boldness of the believers in Omsk has been richly rewarded! The church building was returned, then repaired and renovated by the church members themselves. Over 100 years old and ill-treated for decades, there was much work to be done on it. While the men worked on the main structure and laid a whole new floor, the women redecorated the church throughout and made new chandeliers. These ornate illuminations are special features of many evangelical churches in the CIS. As in Omsk, they are usually handmade by the ladies. In the city of Vinnytsya, Ukraine, Ruth was able to watch new chandeliers in the making, myriads of crystal beads being painstakingly threaded onto giant wire frames. When completed, each individual bead beautifully reflects the lamps while the clusters of beads twinkle and radiate a wonderful galaxy of light. To Ruth, the chandeliers are poignant pictures of individual believers and their churches in a land where reflecting Christ, the Light of lights, has been so clear-cut and eye-catching, even when personally costly for so many.

Ruth returned to the United States on November 21, 1995, feeling deeply challenged by the love and testimony of all those people for the Lord. She prayed that, as a result of her ministry, many would go on to know greater peace with God, or new freedom from sin through fresh faith in Jesus

Christ. Most of all she trusted that some would seek to tap more of the strength of the Holy Spirit — the One *"given to those who obey Him"* (Acts 5:32) — trusting that He would help those dear saints shine ever more brightly for the Lord in their own dark corners of the world.

Even before the end of her second solo ministry journey to the CIS, Ruth was being invited to return for a third. This would be her shortest trip — just under eight weeks from beginning to end — but it would also prove to be the longest in distance, for she was to travel to Belarus and Russia via Pakistan.

During the summer of 1995, Ruth had been invited to spend an evening of fellowship at the home near Wheaton of her dear friend Barbara Christensen, along with a group of other former SGA workers and associates. Excitedly, she related to them some of the wonderful experiences she had had in the CIS. One of the invited guests was a missionary friend on furlough from Pakistan. "Oh Ruth," she had exclaimed, "it would be so great if you could come to Pakistan and tell the Pakistani women about the Christian women in Russia. There are such difficulties living for the Lord in Pakistan! It would be a *real encouragement* for them to hear of some of the things their Russian sisters have had to go through and how the Lord has blessed them. This would give them more courage to go on living for Him."

Ruth immediately warmed to that idea. She was planning her third journey for the beginning of 1996. Yes, she would pray and see how the Lord would lead.

Wichita Bible Church in Wichita, Kansas, is one of the churches which has supported Ruth all through her missionary life since 1950. In order to pray knowledgeably for their needs, this church requests an annual report from all the missionaries it supports. At the bottom of the report form, Ruth found this question: *"If you received a gift of $500 not pertaining to your support, for what special ministry would you use it?"* Ruth immediately phoned the airline agency and asked what additional amount would be needed if she flew to Belarus via Pakistan? Their answer was, "About $600 extra." Explaining her invitation to minister in Pakistan and the additional amount she would need for this, Ruth mailed off the form to the church and left for her fall 1995 missionary trip to the CIS. On returning from Moscow in November, she found a letter from Wichita Bible Church telling her they had sent to the SGA office the extra amount needed for her proposed diversion. The Lord had very clearly answered her prayers for guidance. The means were there for her to go to Pakistan!

Quite unexpectedly, though, one new hurdle arose which would have to be cleared before Ruth could dare set off on such an exacting expedition. Before the end of her previous visit to Eastern Europe in October and November 1995, she had developed a persistent cough!

This cough had been so obstinate and annoying that, immediately on landing back in the United States, Ruth had phoned her friend Pauline Semenchuk from the airport asking if she would arrange an appointment for her at Wheaton Clinic the next morning. Ruth needed professional medical advice. The doctor, after listening to the cough and hearing of Ruth's history of lung problems, said he should obtain copies of her medical reports from her doctor in Ashford, Connecticut. He would request they be faxed to him at once and arranged a further appointment for later on. In the meantime, the doctor said he would give Ruth medication to try to relieve her symptoms. The day before the second appointment, Ruth was still unsure if the Lord wished her to make that next trip to Pakistan and the CIS since her cough was still very troublesome. But there was now great urgency — to obtain affordable advance purchase air tickets, she would have to confirm her reservations within 24 hours!

The same evening, a monthly HCJB prayer meeting was being held in that city. It was a cold, snowy Monday night, but Ruth and others braved the weather. Asked to report on her recent visits to the CIS, Ruth ended her brief talk with a special request for prayer. Even as she was speaking everyone could hear her cough: would they please pray that, if it was His will for her to make that new trip to Pakistan and the CIS, the Lord would heal? She needed to order the tickets IMMEDIATELY!

Returning to the home of son John and his wife Maria, Ruth went to bed. The next morning she awoke feeling "very refreshed and rested." Suddenly she realized that for the first time in weeks she had *not coughed all night!* Neither was she troubled any more by phlegm. Amazed, she asked her son, who had been in the next bedroom, "John, did you hear me coughing last night?"

"No, Mom," came the reply. "I just said to Maria that I didn't hear you cough ONCE!"

Ruth went back to her bedroom and knelt by the bed: "Oh Lord, thank you for taking away my cough. I know I can go to Belarus now. Thank you for guiding me," she marveled. She dressed quickly, then paused to spend more time in prayer. She had been following monthly devotional readings by Dr. Charles F. Stanley. The verses for that day were prophetic, from Daniel 12. And for Ruth, whenever the phrases *"your people"* appeared, they jumped out to read, *"your RUSSIAN people."* By the time she got to verse 3 and read the reference to *"those who lead many to righteousness"* — just what she knew she was called to do — Ruth felt complete peace about making her travel plans. She would go to Pakistan, Belarus and Russia. She longed all the more to encourage Russian women to live for God, come what may!

Phoning the travel agent the moment their office opened, she confirmed the temporary reservations she had made earlier. At 10 a.m. she met the doctor at Wheaton Clinic, as previously planned.

"Well, Mrs. Shalanko," he began, "I have been reviewing all your records and examination reports from your doctor in Connecticut. In view of them and your age and condition, I recommend you do not travel to Russia!"

Ruth looked at him almost with a smile and asked: "What are your exact reasons for this, Doctor? If my coughing stopped, would it be all right to go?"

"Oh, yes, yes," he replied. "I could give you other medication for your underlying conditions."

Startled, he then heard her state: "In that case, Doctor, *I'm on my way.* MY COUGH HAS GONE!"

Ruth left his office convinced that God had once more shown her His will. He was allowing her to return to her work in the CIS. She phoned friends from the prayer meeting with the good news, and proceeded with her preparations for the trip. Enlightened by previous experience, Ruth requested this in a prayer letter dated February 3, 1996:

> "Would you please PRAY FOR ME? Most churches (in Russia and Belarus) cannot afford to heat their buildings. This is an extremely cold winter! Living and travel conditions are difficult."

She could have added that her health was not good . . . that she would travel most of the way alone . . . and that the money in her purse would scarcely cover her most basic foreseeable needs!

When Ruth arrived in Islamabad, Pakistan, it was hot and sticky, even at midnight! For the next 10 days, Ruth was escorted by her missionary friend to several cities for meetings in churches, chapels or private homes. Many things were new to Ruth, particularly the colorful clothes worn by the women. Ruth was given two outfits of these traditional clothes to wear, including gleaming cotton jackets and trousers, and ample head scarves to cover her nose, mouth and even her hair when in public places.

Ruth with Christian ladies in Pakistan.

Describing one of her meetings, Ruth remarks, "What a *delight* to meet the dear Pakistani ladies! From the moment I entered the walled court-yard of the church, left my shoes at the entrance alongside many other pairs, and glanced around the circle of brightly clothed, smiling women, I could feel their love for Christ. Sitting down cross-legged on the mat beside them, I knew I was among friends.

"I did not understand the Scripture they were reading nor the words of the hymns they sang, for everything was in the Urdu language. However, when the ladies started to pray, I suddenly realized I could understand the longings and openness of their hearts before the Lord.

"As I related to them the past and present difficulties experienced by Russian Christian women, they were moved and sympathetic. They related all I said to similar situations in their own lives today! My message seemed to give them encouragement to accept their own difficult roles and to confidently put their complete trust in God — just as Exodus 2 tells us Moses' mother did when she faced the difficult situation of trying to save the life of her baby son."

And that time in Pakistan proved a timely inspiration to Ruth, too, enabling her to better understand the roles of women in yet another corner of the world — a reminder that God can meet the needs of *all* women everywhere, no matter what their food, clothing or culture might be.

Journeying on to meetings in the Moscow region and then to Minsk in Belarus, Ruth found that her descriptions of the difficulties facing fellow believers in Pakistan now drew special sympathy from her more familiar audiences: Russian Christians could empathize, and prayed appropriately! Ruth encouraged them to praise God all the more for their own newfound freedom to live openly for the Lord. Many people she met in the CIS still vividly remembered how they had suffered under communism because of their faith in Jesus Christ. One pastor and his wife who hosted her confirmed they had both served prison sentences. Ruth could understand the pastor's "crime" — preaching the Gospel — but why had his *wife* been sent to prison?

"When the KGB searched my apartment," the wife explained, "they found four Christian books. I was sentenced to one year in prison for each of them, to serve consecutively." And then she smiled: "I spent the whole time witnessing for Christ. It was a *priceless* opportunity, and I saw many accept the Lord!"

On their release from jail, even more priceless opportunities had opened up for that couple in the relatively new town of Salihorsk in Belarus. This had been founded only about 30 years previously, to house workers mining recently discovered salt deposits. When communist rule had ended, the pastor and his wife helped establish a Gospel witness in the district. Souls were saved and a church had been founded in 1990. Ruth expressed her surprise and delight in visiting such a young and vibrant church — where 90 percent of the members had been saved in just the last five years.

Ruth found signs of church growth and spiritual awakening in many of the places she visited in Belarus. Although it was midwinter, her services were very well attended. This was even so in village churches, whose congregations were drawn from wide areas around. One Sunday morning, because of deep snow, Ruth and her companions had to leave their car on the highway and walk a long way to church. But there were still nearly 100 women in the service! The pastor leaned across to Ruth before she rose to speak. "Sister *Ruth Petrovna*," he whispered, "the ladies on the *left* are members of our church. Those on the *right* are not. Most of them have never been in a church before and have never heard of the love of Christ, but they have come to hear you tell of it today!"

Ruth recalls how some of the non-Christians tried to sing the hymns, and all listened intently to her message. How she prayed that their minds, hearts and souls would open to the Lord! She encouraged all to return to that church again after she had gone, and learn more of Him.

In another village in Belarus, the church building was expected to be too small to house everyone who would want to hear this American daughter of a Belarussian couple speak. So the meeting was held in the village hall, which encouraged many unsaved people — men as well as women — to attend. As on her previous journeys, Ruth frankly professed her personal preference to visit the more remote areas, where visiting speakers had been less likely to go. Somehow she felt closest to the country people. "People everywhere eagerly listened to God's Word," she affirms, "but never more so than in the smaller towns and villages, where three quarters of the congregations were our radio listeners."

In the country regions, her audiences were often mixed — men, women, teen-agers, boys and girls. In the larger towns and cities, many of her audiences were female only — sometimes mostly older women, sometimes younger women or even teen-age girls. In the cities of Kobryn and Brest, where she spent several days, she was invited to address meetings of the wives of elders and deacons, young parents, teens, and most memorably, unmarried women. In some ways this last group — which included teen-agers as well as single young ladies and some older spinsters — presented the greatest challenge, for its members seemed the most embarrassed by the kinds of questions they wanted to ask! Ruth hit on an idea. The girls should write their questions down anonymously. Then Ruth would read them aloud and they would discuss them together. It worked! As the debate warmed up, the younger women in particular became more and more eager for Ruth's advice.

In fact, Ruth recalls that this informal meeting also turned out to be among the most lighthearted she had. She aimed to make it instructional for the younger ones, but also encouraging for the older ladies who had never married. There were many laughs and smiles throughout the evening! But Ruth concluded on a serious note, stressing how vital it is to face either marriage or single life following the will of God. The prayers that followed were most sincere, as the young ladies asked God to guide them and show them His will for their future relationships, whatever kind they might be. As she was leaving, they begged her to send them literature on that subject area, for there is very little available on it in the Russian language written especially for women living in the cultural environment of the CIS.

On that journey in early 1996, one of the largest women's meetings Ruth addressed was in the city of Brest in southwest Belarus, not far from its present border with Poland. This was to be her last meeting in the region of her roots. Over 400 women gathered for it from four different churches of that city. The entire meeting was given over to Ruth, who remembers speaking about two hours. At its close, there were many questions from the audience. The first was: "How *old* are you, Sister Ruth?"

With a smile, Ruth told them that in 10 days time she would have her 68th birthday. There were many *oohs* and *aahs* throughout the audience, for women in the CIS retire at 55. But their life is very hard. Many work in factories, on the railroads, or in other manual situations. Then every spring and summer they have to work the fields, gardens and orchards to secure food for their families. Many women give birth to several children, and most are worn out at a relatively young age. Thus, Ruth's audiences were often surprised to see her traveling and speaking at her age — and she was quick to explain that it was only by God's grace and in His care that she was able to stand before them at that time of her life and encourage them in the Lord.

A number of teen-agers wanted to know: "What is there in life for us? If girls don't marry and don't have husbands to provide for them, life is very difficult because there are very few career opportunities for women."

Widows asked: "We cannot live alone on our small pensions. How can we best relate to those whose homes we have to share?"

And an older woman who had had many abortions in her younger days before she heard of the Lord inquired: "How can I go on living, knowing how much I have sinned against God? Can He ever forgive me?"

Ruth did her best to provide Bible-based responses to every such question and every situation. But often it was not easy. "Their lives are so dull, dreary and almost hopeless," she has observed. "But oh, *the believers are so eager to serve Christ!* That was an electrifying meeting in Brest, and one I will never forget!"

Nor will she ever forget meeting once more with her cousin Anastacia in the village of Staramlynia — though this was unforgettable for entirely different reasons. This time the snow was so thick that it was by no means certain she and her relative, Pavel Leonovich, would be able to reach it through the drifts. Fortunately, a tractor had trundled down the final lane a short while before, so their car just made it to the Deyneka home.

As they slithered up to the now familiar, yellow-painted house, there was blind Anastacia standing in the doorway, burdened with a bucket of icy water newly drawn from the well. Ruth jumped out of the car and ran through the snow, calling Anastacia's name. "*Ruthia*," Anastacia cheered up in response, "you said you would come again in February or March, and here you are!" However, after warm hugs and kisses, Anastacia broke unwelcome news: "My husband is drunk, so we cannot go inside. We will have to stay here to talk. I am even not sleeping in the house at night while he is like this, but staying with a neighbor," she ended in a whisper.

So they stood in the yard — Ruth holding Anastacia's rough hands in her own, much smoother ones — as they talked for about half an hour. Ruth gave her cousin the bread she had brought her, with some sausage, oatmeal and other grains, candy, cookies and a little money. A light snow was gently falling. Ruth was glad there was no wind to further sharpen the knife-like cold. Yet again, Ruth

Ruth urging cousin Anastacia to accept Christ, winter 1996.

witnessed to her cousin, and asked if she would accept Christ as her personal Savior. Distressingly, Anastacia would not. "I am *too sinful*," she insisted, shaking her head. "He would never forgive *ME!*"

Ruth was overcome.

"I cried as I stood and talked with her," she confesses. "I knew she was one of my closest relatives on Earth, the daughter of my father's brother. Because of her blindness she could not see me, but I could see her. Her face was weather-beaten, but her features were so like mine. Other things were totally different, though. I was aware of the strong, pungent, smoky smell of her jacket and scarves, the kind of smell that would never wash out. Behind us stood her tiny hut, shared with the chickens. My own life could have been here like this, if God had not called my Papa to do a very special work for Him . . . one which it has been my *great privilege* to carry on.

"I hastened to tell Anastacia that God *had acted to forgive her sins* ALREADY! He wanted to give her a WHOLE NEW LIFE in Him! There were tears in her eyes, as well as mine, as one last time before we parted she insisted she was beyond help, even from God Himself.

"I told her I did not know if I would ever be able to visit her again, but that I would be praying for her, hoping and trusting she would open her heart to the Lord and accept Him. Once more I prayed with her, kissed her face a dozen times, hugged her, then ran back to the waiting car. Tearfully, I left my father's village."

The final meetings of Ruth's third solo speaking tour within a 15-month period were in Kostroma, Russia, an eight-hour bus trip northeast of Moscow. There she was hosted by an American missionary, John Erdel, and his Ecuadorian-born wife, Lorena. Ruth was first invited to speak in a general service at one of the churches on a Tuesday evening. As this ended, another special women's meeting was announced, to be held the next day from 10 a.m. until 2 p.m. Several women who had come in from the surrounding countryside spent the night on the church floor in order to attend that meeting too. When Ruth questioned them, they told her that for years they had only *heard* the voices of the radio missionaries — to *see* one of them again in person was something they did not want to miss!

At the close of the Wednesday meeting, a simple lunch was served for the ladies at the church. Fellowship with that group remains clear in Ruth's memory. In the early 1990s, many missionary societies had joined together for work in Russia under the banner of CoMission. One of its aims is to teach the Word of God to Russian school teachers. Ruth's brother, Peter, was shortly to become president of its second phase, CoMission II.

CoMission was already actively involved with schools in Kostroma, and another meeting was arranged, this one in a home, to allow some of the teachers to meet Ruth informally. As a group of professional educators gathered for it, Ruth became aware that most of them were not yet believers. But all listened intently as she spoke. Afterward, Ruth was introduced to one notary, a member of the Women's Government Committee. This high-class lady looked deep into Ruth's eyes and said, "I never imagined that a woman of your caliber could have such a close personal relationship with God. It is *earth-shaking* to think that such a thing is possible!"

As they all headed for the bus stop on the way home, another lady who had not taken her eyes off Ruth once during her address, linked arms with her and said, "Ruth, hard times are going to come back to us. We have *NO HOPE IN LIFE* other than that hope in God of which you and these CoMission people have been telling us. *If only I had that hope for myself!*"

Ruth encouraged her to attend other meetings which CoMission was organizing, to learn more of how she could receive that hope through faith in Jesus Christ.

As Ruth later reflected on all her recent travels in the CIS, she realized that *encouragement* had been a basic essence of her ministry, especially to the women. Encouragement is needed by believers everywhere. It is greatly needed by believers in the former Soviet Union — even though perhaps in somewhat different ways than elsewhere. Many times Russian Christian women said to Ruth: "All we have is tears! Our life is so hard!" To this she would reply: "Yes, but just as many times as we sow with *tears*, so we expect to reap with JOY! Even though we may weep as we plant the seeds of the Gospel, we will *surely rejoice* as it GROWS UP INTO SPIRITUAL GRAIN!"

By now, Ruth had spent half of the last 500 days traveling through Central and Eastern Europe and Western Asia. She had addressed many thousands of people in almost 200 meetings. Before and after the meetings, she had also given much time and personal counsel to many challenged or troubled souls, in their own homes or on public transport. The exhausting pace of her first solo journey had been matched throughout her second . . . and her third! Together, they would have been an astonishing feat of endurance for anyone in peak physical condition. That a lady in her late 60s had been able to complete them all, and with such evident blessing, joy and success, attests to her own unswerving commitment to the Lord — but much more to the enabling power He grants His chosen emissaries. Neither should we forget that Ruth had been suffering throughout from a breathing problem, long thought to be emphysema. It was not until just after those marathon journeys had been completed that her condition was finally properly diagnosed and treated as asthma!

The fact that Ruth traveled much of the way alone and in the depths of central continental winters further underlines how remarkable those missions were. Together, they must rank among the greatest episodes of female missionary service anywhere in the world in recent years.

Ruth shares: "My ministry to the women of the CIS has been the *greatest experience of my WHOLE life!* I cannot thank God enough for every single service in which I spoke . . . for every single city, town, village and hamlet I visited . . . and for every single lady I was able to counsel, pray with, hug and kiss. I thank God for the BLESSED EXPERIENCE of being able to go to the CIS, and tell the ladies there of *Christ's love for them ALL!*"

CHAPTER 12

Together Again
1995 - 1998

Although Ruth was enjoying her speaking ministries in the CIS, she was becoming conscious of growing older and not being fully fit. How and where might she serve the Lord next? How often we wish we could see into the future! But *"no man knows the future"* (Ecclesiastes 8:7), only God alone — and He was lovingly planning the next chapter of Ruth's life. Even while her own thoughts and preoccupations had been elsewhere, He had been causing key things to happen which in His own good time would both startle and delight her.

Just prior to her second solo speaking mission to the CIS, Ruth had traveled to Illinois to visit her children and their families. She had spent the last day before her flight to Odessa at SGA's U.S. office, now in Loves Park near Rockford, Illinois. Spending some time with Dr. Bob Provost, SGA's president, she reported on the other trips she had made to Eastern Europe since seeing him the year before in Belarus. Bob was full of admiration and praise for all Ruth had achieved . . . but grew increasingly alarmed as she described her intense schedules and the extent of her travels by public transportation at all hours of the day and night. He understood perfectly well from his own wide experience how draining her missions must be, especially in the Russian winters! Even younger, healthier people would have found Ruth's schedules hard to fulfill! With some concern, Bob gently and smilingly counseled that in view of her age he felt it would be better if she did not accept many more invitations for lengthy trips like those.

Ruth then told him of the increasing number of requests she had been receiving from Russian pastors to publish many of the messages she had given on women in the Bible. She also explained her concern for married women in the CIS. There are so many who are sad and lonely because they are believers while their husbands are not. She had met and counseled many single ladies who had not yet married — who might never marry — as well as those, like herself, who had been widowed. All these would benefit from written help and advice from someone who understood Russian mindsets and circumstances.

Bob's response was both immediate and positive: perhaps *writing* was the new type of ministry she should begin to develop as a natural successor to her speaking tours?

Ruth then explained that following the trip she was about to begin, she was already committed to one more, for she had already accepted an invitation from Baptist leaders to minister to women in Belarus in early 1996. Bob gave his assent to this, but then suggested that in view of everything, perhaps it should be her last long journey of that kind.

Ruth recalls: "We ended our discussion with prayer — and peace in both our hearts that this was the *right decision to make.*"

About three months before that meeting with Bob, Ruth had mailed out one of her periodic prayer letters to her family, friends, individuals and supporting churches telling of her imminent visit to Belarus, Moldova, Russia and Ukraine in the fall of 1995. To some of those letters, she had added brief personal notes. One was to a long-standing missionary friend still serving in Ecuador, Dr. Paul Erdel.

But who is Paul Erdel? Born and raised in the Midwest, Paul has served the Lord for many years with the Missionary Church, mainly in Ecuador. The Missionary Church, headquartered in the United States in Fort Wayne, Indiana, traces its origins to late 19th-century groups of Mennonites in the Midwest who felt particularly challenged with regard to leadership training, church planting and missionary outreach. Today, the Missionary Church and its overseas missionary department, World Partners, involves perhaps 80,000 Christian believers in North America, Africa, southern

Asia, western Europe and Latin America — where many are members of thriving Spanish-speaking churches in Ecuador.

After a studious childhood and an early call to Christian missionary work, Paul graduated from Fort Wayne Bible College in 1950 with a bachelor's degree in theology, while simultaneously receiving a B.A. from Taylor University in Upland, Indiana. He also married Chloetta Egly in that singularly unforgettable year! After he completed his master's degree in education at Indiana State University in 1952, Paul and Chloetta set out together for Ecuador in 1953 as World Partners missionaries. From their base in the Pacific coastal city of Esmeraldas, God was to use them over the next 40 years to plant many churches, start a Christian school, and assist in children's Vacation Bible Schools.

Paul has long loved sharing his knowledge of the Lord with others and has done so in almost every imaginable kind of situation in Ecuador — from personal evangelism on the beaches, to lecturing at Pacific Bible Seminary which he founded in Esmeraldas. All his ministries have been practical expressions of a particularly deep passion for lost souls.

In 1965, Paul left Ecuador for eight years to serve as the overseas director of the Missionary Church at its Fort Wayne headquarters. He brought with him his deep conviction that world missions should be the central task of the church and that the Bible tells us how to carry out that task. In 1973, with church planting and leadership training firmly established as the denomination's top priorities, Paul and Chloetta returned to their first love — missionary service in Ecuador. He continued there until his retirement at the end of 1997.

One of Jack Shalanko's many speaking engagements in the 1960s had been to the delegates attending the national conference of the Missionary Church in Ecuador (locally known as *Iglesia Misionera*). His messages were appreciated so much that pastors often invited him back to participate in evangelistic campaigns. Sometimes these fell during school vacations. At such times, Ruth, John and Lydia had all been able to accompany Jack on his visits to the coast and provided the music for the meetings.

When in Esmeraldas, the Shalanko family had always been hosted by Paul and Chloetta Erdel. The Erdel children — Tim, David, John and Ruthie — had also become schoolmates of John and Lydia Shalanko as they had all attended the Alliance Academy in Quito. Thus, warm friendships had grown up between the two families.

While the Shalankos and Erdels shared happy days in the 1960s, they were also to share sad times in the early 1990s. Ruth explains: "In 1991

Chloetta passed away in the United States, following her second heart operation. Paul was devastated, for they had labored together for the Lord for so long. However, two weeks after her funeral, he returned to Ecuador to resume the ministries which they had begun nearly 40 years earlier."

One of the blessings that especially sustained Paul during that period of intense grief was the fact that two of their children were also missionaries in Esmeraldas — son David with his wife Lolly, accompanied by their children, John-Paul, David, Mary and Stephen; and daughter Ruth with her husband Tim Stuck, and their boys, Andrew, Adam and John Michael.

Two years after the death of Chloetta, Paul received through the mail an edition of a journal called *PeriodiQuito*, edited by Ruth's former HCJB friend and colleague, Nancy Woolnough. Prepared twice each year, it features clips from letters written by past or present Christian workers in Ecuador. In that particular edition, Nancy had excerpted some of the thoughts Ruth had circulated following Jack's passage to Heaven in June 1993. As a friend of the family, Paul penned a letter of condolence to Ruth. Having been so recently bereaved of his own spouse, he was able to sympathize with Ruth with special depth, sincerity and understanding. She remarks that: "As Paul ended the letter, he made it clear that no answer was expected. However, I was deeply touched by his message of sympathy. Six months had passed since Jack's death. Consolatory mail from other friends had stopped coming. Paul's letter reminded me of the times we had all spent with his family, and especially of his kindness to his wife Chloetta. He had always been close by to help her, and his quiet spirit and supportiveness had been very evident. With pure gratitude for his letter, I wrote back and thanked him for his kind words. Months later, I received his newsletter from Ecuador with an added handwritten note. I answered this with my own next prayer letter, and so a pattern of communication began."

Thus, in the second half of 1995 it was natural that Ruth should have sent Paul Erdel one of her prayer letters describing her next journey to the CIS — the ministry trip she had so recently discussed with Bob Provost and on which she was soon to embark. In this letter, she also shared that she would soon be revisiting Ecuador for the first time since the early 1980s.

And how had the totally unexpected invitation to do this come about?

Immediately following her first solo period of ministry in the CIS during the first quarter of 1995, Ruth had several opportunities to report to churches in the United States about her various encounters with believers in Belarus, Russia and Ukraine. Returning from Moscow to Chicago in April 1995, Ruth had been happy to stop over for a visit in Wheaton with her son, John, and his wife, Maria. During her stay, a message had come from Joyce and Dwight Peterson who direct the monthly HCJB prayer meeting in that area. Chuck Howard, then HCJB's field director, would be visiting with his wife, Anita. Would the three Shalankos be able to attend? They could, and had gone together.

After Chuck had spoken at the prayer meeting, Joyce Peterson invited Ruth to briefly report on her most recent visit to the CIS. "With a full heart," Ruth says, "I related a little of what had happened. I told of people who had found Christ while listening to HCJB, and families who had been restored as they committed or recommitted themselves to the Lord. I could not finish speaking without tears as I told this group how valuable their prayers were and how missionary radio continued to be a vital part in the life and growth of the Russian church."

At the end of the meeting, Chuck Howard turned to Ruth: "I want to invite you to Quito, to tell the staff about your experiences in the CIS. They need to hear of the results of the radio ministry. As you know, it's easy to get discouraged working only with a microphone! We have a young staff now. Most of them have no idea what has taken place in the Russian language all these past 50 years. Please, will you come?"

Ruth recalls having actually laughed in response: "Chuck, young missionaries don't want to be told by an *elderly lady* how things were in the *olden days!*" But she then turned to Elizabeth Lewshenia, who for so many years had been one of her SGA radio colleagues in Quito, and asked if she thought she ought to go. "Sure, you should go!" was her firm reply.

Getting to his feet, Chuck gave Ruth his business card.

"Will you at least please pray about this?" he said to her. "Then fax me your answer later in the year. I really feel you should come to Quito!"

As Ruth prepared her heart, mind and messages for her next trip to the CIS, due to begin on September 28, her eye often landed on Chuck Howard's card, waiting patiently there on her desk. "Lord, *should I really go back to Quito?*" was the prayer she had found herself repeating every time she saw it, for she still recalled her long ago promise that she would serve Him wherever He would lead.

Finally one day, having developed no negative feelings at all about Quito, she got down on her knees and prayed very specifically for guidance in this matter. Then taking Chuck's card, she faxed him, saying she was willing to go back to Ecuador for that visit *if he still felt it was in the purposes of God.* The very next day, his reply was faxed back: "YES, please come! Give me your dates!" A further flurry of faxes confirmed the trip for November 31 through December 18, 1995.

Ruth began to wonder . . . how would she feel revisiting that country after so many years and in such different circumstances?

In the meantime, however, summer was ending and the CIS was beckoning. It was time to answer her mail and write letters to her family and friends, and to churches which had long and faithfully supported her as a missionary reaching Russians.

There had also been the most recent note from Paul Erdel to answer. Telling him of her planned visit to Ecuador, she put no dates on this for she never thought she would see him. After all, Esmeraldas lies some 200 miles from Quito, over six hours away by bus. In any case, she knew that Paul was temporarily in Mishawaka, Indiana, teaching at the Missionary Church's Bethel College.

To Ruth's great surprise, within one week of telling Paul she would be in Quito, she had received a letter — and a question — back from Paul. He was expecting to be in Ecuador himself in a couple of weeks, as tutor to eight Bethel College students on a Semester Abroad study program. If Ruth was planning to be in Quito between December 1-15, would she, as a veteran missionary, agree to meet and address his students?

She wrote back saying yes.

What did all this mean . . . where would it lead? In December 1995, Ruth found out.

One week after returning home from her fall 1995 speaking tour to the CIS, Ruth boarded an airplane for South America. Later that evening, it landed in Quito. Ruth's immediate response was one of exhilaration: "As I stepped down from the plane, I saw hillsides lit with thousands of lights, like the stars in the sky. I found *my heart was glad,* and a *wave of peace flowed through me.* I began to smile and just could not stop! It was unbelievable! I was back in Ecuador, where I had lived so long and enjoyed so many years of blessing."

Met at the airport by Chuck and Anita Howard, Ruth was taken to stay in the home of her close friend, Helen Broach. The Shalankos, of course, had first met Helen and her husband, Dick, at the language school in San

Jose, Costa Rica, where they had all studied Spanish together. Helen, like Ruth, had been recently widowed, so the two were able not only to recall happy times together, but also fully empathize with each other's recent griefs and trials.

And it was there in Helen's home that Ruth met Paul Erdel again after a gap of 16 years.

First they shared with each other the circumstances surrounding the loss of their spouses. Then they talked of their children . . . and of many mutual friends . . . and of their own individual ministries. Ruth was impressed to learn that in 1985 Paul had earned a doctorate of missiology from Trinity Evangelical Divinity School in Deerfield, Illinois. Ruth and Paul also discovered that each had visited the Holy Land since they had last met, and how each had been moved by the experience. Ruth also learned she and Paul were the same age . . . that they had graduated from high school in the same year . . . and that Paul, when a student, had heard Ruth's father preach at Fort Wayne Bible College. In these and other ways, two hours of animated conversation raced by.

It would be Paul's 68th birthday next week. He invited Ruth to join him and his students for his birthday supper — and then suggested a private meal for just the two of them.

After Paul had gone, Ruth retired to her room. She admits, "I sat on the bed, startled by my feelings. Then I said to myself softly, 'I could really like that man!' But as soon as I admitted that, I dropped to my knees in prayer. I told the Lord how moved I had been with Paul and how I realized I was attracted to him. Yet I did not want to make *any kind* of mistake!"

Ruth promised the Lord she would try not to think of Paul all week. Both she and Paul were lonely. Both wished to continue serving the Lord as actively as possible. Yet if their relationship were to develop further, it would have to be God's doing. He would have to show them both, clearly and unequivocally, that it was His will. Ruth continues: "I saw in Paul a true man of God, with a deep desire to live a holy life. He loved being a missionary. Memories of his kindness and constant help to Chloetta were very vivid to me. BUT I WAS FRIGHTENED lest I step outside God's will for me. I could only leave the matter in His hands. He had *blessed me so much*. He had *opened such unusual doors for me*. He had *given me new opportunities for service* since Jack's death. I did not want to do *ANYTHING* which might displease Him."

Upon her return to HCJB, Ruth went first to the Russian department. Glad to meet again the warmly enthusiastic, Australian-born missionary

Wally Kulakoff, she inquired if she might help in the office between her speaking engagements? Wally replied that they were receiving many interesting letters from listeners in the CIS and elsewhere. Perhaps she could translate some, so their blessings could be shared with others? Ruth began to do so at once, thrilled and excited by the tales they told.

Later, as she enthused over them with Wally, he suddenly asked: "Ruth, what plans do have for next summer? Would you be able to help here with Russian radio for a few months, while Natasha and I are on furlough?"

Ruth says, "My heart just *jumped* at the prospect, for as agreed with Dr. Provost, my last speaking tour to the CIS would end in March! After consulting by e-mail with Bob, I was happy to answer YES!"

To Ruth's continuing astonishment, within one week another man would ask her a question . . . and though this second question would have much deeper implications than Wally's, once again she would answer: "YES, I would be *very* happy to!"

During her stay in Quito, Ruth had several meetings to address. These included a women's Christmas tea, a Bible study for lady workers in the HCJB hospital, and sharing at the weekly gatherings in various HCJB departments and with the large Ecuadorian staff, several of whom she had known when they were much younger. Drawing from her recent visits to the CIS, she rejoiced to be able to confirm that *Russian radio had paid off* and was STILL PAYING OFF. In fact, its results were greater and more far-reaching than anyone had known or imagined! She relayed thanks from the Russian people, pastors and churches for all the programs which had pointed them to Christ . . . thanks for the broadcasts which had helped sustain those people through decades of darkness and persecution . . . thanks for the programs which had encouraged so many and helped them grow since greater freedom had come to their lands. She passed on listener's pleas to the staff to *continue their good work* on behalf of the many Russians who — for one reason or another — cannot read the Bible for themselves or understand it as they would wish, or cannot get to church.

Ruth was also asked to testify at Iñaquito Spanish Church — the one where she and Jack were on the first membership roll, and the construction of whose first church building Jack had supervised way back in 1956. Imagine how Ruth felt as she worshiped in this now great church, with a membership of around 2,000 and a staff of six pastors!

The week sped by. Soon, Friday morning came. Ruth challenged Paul's class to fully turn their lives over to the Lord. She had other appointments in the afternoon. Only when these had been completed did she allow herself thoughts of the private evening and dinner to come. Once more, she committed these to the Lord in prayer.

At 7 p.m. Paul arrived. He took her to a very colorful Ecuadorian restaurant. Musicians in national costume were playing Spanish music. There was much for Ruth and Paul to discuss. Their mutual interests in Ecuador, the Spanish language, missions, and most of all the Lord, readily sustained their conversation. They also talked about their fathers, both of whom had been great men of prayer. "How they would have enjoyed each other," Ruth and Paul agreed.

Ruth completes the story: "As the evening progressed, the interests we shared in our lives and in each other became more and more obvious to us. We had both known deep loneliness and emptiness after our loved ones had died . . . and we were now aware of deep peace and tranquility coming over us. Our values were the same. We had long been friends. Through our work and families, we had shared much in the past. We had similar thoughts of the present and hopes for the future. The love we were feeling for each other was a surprise to both of us — but the peace I had prayed for was definitely there! By the time the evening was over, which we concluded with prayer, we both realized that *it was God who had brought us together* from two continents to meet in Quito . . . TO UNITE US IN MARRIAGE! He was giving us love we had never expected to have again.

"*Only God* could have done this! The signposts were now clear. It was God who had prompted Dr. Provost to counsel me to conclude my solo speaking tours to the CIS. It was He who had put it in Chuck Howard's mind to invite me to Quito. It was He who had led Paul in the preparation of his itinerary, so that he would be in Quito the same time as me. And it was God who had even put it in the mind of Wally Kulakoff to invite me back to Ecuador, where Paul would be for much of 1996. New steps had already been planned for the future path of my life. This was GOD'S DOING! Paul and I were astounded — and smiled when we thought how our engagement would soon flabbergast our families!"

Not only were the Shalanko and Erdel families to be astonished and delighted by that news, but others also who had known Ruth or Paul over the years. Even the Internet was soon spreading it. One to unexpectedly receive Ruth's news was Rev. Philip Somers, pastor of New Castle Bible Church in Mackinaw, Illinois, who had counseled Ruth when Jack was dying. On December 15, 1995, the pastor's 50th birthday, he received a personally addressed e-mail from Ruth. Parts of it read as follows:

> *"Hitherto has the Lord led you,"* Pastor Somers . . . right up to another milestone in your life! God has used you in a wonderful way to preach the true Word of God for all these years. You have been a blessing to many of us, and we thank the Lord for you. I am happy to greet you from Quito, Ecuador.
>
> I truly wish you a very blessed birthday, and this e-mail is SPECIAL to you on this day. But I just have to tell you my own special news. Upon my return to Ecuador, where it has been such a joy to be once again sitting in the Russian office of HCJB reading letters from radio listeners, I met again a missionary with whom I have been acquainted for 40 years. His wife died five years ago. Upon Jack's death, he wrote condolences, and we have corresponded for two years.
>
> Well, we met last week — and something happened to our hearts! After praying, *we decided to get engaged!* We ourselves are just as surprised as you are! Yet our hearts feel such peace from the Lord, for we see how HE worked this out. We thank Him and commit ourselves for future ministry together.
>
> Once again, HAPPY BIRTHDAY, dear servant of God. Warm Christian greetings to you, your wife, and all the dear people at New Castle Bible Church.

But before the wedding could take place, both Ruth and Paul had existing ministry commitments to be honored. While they naturally hoped and expected that the Lord would give them new opportunities to serve Him as a couple, Paul made it very clear he would encourage and support Ruth in any kind of work God gave her, particularly in respect of ministries to women and to her beloved Russian-speaking people. And with good cause, for he already had a keen personal interest in Russia himself — his son John Erdel and his Ecuadorian wife, Lorena, were in missionary service with CoMission in Kostroma, Russia, along with their little daughter, Anna Maria.

Thus, merely one month after her engagement to Paul, Ruth was journeying alone again as previously planned to Belarus and Russia . . . having had no time to agree upon details of the wedding ceremony and reception. Since Ruth and Paul did not expect to be together again until 10 days before that great day, Paul had suggested to Ruth that she make the plans. Yet she would have no time to begin thinking of them until an unusually quiet day for her in Kobryn, Belarus, that February!

The wedding ceremony was held at Pleasant Hill Community Church in Wheaton on June 1, 1996, among 250 guests. Ruth described some of its highlights in a prayer letter dated three weeks later:

> Our five beautiful granddaughters, sons David and Tim Erdel, and Paul and I marched to the song *My Tribute*: *"How can I say THANKS, for the things You have done for me?"* These opening words expressed our feelings of gratitude to the Lord for bringing us together.
>
> The service was led by Rev. Philip Somers, pastor of New Castle Bible Church in Mackinaw, Illinois. The opening congregational hymn was *"To God be the glory, great things He has done."* My cousin, Dr. Alex Leonovich of New Jersey, recounted moving memories of the Deyneka family. Dr. Bob Provost, SGA president, reviewed the history of both families.
>
> Inspirational music was provided by Mrs. Ardie Somers, piano; Nadja (flautist) and Dennis Campbell who sang; and a solo by Marilyn Wong, Paul's niece. First Corinthians 13 was sung in Spanish by missionary Tim Stuck, Paul's son-in-law, and read in English by David Erdel. Ten of our grandchildren lined up to sing *Jesus Loves Me* in English and Spanish. Tim Erdel read excerpted verses from the biblical book of Ruth, while John and Maria Shalanko read Proverbs 31:10-31.

The Shalanko and Erdel families at their wedding ceremony on June 1, 1996.

After the marriage sermon on TOGETHERNESS, our wedding service concluded with the congregation singing *"Praise God from whom all blessings flow!"* We are truly thankful to the Lord for uniting us. We are so happy!

Was this a typical American wedding? Ruth responds: "Not at all! It was not like *any* wedding before, but put together to express as much as possible my heartfelt praise to God for giving me another wonderful companion on the path of my life. I doubt if a wedding quite like ours will ever be seen again!" Indeed, there were many ways in which it was unusual, even for these days of eschewing tradition. For one thing, it was followed not by one reception but two — the first at the Pleasant Hill Church that same afternoon, and the second a few days later in Ashford, Connecticut. Here, Ruth's friends at Gilead Home, who had been unable to travel to the wedding, arranged a reception of their own, complete with wedding cake and money tree as expressions of their love for their former manager and her new spouse.

For another thing, Ruth's wedding dress was most unusual too. It has been rightly said that missionaries are one of those groups in society least likely to become millionaires — or even get close! Working on a very tight budget, Ruth was especially thrilled that she managed to get married in an *$8 dress!* She explains:

"Every bride thinks carefully about what she will wear for the ceremony. In my mind I envisioned a dress in pink or rose, colors I'm fond of. I walked around a few shops to see what I might be able to purchase, but there was absolutely nothing that satisfied me or even merited consideration — mainly due to the price tags on that kind of garment. Then, because of my upbringing and my general interest in clothes worn before by other people, I began to visit used-clothing shops. One rainy day I visited such a shop in Wheaton. There, on the rack of specialty dresses, was a *dark rose-pink dress.* I became excited! It seemed to be my size. I looked at the price tag. It read: "$8 — AS IS WITH SPOTS!"

"I looked for the spots, and knew they could be easily washed out. I tried it on. It fit perfectly. I stood and looked at it in the mirror, and thought to myself, 'How is it possible to buy one's wedding dress for just $8?'

"So I bought it, thinking 'I can't lose.' At home, a good bottle of liquid soap removed the spots and refreshed the dress . . . and I enjoyed wearing it for my wedding ceremony!

"When Paul heard about how I had bought my dress, he wanted to get his wedding suit from the same shop! But I insisted that after all his years of frugal living in Ecuador, he deserved a new dark navy suit; so we bought one elsewhere."

And what advice were this bride and groom given at their wedding? Pastor Somers began his message with reference to that unexpected e-mail he received from Ruth on his 50th birthday. He then continued, elaborating a principle intended by God to be at the center of any marriage:

> Not long ago Ruth shared with us the joyous news that God had, in His own sweet way, provided a companion for the rest of life's journey. That prompted an immediate response of gratitude to God, from whom all blessings flow. In that first exchange and later in a phone conversation, Ruth used the phrase: "The Lord brought us together." For whatever reason, the word TOGETHER lingered in my mind. The morning following our phone conversation, my Bible reading included a TOGETHER and I made note of it, wondering if the Lord was stirring me.
>
> Since that day, I've bumped into so many TOGETHERS that it seemed only right that a couple who have been brought TOGETHER into a TOGETHER relationship ought to give some consideration to a TOGETHER message from the Lord they serve.
>
> The Old Testament prophet Amos wrote the defining truth about TOGETHER when he penned the question, "*Can two walk TOGETHER except they be agreed?*" The answer to that rhetorical question is, "No, they cannot." And the observations drawn from that question remind us that we must be walking toward the same destination . . . at the same time . . . at the same speed . . . if we are to truly walk TOGETHER.
>
> God has TOGETHER plans for His children. Ephesians is rich in TOGETHER instructions and says that we are "*quickened TOGETHER*" and "*raised up TOGETHER*" to "*sit TOGETHER*" as people who have been "*joined TOGETHER*" and "*built up TOGETHER*"

for a dwelling place of God. Colossians 2 further declares that we are *"knit TOGETHER"* and *"made alive TOGETHER."*

I have learned that God has a TOGETHER plan for the prayer life of the saints, so that where two or three are *"gathered TOGETHER in His name, He is in the midst of them."*

That isn't all. When believers in Jesus begin TOGETHER they work TOGETHER. Paul told the Corinthian believers they could *"help TOGETHER by prayer"* and he told the Philippian Christians they were *"workers TOGETHER with Him."* In John 4, Jesus taught that both the one who sows and the one who reaps would *"rejoice TOGETHER"* at the harvest, which points us to the glorious subject of missions TOGETHER.

God's Word plainly teaches that we are not to be *"unequally yoked TOGETHER"* with unbelievers. Instead, what God hath *"joined TOGETHER"* no man is to put asunder. The result of that truth is that Peter tells us that we become *"heirs TOGETHER"* of the grace of life, and our prayers have great power and cannot be hindered. Under those circumstances, Philippians 1 becomes so very true — we are actually *"striving TOGETHER"* for the faith of the Gospel!

The future of the saints who love TOGETHER and pray TOGETHER and serve TOGETHER and walk TOGETHER is quite clear. Thessalonians tells us that *"whether we wake or sleep, we are to live TOGETHER with Him"* as we wait to be *"caught up TOGETHER"* to meet the Lord in the air.

So, the whole story of this TOGETHER romance and this TOGETHER relationship is the story of our Lord's TOGETHER romance and TOGETHER relationship with His own bride, the Church. By the indwelling Spirit he is linking TOGETHER and leading TOGETHER those who love Him, so that all things will then *"work TOGETHER"* for their good and they will know they are called according to His purpose.

Paul and Ruth, from this moment on, until you stand before the Savior you serve . . . DO IT TOGETHER!

Ruth and Paul needed no further encouragement. Already sharing so many overlapping interests, it was a delight to serve God together. In early

July, they were thrilled to fly to Quito. Ruth's task that summer was to honor the promise she had made to Wally Kulakoff the year before, to cover for him as he took a much-needed furlough. Paul's first task was to begin preparing to lead a further group of Bethel College Semester Abroad students. One week after the new Erdel couple arrived in Quito, a new limited edition journal was launched. In the first, Ruth explained:

> It's a new couple, it's a new life, it's a new land, and a unifying of a new family circle, so we decided to begin this new publication, *The Erdel Monday Memo*. This is issue number one.
>
> It feels natural to be in Quito. Working again in the Russian department of HCJB seems to have melted 16 years away. The big differences are a new office, new buildings, new shopping malls, new people, and even a new husband! I accept all of the above, and must say how happy I am to be involved in this ministry.
>
> We both feel very fortunate to have inherited a new family each, and wonderful new friends. We have learned to love you ALL and wish for you God's special blessings. Please keep praying for us. We are remembering you each morning in our special time together. Bye for now from the land of beautiful mountains, palm trees, green grass, and lack of oxygen. HA!
>
> Love,
>
> *Ruth*

The next week's Monday missive told of Ruth's first trip to Esmeraldas after many years, to visit Paul at his mission base. Ruth wrote:

> THURSDAY, JULY 19: Such charming countryside — sheep and shepherds, goats and cows, horses and mules, chickens, patches of farmland, much green vegetation, and palms and banana plantations between Santo Domingo and Esmeraldas!
>
> Upon arriving at the two mission homes, Paul was excited to show me his book-lined room — his domain for the past five years.
>
> SUNDAY, JULY 22: In the morning we went for a flying visit to all seven *Iglesia Misionera* churches in Esmeraldas. Paul introduced me and asked me to say a word in four of them. Not having been alerted before, I practiced my Spanish on the spot . . . but was re-

warded by smiling black faces and juicy kisses from several ladies.

Today, WEDNESDAY, JULY 25: Paul was up early to finish his lesson plans on U.S. history for the Bethel College students. BIG JOB, well done! He continues preparing other lessons.

This week I assisted Elena Ralek in a radio program, then read and translated letters from Russian radio listeners. I laughed, cried, and contemplated the path of life many have to take . . . so different and much harder than in North America. I'm excited to be part of this ministry again.

In early August, another letter was mailed out. A few brief snips from it give further glimpses of God's great blessings on both past and present ministries by the Shalankos and Erdels in Ecuador — and of His master stroke in bringing Ruth and Paul together in their later years:

> On Saturday, July 27, we joined thousands of Ecuadorians at La Carolina Park in Quito. For over two hours we participated in the special outdoor celebration commemorating 100 years since the Gospel entered Ecuador in 1896.
>
> We were given a special invitation to attend, as it seems we were the "oldest North American missionaries around!" They read the names of those who had made special contributions in evangelizing Ecuador. It was very heartwarming to hear Jack's name mentioned, and then the mention of Paul's presence and his many years of ministry in Ecuador. Great advancement in the Gospel has been made in the over 40 years since we arrived in this land.
>
> My work in the Russian office is such a challenge . . . I find the day ends too soon! Am putting together a new program we hope to record in a couple of weeks. One needs to have six scripts ready before beginning to record.
>
> Paul keeps busy preparing for the Bethel students. He leaves for Mishawaka on August 16 and plans to return with them on September 13, when I look forward to greeting them all.

Yes, Ruth and Paul's first separation since their marriage was approaching fast. For despite their new commitment to togetherness, both had scheduled dates which would soon mean long times apart. Initially, much of the period from mid-August to mid-December 1996 was spent that way.

Paul's work was mostly in Esmeraldas and elsewhere in Ecuador, in keeping with his deep desire to challenge young people to actively participate in missions. As befits its name, the Missionary Church maintains its original high level of enthusiasm for outreach, both local and far afield. Its Semester Abroad program for students from Bethel College is designed to encourage this. The program places selected students with a tutor in a foreign country for three months. While continuing their course work, the students are exposed to new locations, different people groups, and unfamiliar cultures. They also witness mission work in the country they visit. With Paul in Ecuador, they would see and discuss educational, medical and radio ministries; literature distribution; church planting; open air and one-to-one evangelism; and much more. They would be taken by Paul to visit the whole range of missionary situations — from cities like Quito and Esmeraldas, to villages in the mountains and at the edge of the jungle.

Meanwhile, Ruth stayed in Quito, busy at HCJB, mainly translating and answering letters from Russian listeners, as well as recording editions of the new prayer programs. In sharp contrast to her earlier years with Voice of the Andes, she found the correspondents from the former Soviet Union now able and eager to write freely, openly expressing not only their personal situations and needs, but also describing how much the radio broadcasts meant to them.

Ruth at her desk in Quito, Ecuador.

Ruth and Paul kept in touch with each other as best they could, mainly by letters, occasional phone calls, and even a couple of weekend visits. She helped with the training of his students too, not only in Quito the first week after they had arrived, but also with the Bethel College girls in arranging Vacation Bible School classes for over 70 children in the village of Same in November. Then in December 1996, when her commitment at HCJB had ended and Paul's students had left, the Erdels returned to Esmeraldas together for the next three months. Their December newsletter began in this way:

What a joy for Paul and me to wish you a BLESSED CHRISTMAS! Early one morning last week, it was so peaceful to sit on a warm Pacific Ocean beach to read God's Word and pray together. We thank the Lord for our happy life and good marriage.

Returning to the United States in the spring of 1997, Ruth and Paul had a new and important decision to make: where to set up their new home together. Prayerfully, the city of Mishawaka, Indiana, was chosen. This is within a half-day's drive of both the SGA office in Loves Park, Illinois, and the handful of homes of Ruth's brother, sister, children, and several grand-children, all of which are in the greater Chicago area. The new Erdel do-main is also very close to that of Paul's son Tim, his wife Sally, and their three children, Sarah, Rachel and Matthew — as well as being just a mere stone's throw from Bethel College itself, providing opportunities for in-formal and fruitful contacts with the student body.

Ruth and Paul then paid their first, albeit brief, visit to Russia together, embracing St. Petersburg, Yaroslavl and Moscow. Meanwhile, John and Lorena Erdel and their family — home on furlough from their CoMission work in Russia — could conveniently house-sit and relax in the new Erdel home in Mishawaka. Ruth explains why she and Paul went to Russia at that time: "I had talked so much about Russia to Paul. I had tried to explain it and he had tried to envision it, but now he was able to see it with his own eyes. He was able to see the land of my forefathers, to meet people I had met, and to understand more of my life and love for the Russian-speaking peo-ple. Paul was also able to witness for himself the hunger that so many Rus-sians have for the Lord. In Moscow, Natalya, who is in charge of women's groups in churches in that region, met us specifically to ask if I could re-turn in the future to speak at special meetings. She wished to have her pic-ture taken with us so that she could show the other sisters the new hus-band God has given me!"

Only one week after receiving that new invitation to minister again in Russia, Ruth was speaking in a Russian meeting every day — though not in Russia, but back in Ashford at the 1997 Russian summer camp pro-gram at the RUEBU center.

"It was as if we were still in Russia," exclaims Ruth, "for the camp pro-gram was held in the Russian language. A wonderful group of about 200 kids had gathered for it. The prayers of their parents were that they would be strengthened in the spiritual truths they had learned in their own homes, and that those who were without the Lord would come to know Him."

Thus, by August 1997, Ruth and Paul had been able to enjoy a period of nearly nine months of almost uninterrupted togetherness — before this gave way to their next spell of four months largely apart. Ruth, further developing her newfound reputation as furlough facilitator at HCJB, had agreed to work another term in Quito, this time to relieve Andres and Elena Ralek, Slavic missionaries from Argentina. Simultaneously, Paul would be tutoring another batch of Bethel College students in Ecuador, the sixth successive year he had done this.

But despite her separation from Paul, Ruth was very happy in her work at HCJB: "I would say that the joy of my day was going to the post office box, unlocking it, and seeing where the mail had come from," she affirms. "As I read the sender's addresses and recognized a city, town or village I had visited, it was like meeting old friends again. Day after day, as I went to the office early and stayed all day until after 6 p.m. in the evening, I felt that supreme happiness that comes from knowing what God has for you."

In particular, Ruth had decided to answer as many letters as personally as possible, using carefully selected Bible verses to address the many different questions their writers raised. And she felt particularly led to encourage those young women — particularly single mothers — who agonized for advice and help. One such mother, when plagued by desperate financial problems and poor health, had sought and found the Lord as her personal Savior. Now she was trying to raise her child in a Christian way but was finding this difficult. Radio programs were the "spiritual breakfast" which gave her the strength to start each day living for the Lord.

Ruth answered letters from men, too — even ones which took a long time to read, like the 22-page bundle from an area she did not know. In a nutshell, the writer described how he had been brash, crude, bossy, and therefore an unhappy "man of the world," while his wife had been kind, sweet and gentle, a faithful worshipper in the Orthodox Church. Quite unexpectedly one day, he chanced upon a Russian broadcast from Quito. Initially attracted by the music and poetry, he and his wife soon began listening regularly to Voice of the Andes programs. Now three years later, he was writing to the station for the first time. He had come to love the Bible. Even the Orthodox priest had remarked on how much he had changed as a person, for as the man himself put it: "I no longer shout at my wife. I am trying to be a kind man. Your teaching on the radio has brought about these changes in my life."

And there were some whom Ruth counseled to commit themselves to Jesus Christ and find real purpose in living. One was 21-year-old Vlachislav, who wrote: "I have not listened to you for two years as I have been serving in the Army. I've come home different! I'm mean, irritable, and have begun to drink. When my father reprimanded me, I hit him. I don't want to be this way, and long to change. *I need help!*"

In October, Ruth traveled to the coast of Ecuador to join Paul for a few days. On that occasion, she also served as one of the speakers at the Missionary Church women's convention in the same city where Paul and his students were studying. Ruth confesses: "I was afraid to use my Spanish in such a public ministry, particularly after being away from Ecuador so long. But the Lord helped me all three times that I addressed the Ecuadorian ladies. The other speaker was Paul's daughter, Ruthie Stuck, who speaks perfect Spanish. We all agreed it was wonderful to serve the Lord together."

Two brief years have brought both unexpected changes and new delights into the lives of Ruth and Paul. According to Ruth's own description, they are "Grandma and Grandpa missionaries." In the first quarter of 1998, both turned 70 years old. If neither lifted another finger for the Lord but fully retired, each should still richly merit His eventual commendation at the gates of Heaven: "*WELL DONE, good and faithful servant.*"

Celebrating Ruth's 70th birthday: (at back left to right) Lydia; her husband, Steve; their daughter, Gemma; John's wife, Maria; John; (in front) John and Maria's daughter, Katrina, on Ruth's lap; Lydia and Steve's daughter, Gracia, on Paul's lap.

But retirement is not in the picture yet! Ruth speaks of "seeing what further opportunities there may be for reaching Russians." She also "longs to write for Russian women," and now has at least three specific book projects already forming in her mind. As much as possible, she hopes to be close together with Paul, but they both intend that "in EVERYTHING He might have the supremacy" (Colossians 1:18).

Ruth concludes: "As I look BACK on my life, I am thankful for all God has sent my way. I thank Him for my parents, for their deep love, for my upbringing, for teaching me to love Christ, and for showing me their burden to reach the Russian people with the Gospel. In turn, this inspired me. My life as a missionary has been a joyous one and very fulfilling.

"I am also thankful for every tear and for dark days of trials and misunderstandings. And I thank the Lord for taking away things that were very dear to me so *I could see HIS face more clearly.*

"Now, I look FORWARD. Whatever God has for me in the future, I am willing to accept. My dearest friend recently said to me, 'Ruth, when are you going to *stop*? When are you going to *settle down*?'

"I looked at her, and tears came to my eyes as I answered, 'Camille, I just cannot 'stop' the burden I have for my Russian people! The greatest joy of my life is serving Christ. As long as He gives me health and strength, my joy in life is to keep working for Him. This is my purpose for living — *to reach my Russian people for the Lord Jesus Christ!*'"

Epilogue

This has been the story of Ruth's remarkable life, thus far. But one thing remains to be done — to reflect on it, for many lessons from her life are worth relating to our own.

How do others reflect on Ruth's life and ministry? Early in 1996, as part of our information gathering for this book, we invited comments on Ruth from a range of people who had known her well, in many cases longer and better than we ourselves. Many of their replies have already been woven into the text. But others we have reserved until this point, for they provide some particularly intimate and illuminating glimpses of Ruth, pertinent to filling out her personal profile. And as we appraise her ministry and its impact on others, these glimpses also glorify the Lord.

First, some additional observations from Mary Beechik Fewchuk. This lifelong friend of Ruth had been her youth group leader and one of her music teachers at the Crystal Street church in Chicago during the 1940s. Mary remarks that:

> Ruth greatly admired and always obeyed her parents. The Chicago young people marveled at this! Ruth was always willing to serve the Lord, and later it thrilled me how God was using her musically on the radio — playing the accordion and piano, and singing in duets and trios.
>
> For many years, I was an SGA missionary in Argentina, Paraguay and Uruguay. It was *so very good for me* to hear Ruth and Jack

singing on the radio. Their songs helped me so very much at a very discouraging time.

When Jack became ill, Ruth cared for him so tenderly, together with her dear widowed mother in the Russian aged people's home. Later, when she was put in charge of this home, she humbly and lovingly took on this task. She surely *deserves every good thing* the Lord has in store for her!

Stella Jarema, a colleague of Ruth's in the Russian-language department of HCJB, writes about the long period Ruth and she spent together in missionary service in South America:

I first met Ruth in Toronto in January 1953. Mr. Deyneka Sr. was the speaker at Youth for Christ in Toronto, and I was asked to come and be the soloist. That's when I was first introduced to Ruth's many talents as an accomplished pianist and a dynamic and impressive speaker. She is a *natural* at speaking — truly having a gift from God! In this regard, Ruth is *very much like her Dad!*

It was during one of the Shalanko's furloughs, when I was working with SGA in Chicago, that they asked me about coming to Ecuador to record Russian and Ukrainian music for the Russian radio programs at HCJB. I went as a short term worker for one year — and stayed for 23 years!

I had the privilege of singing in duets and trios (Russian recordings) with Ruth. In those wonderful days in Quito, we also shared in the joys of singing in the HCJB choir on TV, radio and in the Quito Day concerts — in English and Spanish. I traveled with the Shalankos to the coastal city of Guayaquil, where Jack spoke in churches and at conferences where Ruth and I furnished the music. Ruth was chosen very often to sing in special musical groups because of her gift of reading music well and blending in nicely with other voices.

Ruth is a firm believer in prayer. As long as I've know her, she has taken everything to the Lord in prayer. In the Russian department, we prayed for our listeners' special requests sent in the mail, and for the programs. When we recorded Russian songs on Thursday mornings, we prayed before the recordings and especially prayed that each song would be a blessing to our listeners. As a new missionary, praying about everything *really impressed* me!

Ruth is very outgoing, friendly and generous, and quickly became a true friend. We spent many hours in each other's homes around the dinner table sharing, and often just having a fun time. She is also a fine seamstress — even making a few dresses for me! In Quito, she was always willing to help and give suggestions to those who came up with a problem in their sewing. As long as I can remember, Ruth has *never been idle* — she always found something to do, whether it was cooking for her family and friends, sewing, answering listener mail, counseling, sharing or praying. Ruth has always been a devoted wife and mother. I love her!

Joseph Springer, one of the talented musicians at HCJB to whom Ruth refers in Chapter 5, has remained, like his wife Betty, one of Ruth's dearest friends from her earliest days in HCJB to the present time. He writes:

Ruth and Jack Shalanko were delightful missionary colleagues who, as well as being devoted personnel on their Russian programs, worked with us on English broadcasts and several of HCJB's long-play records. Their children were about the same age as ours and we had many times of fellowship on a social level.

Ruth accompanied us not long ago on a *Friends of Ecuador* cruise to the Caribbean and was a delightful addition to our group. We also had the privilege of traveling with her to Russia. We were *overwhelmed* to see the appreciation of the Russians for her radio ministry to them from HCJB!

Helen Caldwell, of Miami, Florida, is retired after 36 years of service with the former Eastern Air Lines company. How did she get acquainted with Ruth? Helen explains that she first met Ruth when the Deynekas called for some flight reservations. Since that time, she has "had the privilege of supporting Ruth ever since she went to the field, many years ago." Helen explains further, making some well-focused observations on the differences between missionary senders and those being sent:

They (Peter Sr. and Ruth) came into my office on the ground floor of the Columbus Hotel on Biscayne Boulevard in Miami. As he spoke with me at the counter, she stood over by the door, quietly waiting for him to finish his business. Then he called her over and introduced her to me. She was so quiet and shy, my first impression was that she'd better perk up a bit if she wanted to be a successful missionary like her energetic and forceful father! WAS I EVER WRONG!

I had the pleasure of visiting Ruth twice while she and Jack were there at HCJB. What a lot I learned about the work of a missionary! She took me all around the HCJB compound and to see the huge antenna towers at Pifo. We went down to Shell Mera to take a MAF plane into the jungle to visit a British missionary, Mary Skinner, living alone in a tiny jungle village. We stayed there three days. Ruth just reveled in every minute of it, but I couldn't wait to get back to civilization! These trips showed me we are not all cut out to do the same work, and I was glad she had been called to do a work I wasn't capable of! I voiced this lack in my character to Ruth. She reminded me that *she* wouldn't be where she was if I wasn't where I was — helping to SEND her! She was *such an encouragement* in this way, never making me feel she was superior, out on the front lines, doing the "hard stuff."

Although God and the work He had given her always came first, she did not neglect her family. She was so capable as a wife and mother. She was able to strike a balance few are able to achieve.

Ruth has come to visit us a few times at our home in Miami. We've gotten big kicks out of the fact that she has often been so tired out that she has fallen asleep practically in the middle of a sentence! I have followed Ruth's itineraries these past few years with much prayer, wondering how she could possibly do so much. What *joy* she has gotten out of it, though. And how many people's lives (especially women's) she has touched, we will never know until we get to Heaven!

Ruth is a personification of Romans 8:28. We all quote this verse, but few of us *live* it as if we really BELIEVE it! I have never seen Ruth down or discouraged. Tired to the bone, yes, but never doubting that God would give her the strength for the next task He gave her and never questioning His love and goodness. I know there have been discouraging times for her, but she never takes them to people — *she takes them to the Lord.*

Barbara Christensen, secretary for more than 10 years to SGA's radio department in Wheaton, Illinois, met Ruth just after Ruth and Jack's relocation to Wheaton from Quito in 1980. Barbara reflects on their friendship:

Besides working in the SGA radio department together, we spent times sharing our problems and concerns about our children and families. We would pray together, support each other, listen to each other, cry together, and laugh together. So we developed a very close personal friendship, and I grew to respect very much this woman of God.

I greatly admire Ruth. She is totally committed to her ministry: faithful, honest, and devoted to sharing the Gospel with a lost nation. She is loving, caring and giving — someone I would very much like to be close to always. Ruth is the kind of person I would like to grow into.

My friendship with Ruth is something I feel God has graciously given me. I thank Him for the opportunity of knowing her!

Rev. Philip Somers leads New Castle Bible Church in Mackinaw, Illinois. This church still supports Ruth in many different ways, as it did Jack when he was alive. Pastor Somers explains:

When I became pastor of this church, I began writing to all the missionaries it supported and found kindred spirits in the Shalankos. They used to come to our big Christmas dinner here and share. No one will ever forget hearing Ruth and Jack sing in Russian *When His Glory Paints the Sky* — it moves me to tears just to write this.

When Jack could no longer speak easily, if asked to pray in Russian he would still take your heart to the throne. He would stir your soul! Something glorious was happening when he began to talk with the Lord in his native language.

When he lay dying, I encouraged Ruth to talk to him as if he was wide awake — to read the Word to him, and pray out loud with him. She did and was much blessed.

Ruth Shalanko is a princess in the kingdom of God. She is one of God's best! Her heart for missions and the poor knows no bounds. Her trips to the CIS and Pakistan have focused on little towns and the quiet, neglected people. She literally chooses to walk in *Christ's* light, not the limelight! She is bold in speaking of Him, quick to reach out in love, creative in explaining God's Word to those who know so little of it, and is talented beyond measure. She adorns the work of the Lord!

Lydia Felter is Ruth's younger sister — the one whom Ruth confessed she had never known very well until the Shalankos moved to Wheaton in 1980. She has now come to appreciate her big sister very much:

> Ruth is a very dedicated person, dedicated to God, to serving Him, and to all who come along her way. She has a very outgoing personality, and loves to keep busy whether speaking, helping, or just being a friend in time of need. She is a strong person, generous and friendly. She is well-liked by everyone who knows her.

Anita Deyneka, Ruth's sister-in-law, speaks on behalf of herself and Ruth's brother, Peter. Anita confirms how highly Ruth's close and extended families think of her:

> From his early years, Peter doesn't remember sibling conflicts (as are usual between brothers and sisters!), but recollects Ruth being a good sister.
>
> Regarding her ministry, I'm sure you already know how exceptional this has been — first in Europe among displaced persons, then in Ecuador, in Wheaton, in Ashford, and over much of the former Soviet Union.
>
> She is a godly, dedicated missionary who has brought the Gospel and help to people's lives wherever she has been, and under all kinds of circumstances . . . people from all over the world would confirm this.
>
> It is important to emphasize Ruth's energy and how much she has been able to achieve. Both are remarkable! Despite her asthma, she has traveled all over the former Soviet Union, even to the remotest places in the worst weather.
>
> As for family, there could not have been a more wonderful sister or sister-in-law in the world than Ruth! We love her very much! In addition to being very close to her own children, she has always been a tower of strength for the extended family. She really cares about people and goes out of her way to help them. She is also *fun* to be around.

Last, but by no means least, her now grown-up children, John and Lydia, should have a final say. How do they sum up their mother? John has already been quoted in Chapter 5, but adds this:

From our childhood, I always remember Mom as a very giving person. It seemed like she thought of everybody else first and saved anything else for herself last. She just wanted to glorify and worship God in all that she, and we, did.

One particular thing comes to mind. Our parents always supported us in what we did. As I currently coach youth teams, many times I do not see the parents of the children attending the games. In contrast I have had kids say, "Oh, this is the first game my mother or father has attended in two or three years!" I think this is why so many kids are struggling in today's society and having problems. I really appreciated Mom being there for me, and hope to do the same for my own daughter, Katrina.

Through all the years, she stressed over and over *how the Lord answers prayer* and how if we trust Him, He will show us the way. I think this is one of the reasons why she has been so effective in her ministry, because she has continued to maintain this faith.

We had a lot of love in our home — and her love for the Russian people has been very obvious too. She has not only loved those near and dear to her, as her family is, but also so many others who, in her eyes, are children of God. She loves them very, very much. That's why she has wanted to reach them for the Lord and give them the message of the Bible!

Meanwhile, daughter Lydia's final comment is very brief and to the point. She wishes to say no more, and need not, for she sums up everything in her six-word description of Ruth: "My mother, *who is a SAINT!*"

On her way to Pakistan in February 1996, Ruth stopped off in England to see us for what was to be the genesis of this book. A few days later, when we returned her to the train station on a frost-whitened British morning, no one could have guessed that this tall, slender, elderly lady had already traveled 4,000 miles to be with us — or that she would travel 20,000 more before she returned home to the United States two months later! For although she was wearing a sensible, brown winter coat, she carried only two small bags.

Ruth was not setting out on a vacation. Indeed, none but the most adventurous would choose her arduous journey for fun, even in warmer months of the year! No, she was calmly embarking for the third time in just over one year on one of those special missionary journeys to minister to women in the CIS.

Reflecting now on Ruth's brief stay with us and the mode of her departure, several related things comprise a cameo of her whole life.

First and foremost there was her *quiet acceptance* of the demanding path that lay ahead. Convinced that the Lord had called her to minister in Pakistan and the CIS, she was determined to go — despite the apprehension of an average of one meeting every day for two months, interspersed by tiring, long-distance travel in some of the harshest regions in the world. Furthermore, she would often stay in simple homes with few or no modern conveniences. And she would have so very little time to herself. She had been on such missions before. She generally knew what to expect — and was clearly daunted by the prospect! Yet because the Lord was leading her, unquestionably she would follow!

Why, we may ask, was she so ready to accept the revealed will of the Lord if this was so tough? Because of her *total commitment* to Him! We know how He had become her personal Savior and Lord at the tender age of nine, and how He had clearly called her at the only slightly less tender age of 13 to serve Him among the Russian people. For Ruth, it is no cliché to say that these had been truly defining moments in her life. We recalled earlier the words of Jesus who once said: *"No one who puts his hand to the plow and looks back is fit for the kingdom of Heaven"* (Luke 9:62). Unlike so many who have served God for a while, Ruth has never seriously looked back. Time after time, she has renewed her commitment to her life's calling. Each recommitment further buttressed her unshakable resolve to serve her Heavenly Master, and Him alone.

Such commitment is *very rare* in the modern world. As we reflect on her life and its challenges, we should consider how different the Church of Jesus Christ might be in our own land and locality if more of us were as fully and consistently committed to Him and His cause as Ruth!

The next of Ruth's characteristics that was strongly evident during that February visit was her *complete trust* in her Savior. Because her planned route to Pakistan holds no appeal for the mass travel market, her tickets were expensive. Gifts from friends and churches had covered them, but there had been very little to spare! What would Ruth do if unexpected additional expenses arose, say if — as actually turned out to be the case — her itinerary had to be changed after it had begun? Ruth showed no signs at all of concern about such things as she prepared for her journey. Had not her Master revealed Himself to servants of old as Jehovah Jireh — the Lord who provides? Ruth trusts in an UNCHANGING God!

If we consider, too, the possible perils Ruth might encounter on such a long trip through countries with uncertain attitudes toward single, foreign women traveling alone, it is clear that *outstanding bravery* also clearly characterizes her. We knew there had been previous times when she had been concerned for her own personal safety and welfare. She was often unaccompanied on her journeys. Local arrangements did not always work out precisely as planned. But her trust was always consciously in the God who had promised Joshua: *"I will be with you wherever you go"* (Joshua 1:9). And had He not memorably calmed her own fears in Quito, as husband Jack had prepared to venture on foot into killer Auca territory? She had found Him true to that promise all her life! There was, therefore, every cause to trust Him for that promise, again and again. Indeed, the Lord had especially reminded Ruth before her previous trip to the CIS of His historic commitment to Joshua — and had confirmed that He would similarly bless journeys of her own.

What had probably given us the most concern during the short time she had spent in our home had been something different still — her state of health. From the moment we had greeted her three days before, we had been astonished at how little luggage she was carrying — just those two small bags. It was so much less than we would have expected of anyone traveling so far in winter, for so long! Only in reply to our gentle expressions of surprise did the major reason for this become clear: she was *not well enough* to carry more, even if she had wished. Furthermore, she would be 68 years old the next month. She is a lady of *amazing resilience!*

It might be supposed that immediately after one journey of a few thousand miles across six time zones and with another to follow just as long, Ruth's three short days with us in England would have been spent recovering. Not a bit of it! She spent much of that time on SGA business. And she gladly accepted our hesitant invitations to speak at two small meetings while in the Bristol area. Yet her talks were given with as much application and intensity as she could have mustered to large congregations such as Moscow Central Baptist Church! It enormously impressed us that this first-class speaker, whose messages and platform presence rivet her audiences, should be so concerned for these little groups of British believers.

Ruth is indeed a person of *great humility*. She frequently protested to us that another book about her beloved father would have been much more interesting and appropriate than one about herself. We also recall late November 1977, when Ruth and her husband Jack spent a weekend with us to participate in the annual missionary convention in Bristol's Kensington Baptist Church. While Jack had preached the Word in the Sunday morning and evening services, Ruth had been content — as ever in her married life — to play the supporting role, briefly describing their missionary radio ministries and joining Jack in duets. For as others have remarked in this book, Ruth has never sought the center stage. Is it not much better to obey every call from the Lord than to leap to the echo of one's own voice?

From 1977-1992, we frequently visited SGA's U.S. office in connection with the Radio Academy of Science (RADAS) program. During those years, we met often with Ruth and Jack and enjoyed meals in their home. One of our favorite childhood pictures of our then-small daughter, Stella, shows her sitting on the front steps of the SGA building with a large Band Aid on one knee and her favorite blonde dolly, Lydia, sitting on the other. At Stella's side was Ruth's daughter, Lydia Shalanko — the lovely, fair-haired young lady after whom the dolly had been named because Stella adored the real-life Lydia so much!

Some of our warmest and most grateful memories of Ruth are of the occasions she volunteered to take Stella and our son Andrew out for the day while we were busy working in the Wheaton office. Fortunately, Ruth herself seemed to enjoy those outings as much as our children did — to local parks, museums, or even downtown Chicago and onto Lake Michigan. But we marveled then, and still do, at the unexpected thoughtfulness of one whom we already held in such high esteem. After all, Ruth was a senior missionary in her own right, with a full schedule of responsibilities in the SGA office, and much sought after for ministry in local churches. Yet she still took the time to share herself with our family. Therefore, to Ruth's other characteristics we must add *natural warmth*, *kindness* and a *strong sharing instinct!*

And this is not all. We have seen how Ruth, and so many of her friends, relatives and colleagues, have long swum against the ever-rising tide of trust in material fortunes. Through self-giving, God-honoring lives, they have been storing up instead *priceless treasures of their own in Heaven.* One of the most beautiful paradoxes of the Christian life is that the more we give of ourselves in serving others, the more the Lord credits to our own heavenly accounts.

For Ruth and her close associates around the world, the greatest thrill of all in life has been to see the growth of the Lord's *great treasure store of souls,* as one by one others have come to faith in Jesus Christ or entered a deeper knowledge of Him. And the nearer we approached the end of this two-year writing task to honor God through this testimony of His chosen daughter, the more we came to appreciate the richness of God's grace not only for Russians, but for all people everywhere.

What a life! What an EXAMPLE! This is the story of one of the greatest lady missionaries of the second half of the 20th century. We would all do well to reflect upon it . . . and adjust our own lives accordingly.

APPENDIX 1

Calendar of Key Events

March 29, 1928   Born Ruth Faith (Vera) Deyneka in Chicago, first child of Rev. Peter and Mrs. Vera Deyneka.

March 30, 1937   Born again, at home at her father's knee.

March 1941   Hears her father, Peter Deyneka Sr., make first international Russian-language Christian radio broadcast from HCJB.

April 1941   Responds to call for commitment to full-time missionary service after sermon by her father at Russian Evangelical Christian Church in Chicago.

June 1945   Graduates from Schurz High School in Chicago.

May 1950   Graduates with bachelor of arts degree from Bob Jones University, Greenville, South Carolina.

July 7, 1950   Leaves United States for missionary work with SGA among displaced persons in Europe.

August 1952   Meets Rev. Jack Shalanko in displaced persons camp in Trieste (now Italy).

November 21, 1953   Marries Jack Shalanko.

December 31, 1953   Leaves United States with her husband for Spanish-language training in Costa Rica.

November 26, 1954   Son John Shalanko born in San Jose, Costa Rica.

December 24, 1954   Arrives to begin work in the Russian radio department of HCJB in Quito, Ecuador. Participates in various Russian, Spanish and English ministries by radio and TV, ministers in music in local Ecuadorian churches, and undertakes several overseas tours for HCJB with husband Jack — continuing for 27 years until April 1980.

May 6, 1956   Daughter Lydia Vera Shalanko born in Quito, Ecuador.

April 30, 1980   Relocates to the SGA office in Wheaton, Illinois. Participates in various radio, literature and deputation ministries of SGA, and Spanish church ministries in Wheaton and West Chicago, Illinois — continuing until May 1989.

April 1985   Pays her first visit to the U.S.S.R.

July 26, 1987   Death of her father, Rev. Peter Deyneka Sr. (age 89).

May 1989   Moves to Ashford, Connecticut, to care for her mother, Vera Deyneka, and continues ministry of translating and answering letters from Russia.

September 1989   Husband Jack Shalanko retires from SGA radio ministry due to ill health.

January 1, 1992   Begins service as manager of Gilead Home, Ashford, Connecticut — continuing until December 31, 1994.

February 15, 1993   Death of her mother, Vera Deyneka (age 88).

June 13, 1993   Death of her husband, Rev. Jack Shalanko (age 68).

May 1993   Commences seven extended missionary journeys (continuing until March 1996) to several republics created from the former U.S.S.R., including one visit to Pakistan, for speaking ministries to women:

May 28 - June 11, 1993 — Belarus, Russia, Ukraine (prematurely terminated because of Jack's illness).

October 6 - 24, 1993 — Ukraine.

August 8 - 22, 1994 — Kiev and Rovno, Ukraine.

September 9 - 30, 1994 — Belarus, Ukraine.

January 5 - April 4, 1995 — Belarus, Russia, Ukraine.

September 26 - November 22, 1995 — Moldova, Russia (including Siberia), Ukraine.

February 5 - March 26, 1996 — Pakistan, Belarus, Russia.

June 1, 1996   Marries Dr. Paul Erdel in Wheaton, Illinois.

July 8, 1996   Returns to work in the Russian department of HCJB, Quito, Ecuador, for over three months, then joins Paul in Esmeraldas, Ecuador, in Spanish ministries — continuing until February 14, 1997.

June 21 - July 2, 1997   Revisits Russia, the first time with husband Paul.

August 7, 1997   Returns to work in the Russian department of HCJB in Quito, while Paul teaches in the Esmeraldas-based Semester Abroad program of Bethel College in Mishawaka, Indiana, until December 18, 1997.

March 29, 1998   Celebrates 70th birthday in Wheaton, Illinois.

Geographical and Political Definitions

BELARUS

Formerly the Soviet state of Belorussia (White Russia), Belarus has been an independent republic within the CIS since 1991 with a population of over 10 million. Its indigenous people and language are both very closely related to those of Russia itself. Historically, from the Middle Ages it has been ruled in succession by several of its neighbors, including Lithuania, Poland, Germany and Russia. Its borders were then substantially altered by World Wars I and II, where a large tract became occupied by Poland after the end of World War I and remained so until World War II. Its capital, Minsk, has been described as: "Unique among the capital cities of the (former) Soviet Union for having been ruined over and over again, and yet still dominating its region" (V. & J. Louis, 1976).

COMMONWEALTH OF INDEPENDENT STATES (CIS)

The name adopted by 11 of the 15 former Soviet republics in December 1991 as they became newly independent of the U.S.S.R. The CIS excludes the four states of the former U.S.S.R. not joining the CIS — namely the Baltic republics of Estonia, Latvia and Lithuania, and the Black Sea coast republic of Georgia. The CIS Union Treaty is based on international standards of human rights and freedoms, including much greater freedom for religious beliefs and practices. Most, if not all, of these new nation states have struggled economically to switch from centralized economic planning to differing degrees of market economics.

FORMER SOVIET UNION OR FORMER U.S.S.R.

A convenience name given to the entire area of the old U.S.S.R. after its breakup in the early 1990s.

RUSSIA

Historically the homeland of the Russians, modern Russia is now the largest single country to emerge from the former Soviet Union. First recognized separately in the Middle Ages, Russia grew territorially, mainly northward and eastward, from its origins in the Volga River basin to the Pacific coasts of Asia in the mid-19th century. Outposts in North America (Alaska and parts of California) were sold to the United States in 1867. Before the Russian Revolution in 1917 which overthrew the Tsarist ruling family, most Russians were still peasants and the state religion was Russian Orthodoxy, though Protestant churches had spread widely since the middle of the 19th century. Modern Russia has a population of about 150 million, of which ethnic Russians account for about four-fifths. Some 25 million ethnic Russians were living in other parts of the former Soviet Union upon its collapse in 1991, many in the newly independent neighboring nations of Belarus and Ukraine.

RUSSIAN FEDERATION

This was the largest of the republics of the U.S.S.R., occupying over five-sixths of its area and containing about half its population. However, its greatest importance was to be neither geographical nor economic, but political. As the source and heartland of atheistic materialism, its principles were exported to many other countries of the world until the long-predicted and sudden collapse of the communist system in the late 1980s and early 1990s — and the demise of the U.S.S.R. itself in 1991.

SOVIET UNION

An abbreviated name for the U.S.S.R.

UKRAINE

After Russia and Kazakhstan, this was the third largest republic in the U.S.S.R. in terms of area, and the second most populous after Russia. It was in its capital, Kiev, that Christianity first came to the region — Prince Vladimir had his subjects baptized in the Dnieper River in 988 A.D. During the Middle Ages, Ukraine developed its own language and culture, but did not become an independent state until December 1917. Less than five years later, it joined the young U.S.S.R., being one of its four founding members. It regained its independence in 1991. Its present population is over 50 million. It is quite rich in natural resources and is intrinsically more viable than several of the other states within the CIS.

U.S.S.R.

The Union of Soviet Socialist Republics. In its day, this was the world's biggest nation in terms of territory, stretching from the Baltic Sea in the west to the Pacific Ocean in the east and from the Arctic Ocean to the Himalayas. With nearly 300 million citizens, it was also the world's third most populous (after China and India). Founded in 1917 following the October Socialist Revolution led by Vladimir Lenin's Communist Party, the U.S.S.R. — the world's first socialist (communist) state — sought to actively spread the basic tenets and values of socialism throughout the globe. At home its welfare provisions were highly advanced, but freedoms of the individual — particularly in respect of religion — became severely curtailed. The U.S.S.R. was formally abolished on December 31, 1991. At that time, ethnic Russians accounted for just over half of its total population.

Topics for Thought and Discussion

This section has been prepared to encourage readers — whether alone or in groups — to explore the text for lessons which have a much broader relevance than to the situations it describes alone. The lists of questions set out below are by no means exhaustive, but include some intriguing points for thought, meditation and prayer which suggest themselves from a careful reading of each chapter.

At the end of many of the questions listed below, a few leading Scripture references are cited. These have been chosen to throw some initial light on the questions. They are suggested starting points for discussion of the Scriptural principles which have guided Ruth's life, and which could beneficially influence our lives as well.

CHAPTER 1

1. Many of the problems facing Christians in Russia as they seek to serve the Lord today are different from those of the communist era. Discuss the problems of both eras. How do these problems relate to the Christians in your country today?

2. Ruth inquired at what time the home meeting in Vinzili would end. Her expectation was different from that of her audience. What are some benefits of extended time spent in corporate worship? (Nehemiah 8:1-3; Acts 20:7-12; Hebrews 10:19-25)

3.   Peter Deyneka Jr. urged relatives and other villagers in Staramlynia to trust Christ as their compatriots Peter Sr. and Vera had done. What are some ways we might best witness for Jesus Christ to our relatives and friends?
     (Matthew 5:16; John 1:35-51; Ephesians 4:17-32)

4.   If God called us, would we be prepared, as Ruth has been, to go to the other side of the world to serve Him?
     (Isaiah 6:8; Matthew 28:19-20; Acts 13:1-3, 16:9-10)

CHAPTER 2

1.   At a young age, Ruth became conscious that her family was different from many others in the United States. If we are followers of Jesus Christ today, how different should we be from others?
     (Matthew 5:3-10; Romans 12:2; Colossians 3:1-17; 1 Peter 1:14-16)

2.   How did you react to Peter Sr. and Vera's approach to domestic budgeting? What budgeting principles should apply to Christians — including those who rely on gifts from others for their livelihood?
     (Matthew 6:19-21; Acts 4:32-37; 2 Corinthians 8:1-15)

3.   Do we need to spend money on others to show that we love them? How does what we give relate to our demonstration of love for God?
     (Genesis 37:3-4; Mark 12:41-44; John 12:1-8)

4.   If "much prayer" is "much POWER" and "little prayer" is "little power," how might we enjoy more fruits of that power in our lives, our families, churches and missions?
     (1 Chronicles 5:20; Proverbs 15:29; Luke 18:1; Ephesians 6:18)

5.   How may Christian parents encourage their children to become Christians too?
     (Deuteronomy 6:5-9; Proverbs 22:6; Matthew 18:1-5; Ephesians 6:4)

CHAPTER 3

1.   How early in life may someone hear God's call to a particular type of service for Him? Do those who receive a clear call at a relatively young age face any particular problems?
     (1 Samuel 3:1-10, 17:34-37; 1 Timothy 4:12-16; 2 Timothy 2:22-26)

2. "But who would be listening?" was Peter Deyneka Sr.'s response to the invitation from Dr. Clarence Jones to preach the Gospel in the Russian language over the radio to North America. "Speak and we'll find out!" was the reply. What role can experimentation play in proclaiming the Gospel locally and further afield?
   (Ecclesiastes 11:1-6; 1 Corinthians 9:19-23)

3. In Chapter 3 the assertion is made that while Ruth was in her teens, young people from Christian homes generally lived much more protected, sheltered lives than they do today. What might be the benefits and disadvantages of the greater personal freedom Christian teenagers expect outside home and church today?
   (1 Corinthians 6:12-17, 10:23-33; Ephesians 6:1-3; Galatians 5:13-15)

4. Ruth's friend Pauline Mazur Semenchuk suggests that in the days before television, Christians were much less exposed to temptations which invade the home than they are today. What are these temptations and how can we resist them?
   (Luke 4:1-13; 1 Corinthians 10:6-14; 1 Timothy 6:9-11)

5. At college, Ruth's public prayers at first lacked their previous fluency. What factors may hinder our own public prayer lives?
   (Psalm 51; Isaiah 1:15-17; Matthew 6:5-8; 1 Peter 3:7)

6. How can Christians guard against the development of romantic relationships which may not be in line with God's will?
   (Psalm 119:9-16; 2 Corinthians 6:14-17; Hebrews 13:4-8)

7. Do personal wishes ever conflict with our instructions as Christians to obey God and His Word? What role might advice from more experienced Christian friends play in our decision-making processes?
   (Proverbs 2:1-6; Titus 2:1-14; 1 Peter 5:1-9)

CHAPTER 4

1. Once Ruth had recovered peace of mind after her "little romantic episode," her parents never referred to it again. What should we do with our memories of the battles fought and won by ourselves and other Christians? Do we ever bring up problems they themselves have left behind? (Philippians 3:12-14; Colossians 3:1-20)

2. Ruth's courage in wishing to stay in Europe as a 22-year-old missionary with only $10 in her pocketbook touched Peter Sr.'s heart. Discuss her undoubted courage. (Luke 9:57-62)

3. On the mission field in Europe, Ruth and co-worker Roz Kucher Leonovich were soon confronted with situations for which their Christian ministry training had neither prepared them nor even led them to expect. What should we do if such situations confront us? (Joshua 1:6-9; James 1:2-5,12; 1 Peter 3:13-17)

4. How might we encourage young people to see that they need salvation through faith in Jesus Christ as much as older people? (Deuteronomy 4:9, 11:18-21; Proverbs 1:8-9; Ecclesiastes 12:1)

5. A Russian lady living in France wrote to SGA saying of Ruth: "This is the first time I met a girl who is so consecrated to the Lord." What does consecration entail? (Romans 12:1-3; 2 Peter 1:4-8)

6. Ruth professed to "such a burden" for young people without Christ in the DP camps of Western and Central Europe. How is it that some Christians become concerned for the spiritual needs of others and act accordingly, while others become seemingly "so placid and content with everyday living?"

7. Ruth continually prayed for guidance from God in respect to every major decision she had to make. How and when does God provide guidance to His children? (Psalm 119:97-104; James 4:13-15)

CHAPTER 5

1. Ruth and Jack neither wished to learn Spanish nor to stay in Costa Rica as long as they did — yet God rewarded them for both. What are our reactions to unexpected situations in which we seem to be prisoners of circumstance? (Acts 28:17-20,30-31; Philippians 4:12-13)

2. What should be the Christian's response to health problems? (Job 2:6-10; Luke 17:11-19; 2 Corinthians 12:7)

3. In our planning for the future (lives, ministries, projects etc.), what are the relative values of logic, impulse, and the will of God? (Proverbs 19:21; Acts 8:26-31, 16:6-10)

CHAPTER 6

1. Jack wrote that when he volunteered to go on the expedition into Auca territory, "Ruth took it like a good soldier." What do you think he meant by this? How should we respond if a loved one of ours felt called of God to enter some difficult or even dangerous situation? (Psalm 46; 1 Peter 5:6-7)

2. Jack was indelibly impressed by the sight of the martyred missionaries and their burial at Palm Beach, and consequently rededicated himself to the service of God. Was this a natural reaction to all he saw? In what other ways might he have responded?

3. Jack wrote of the Palm Beach martyrs: "They so willingly and courageously gave their lives, while many of us are afraid even to open our mouths to witness for Him where no danger at all confronts us." What do we fear when opportunities for Christian witness arise? How may we overcome such fears? (Daniel 3:16-18; Romans 8:31-39)

4. Relatives of the martyrs readily forgave those who had murdered their loved ones. Are there lessons in this for us? (Matthew 8:21-35; Ephesians 4:29-32)

5. Should we be concerned if entire tribes or peoples have not yet heard the Gospel of Jesus Christ? To what lengths should we go to share this Gospel with them, even in remote and possibly dangerous situations? (Matthew 18:12-14; Romans 10:1-4)

CHAPTER 7

1. Ruth and Jack were involved in the infancy of Christian radio and TV. How important are these media ministries today and why?

2. How are we able to best encourage fellow believers in other countries where there is much opposition to the Gospel? (Acts 20:1-4; 1 Corinthians 16:1-4; Ephesians 3:14-21)

3. Many missionary visitors to the former Soviet Union have reported on intense hunger for the Word of God. What are the characteristics of such hunger?
   (Job 23:8-14; Nehemiah 8; Acts 10:1-8,24-48, 17:10-12)

4. Early Russian radio missionaries received little or no listener's response. If we don't get positive feedback from the work we do, how can we continue the work?
   (Psalm 37:3-11; Isaiah 55:9-11; Ezekiel 2:1-5; 3 John:3-5)

CHAPTER 8

1. Ruth was initially upset when she had to leave her "little nest" in Quito behind, as well as many of her friends. List your own most treasured possessions? How would you react if you became separated from them?
   (Job 1; Psalm 112; Matthew 6:19-24)

2. Chapter 8 asserts that "without due care, even work for the Lord can lessen our love for Him as a person." If this became so in our experience, how should we respond?
   (John 21:15-19; Revelation 2:1-5)

3. Would we appreciate the Bible more if copies of it in our country were scarce? Why?
   (Psalm 119; Proverbs 25:25)

4. Christians behind the Iron Curtain ran many risks as they sought to live for God. Do we run any risks by being Christians? How should we view such risks and respond to them?
   (Matthew 5:11-12,43-45; Acts 5:40-42; Romans 8:31-39)

CHAPTER 9

1. How can those of advancing years be best helped with their natural frustration as illness or physical weakness takes its toll?

2. Ruth-the-manager helped Ruth-the-patient find peace with God the day she died. Statistically, very few people come to faith in God when they are old. Why may this be so?
   (Proverbs 28:14; Ephesians 4:17-19)

3. Within six years, Ruth suffered the loss of her father, mother and husband. How might her responses to the deaths of her loved ones be models for us as Christians?

4. Vera Deyneka "had always been ready to serve the Lord simply and unobtrusively, and thus to very great effect." What are the keys to this type of effective Christian service?
(Joshua 22:1-5; Psalm 2:7-12; Matthew 6:24; Acts 20:17-19; 1 Corinthians 12:1-11; 1 Timothy 4:14-16)

5. What does the Bible have to say to about widows and widowers?
(1 Corinthians 7:8-9; 1 Timothy 5:3-16; James 1·27)

CHAPTER 10
1. In Ashford, Connecticut, Ruth often did more for the residents of Gilead Home than her circumstances required. Are we prepared to go the second mile to make things nicer for others?
(Matthew 5:38-42; Mark 14:3-9; Luke 21:1-4; Colossians 3:23-24)

2. Ruth was not always happy with her chance companions when travelling. What can we do when we find ourselves in new situations of which we are fearful?
(Deuteronomy 1:26-31; Psalm 61; Matthew 10:24-31; 2 Timothy 1:8-12, 4:16-18)

3. After agreeing to become manager of Gilead Home, Ruth found herself carrying responsibilities for which she was not trained. Discuss the role of teamwork in Christian circles.
(1 Corinthians 3:1-9; 2 Corinthians 8:10-15; 1 Peter 4:10-11)

4. After Vera died, Ruth found herself suddenly available for new types of Christian service. How do we react to unwelcome crossroads in our Christian lives?

5. Ruth has never given up praying that her cousin Anastacia would come to know the Lord. Should we, and do we, persist in prayer for nonbelievers as well as our Christian friends?
(Mark 11:20-26; Luke 18:1-8; Colossians 1:9-14)

CHAPTER 11

1. Ruth repeatedly encouraged her listeners to apply God's Word to their own lives. On what basis do we select passages of the Bible to help us live for Him?
   (Psalm 119:121-128; Matthew 13:1-23; 2 Timothy 3:16-17)

2. Ruth prepared many messages based on women in the Bible. What principles should guide us as we try to learn from people in the Bible?
   (Hebrews 11:1-12; Romans 15:4-6)

3. How may Christian workers remain fresh in the face of heavy ministry schedules?
   (Psalm 23; Isaiah 40:27-31; Mark 6:30-31; 1 Peter 5:1-11)

4. How may Christian weddings and funerals be opportunities of witness to unbelievers?
   (Psalm 116:15; Ephesians 5:21-33)

CHAPTER 12

1. When should Christians decline new invitations for ministry?
   (Acts 16:5-9, 18:18-22)

2. Does our desire to please the Lord outweigh other personal desires?
   (Psalms 37:3-5, 145:17-20; Romans 7:14-25; Galatians 5:13-26; Philippians 1:21-26)

3. Should a Christian retire from active service for the Lord?
   (Psalm 92:12-15; Acts 2:17-21; Hebrews 11:11-12)

4. Why engage in missionary activities when there are so many needs right here at home?
   (Isaiah 49:1-6; Mark 16:15-16; Luke 24:45-47; Acts 1:1-8)

5. Does God always meet all the needs of His children?
   (Luke 12:22-34; John 6:25-35; Philippians 4:10-19)

APPENDIX 4

Reference List and Selected Bibliography

Barrett, E.C., *Prime Target: Part of the Story of the Slavic Gospel Association*, SGA, Eastbourne, United Kingdom, 1972

Barrett, E.C. & Fisher, D., *Scientists Who Believe*, Moody Press, Chicago, Illinois, United States, 1984

Barrett, E.C., *Scientists Who Find God*, SGA, Eastbourne, United Kingdom, 1996

Bater, J.H., *Russia and the Post-Soviet Scene*, Arnold, London, United Kingdom, 1996

Bergman, S. (ed.), *Martyrs: Contemporary Writers on Modern Lives of Faith*, Harper, San Francisco, California, United States, 1997

Bershadsky, L., with Millington, A., *I Know His Touch*, Crossway Books, Westchester, Illinois, United States, 1984

Bourdeaux, M., *Faith on Trial in Russia*, Hodder & Stoughton, London, United Kingdom, 1971

de Chalandeau, A., *The Christians in the U.S.S.R.*, Harper, Chicago, Illinois, United States, 1978

Dalziel, S., *The Rise and Fall of the Soviet Empire*, Smithmark, New York, New York, United States, 1993.

Deyneka, P., *Twice Born Russian: An Autobiography*, Zondervan, Grand Rapids, Michigan, United States, 1944

Deyneka, P., *Much Prayer, Much Power!*, Zondervan, Grand Rapids, Michigan, United States, 1958

Deyneka, P. Jr., *Christians in the Shadow of the Kremlin*, Hodder and Stoughton, London, United Kingdom, 1974

Elliot, E., *Through Gates of Splendor*, Harper and Bros., New York, New York, United States, 1957

Evans, D., *Communist Faith and Christian Faith*, SCM Press, London, United Kingdom, 1965

Freed, P.E., *Let the Earth Hear*, Nelson, Nashville, Tennessee, United States, 1980

Harris, T., *Moving God's Finger*, SGA, Eastbourne, United Kingdom, 1991

Louis, V. & J., *The Complete Guide to the Soviet Union*, Michael Joseph, London, United Kingdom, 1976

Neeley, L., *Come Up to This Mountain: The Miracle of Clarence W. Jones and HCJB*, Tyndale House, Wheaton, Illinois, United States, 1980

Noble, J., *I Found God in Soviet Russia*, Oliphants, London, United Kingdom, 1959

Philip's, *Philip's Atlas of the World*, George Philip, London, United Kingdom, 1996

Pollock, J.C., *The Christians from Siberia*, Hodder & Stoughton, London, United Kingdom, 1964

Portal, R., *The Slavs: A Cultural, Historical Survey of the Slavonic Peoples*, (English translation from the original French), Weidenfeld & Nicolson, London, United Kingdom, 1969

Rohrer, N.B. & Deyneka, P. Jr., *Peter Dynamite: Twice Born Russian*, Baker, Grand Rapids, Michigan, United States, 1975

Warburton, M., *I Would Rather Be . . .* , SGA, Eastbourne, United Kingdom, 1975

Warburton, M., *A Kingdom Which Cannot be Shaken*, SGA, Eastbourne, United Kingdom, 1978

Woodbridge, J.D. (ed.), *Ambassadors for Christ: Distinguished Representatives of the Message Throughout the World*, Moody Press, Chicago, Illinois, United States, 1994

APPENDIX 5

Slavic Gospel Association

SGA is a global, nondenominational, evangelical mission organization, founded in 1934 by Peter Deyneka Sr., a Russian immigrant with a deep concern for the spiritual well-being of his compatriots wherever they were to be found. After the fall of the Iron Curtain, profound political and economic changes spread across the former Soviet Union and Central and Eastern Europe. Today, SGA's ministries are concentrated in these regions with the aim of serving the local, indigenous, evangelical churches to bring the Gospel of Jesus Christ to their own peoples. Through a unified strategy, SGA ministries in Australia, Canada, France, New Zealand, the United Kingdom and the United States work together to that end.

SGA carries out a multifaceted range of missionary outreach including media ministries (literature, radio and TV) based increasingly within the target countries themselves, training of nationals for pastoral ministries and church planting, sponsorship of church planters, pastor training conferences and youth camps, children's work, prison ministries, church construction assistance, and the provision of humanitarian aid which is distributed by the local churches. Six Regional Ministry Centers are maintained in Moscow, Omsk and Khabarovsk (Russia), Minsk (Belarus), Kiev (Ukraine) and Almaty (Kazakhstan) to support the outreach of national churches in the former Soviet Union.

In the fall of 1997, SGA accepted the invitation of the Union of Evangelical Christians-Baptists (UECB) of Russia to become their official representative in the United States, Australia, Canada and New Zealand. Training, equipping and supporting ministries are simultaneously taking place in Poland, the Czech and Slovak Republics, Hungary, Romania, Moldova, Bulgaria, Croatia, Serbia and Macedonia.

If you would like to learn more about SGA and its many ministries, please contact:

AUSTRALIA
Slavic Gospel Association
P.O. Box 396, Noble Park, Victoria 3174

CANADA
Slavic Gospel Association
205-2476 Argentia Road, Mississauga, Ontario L5N 6M1

FRANCE
Association Evangelique Slave
Rue de Mauberge, 59164 Marpent

NEW ZEALAND
Slavic Gospel Association
P.O. Box 10-156, 591 Dominion Road, Auckland 4

UNITED KINGDOM
Slavic Gospel Association
37A The Goffs, Eastbourne, East Sussex BN21 1HF

UNITED STATES
Slavic Gospel Association
6151 Commonwealth Drive, Loves Park, Illinois 61111

About the Authors

ERIC AND GILLIAN BARRETT have served as volunteer SGA representatives in the United Kingdom since 1967, through speaking, writing, and (in Gillian's case) singing ministries, as well as practical mission team leadership in Western and Central Europe. In the late 1970s, Dr. Barrett — an internationally honored space scientist and author — designed SGA's evangelistic *Radio Academy of Science* (RADAS) program, and regularly wrote scripts for the series from 1980 to 1993. He has also edited two volumes of testimonies originally used in these programs — *Scientists Who Believe* (with David Fisher, Moody Press, Chicago, 1984), and *Scientists Who Find God* (SGA, Eastbourne, United Kingdom, 1997).